Philadelphia

COMPARATIVE AMERICAN CITIES

A series edited by Joe T. Darden

Philadelphia

Neighborhoods, Division, and Conflict in a Postindustrial City

Carolyn Adams

David Bartelt

David Elesh

Ira Goldstein

Nancy Kleniewski

and William Yancey

Temple University Press · Philadelphia

This book is dedicated to the people and communities of Philadelphia, struggling to shape their future together.

Temple University Press, Philadelphia 19122

Copyright © 1991 by Temple University.

All rights reserved

Published 1991

Printed in the United States of America

Publication of this book was assisted by a grant from the Samuel S. Fels Fund.

⊗ The paper used in this publication meets the minimum requirements of American National Standard for Information Sciences—Permanence of Paper for Printed Library Materials, ANSI Z39.48-1984

Library of Congress Cataloging-in-Publication Data
Philadelphia : neighborhoods, division, and conflict in a
postindustrial city / Carolyn Adams ... [et al.].
    p.   cm. — (Comparative American cities)
  Includes bibliographical references and index.
  ISBN 0-87722-842-6 (alk. paper)
  1. Community development, Urban—Pennsylvania—
Philadelphia Metropolitan Area.   2. Inner cities—Pennsylvania
—Philadelphia Metropolitan Area.   3. Neighborhood—
Pennsylvania—Philadelphia Metropolitan Area.
4. Gentrification—Pennsylvania—Philadelphia Metropolitan
Area.   5. Philadelphia Metropolitan Area (Pa.)—Race relations.
6. Philadelphia Metropolitan Area (Pa.)—Economic conditions.
7. Urban renewal—Pennsylvania—Philadelphia Metropolitan
Area.   8. Regional planning—Pennsylvania.   I. Adams,
Carolyn Teich.   II. Series.
HN80.P5P477   1991
307.1′416′0974811—dc20   91-7571

Contents

List of Tables and Figures

Tables

Figures

Preface

This book has been a unique and complex endeavor, linking the specialties and academic styles of six coauthors across several disciplines and interest areas. What united us on this task was the central goal of the book—to explain as completely as possible what has happened to Philadelphia and its metropolitan area in the past four decades. At once both historical and sociological, it focuses on the centrality of economic change and corresponding political, demographic, and social movements with the region.

Philadelphia is a city wracked by conflict and facing a difficult future. Its civic and political life often threatens to devolve into casting blame on one group or another for its current difficulties. If there is one message that resonates throughout this book, it is simply this—that the city and its surrounding communities are caught in the throes of a wrenching social and economic shift that must be confronted head on. Above all, this struggle must not be overwhelmed by internecine struggles between various constituencies, communities, or neighborhoods for a larger slice of a shrinking pie. The forces of economic change have transformed an industrial city into a postindustrial metropolis—and have, we would argue, increased the payoff for coordinated regional actions while simultaneously dividing one neighborhood from the other, one ethnic group from another, and one gender from the other.

This divided metropolis faces a tenuous future, yet we know that it will survive—the only question is in what form. If this book helps focus discussions of alternatives for the city and the region, we will be gratified. If we have increased our readers' understanding of the current social frameworks of their day-to-day situations, we will be similarly gratified. For this volume is both an academic treatise and a labor of love and concern for this city.

In any coauthored work some means of identifying the specific responsibilities of each of the authors is needed. Carolyn Adams and David Bartelt alternated responsibility for pushing the project from beginning to end. They jointly wrote the introductory chapter, with contributions from David Elesh. Adams also prepared Chapter 5, dealing with the political changes in Philadelphia, and was responsible for Chapters 6 and 7.

Bartelt was responsible for the housing chapter (Chapter 3) and was assisted by Ira Goldstein, who did much of the analysis dealing with gentrification, and Bill Yancey, who focused on issues of desegregation. David Elesh analyzed Philadelphia's economic transformation in Chapter 2, and he and Bill Yancey developed the analysis of the effects of the transformation on income shifts also found in that chapter. The examination of these changes—the basis for much of the rest of this book—originally occupied two much longer chapters and was molded into one by Bartelt and Elesh. Finally, Nancy Kleniewski was responsible for the analysis of urban renewal, found in Chapter 4.

We are several authors, but we have been united in sharing a basic theme of the book, that economic changes and the political and social responses to them often reproduce and magnify existing social divisions. As much as individual authors took on specific responsibilities, this was indeed a collective effort. All of the authors provided substantial constructive criticism over the life of the project, giving the various book meetings the sobriquet of "psychiatric sessions." We deliver our work to our readers with the hope that these sessions have indeed improved the final book.

A special note of thanks goes to the very patient and extremely helpful work of B. J. Urso, the person most responsible for transforming the wide variety of manuscript drafts, disks, tables, and figures into a coherent manuscript. Mark Mattson, coordinator of the Geography and Urban Studies Department's Cartographic Lab, prepared the figures and maps for the book with his usual high standards and impeccable quality. Scott Fort assisted in this effort. Fred Miller, who was then Director of Temple's Urban Archives, provided documents and helped interpret the history of urban renewal in Philadelphia.

There was, as always, a personal support network beyond the coauthors that needs to be specifically acknowledged. Tim Adams, Pearl Bartelt, Bill Davis, Estella Elesh, Linda Samost Goldstein, and Pat Wisch have all both tolerated and encouraged the work that has gone into this book, often reading, criticizing, and generally facilitating the project. It has been this continued support that has helped this book move from idea to reality.

Finally, a special mention goes to Janet Francendese at Temple University Press. Though this work has benefited from the support of the entire staff of the Press, it has been Janet's editorial supervision and gentle prodding that have helped make this book emerge from its first tentative outline. Joe Darden, the series editor, has also been instrumental in moving this project along and in ensuring that it forms a part of the overall comparative cities series of the Press.

Series Preface

The Comparative American Cities series grew out of a need for more comparative scholarly works on America's urban areas in the post–World War II era. American cities are storehouses of potential assets and liabilities for their residents and for society as a whole. It is important that scholars examine the nation's metropolitan areas to assess trends that may affect economic and political decision-making in the future.

The books have a contemporary approach, with the post–World War II period providing historical antecedents for current concerns. Each book generally addresses the same issues, although the peculiarities of the local environments necessarily shape each account. The major areas of concern include uneven regional development, white middle-class suburbanization, residential segregation of races and classes, and central-city issues such as economic disinvestment, black political power, and the concentration of blacks, Hispanics, and the poor. Each city in the series is viewed within the context of its metropolitan area as a whole. Taken together, these studies describe the spatial redistribution of wealth within the metropolises—the economic decline of central cities and the economic rise of the suburbs—a redistribution facilitated by the massive construction of interstate highways in the 1950s, 1960s, and 1970s.

Since World War II the metropolitan areas included in this series have been increasingly affected by uneven economic and social development and by conflict between cities and suburbs and between the white majority and the growing nonwhite minority. The central cities of each metropolitan area have also been losing jobs to the suburbs. There has been a tendency toward growing income inequality between cities and suburbs and between blacks and whites. Economic growth and decline have followed closely the racial composition of neighborhoods—that is, black neighborhoods have declined, while white neighborhoods have generally grown.

All of these studies asses the ways central-city governments have responded to these issues. In recent years most central-city elected officials have attempted to provide services and employment opportunities on a more equitable basis and to implement a more balanced and progressive economic development agenda. Most central-city mayors have been elected with the strong support of minorities, and the mayors have often cooperated with the business elite in attempts to stimulate more economic growth and to save the cities from further economic decline. Since this decline is related to structural changes in the economy within the context of uneven development, however, attempts at preventing the flow of jobs to the suburbs have largely failed, and the economic and social gap continues to widen.

There are no quick solutions to the economic, racial, and political problems of the cities in these studies. Though high-technology industries may play a part in each city's future, it is unlikely that they will produce as many jobs as are needed, or reduce the racial differences in unemployment rates. Blacks and other minorities who have limited spatial access to the areas of high-tech industries may not receive a fair share of their benefits.

Each city's plight is deeply rooted in America's problems of free-market economic investment, racial prejudice and discrimination, and the outmoded political structure that continues to separate the city from the suburbs, one suburb from another, the rich from the poor, and blacks from whites. As long as this structure remains, there is a strong probability that the situation will worsen, as population mobility continues to reinforce patterns of economic, social, and racial inequality, contributing to more racial and class conflict.

The problems of urban America require the immediate attention of government officials and the citizenry of this nation. New solutions involving changes in the political structure are long overdue. Our hope is that comparative studies such as these might provide the impetus for informed decisions and policies that will address the underlying problems besetting America's major urban areas.

Joe T. Darden, Series Editor
Comparative American Cities

Philadelphia

1

The Legacy of the Industrial City

Like most American cities, Philadelphia combines many contradictory realities. Its public images range from the stodgy WASP fiefdom portrayed in *The Philadelphia Story*, to political graft and police payoffs, to bombed-out neighborhoods, to a gentrified, phoenix-like creature rising from the ashes of its past. None of these images is complete, yet each is a part of the total picture of the city. The contradictions arise partly from a clash between the city's past and its present; although the city was created in response to the political and economic environments of the seventeenth century, it has been recreated repeatedly as those environments have changed. Each re-creation has been incomplete, leaving in place many elements from the past, yet each laid the groundwork on which future changes would have to be based. This book shows how past patterns of work, residence, and public policy created the arena in which the current changing social and economic order makes its own imprint.

A basic premise of the book and of the series of which it is a part is that, to some extent, each city's history needs to be told in its own terms. There is no simple developmental scheme here, no attempt to understand all urban issues as the result of a few universal laws. Although we assume that the local economy operates largely within national and international market-places, we understand that the general economic principles at work can produce different patterns in different places. What has happened in Philadelphia is only one of a number of outcomes that could have occurred. For that reason, a substantial part of the task of this book is to understand how Philadelphia's past has interacted with national and international trends to produce particular local patterns.

Yet if our objectives were limited to explaining what has happened in Philadelphia, this book would be of only parochial interest. What makes a study of Philadelphia worthy of broader attention is the extent to which explanations of its development apply to other cities as well. We write of Philadelphia but we believe many of our interpretations can be generalized to other older cities that, like Philadelphia, have deep roots in manufacturing and diverse populations. The challenge of the book is to display the contours of the broader processes shaping Philadelphia's development in the particulars of its history.

In specific terms, this means that we begin our analysis of Philadelphia with an appreciation of the historical interplay between private enterprise and public policy that shaped its economic development, an interplay that shifted the types and locations of economic activity in the metropolitan region and continually redefined the opportunity structure for the region and its people. In theoretical terms, we see Philadelphia's development as defined by a capitalism constrained, aided, and redefined by public policies that create, limit, and reorganize markets for labor and goods and services.

The fact that capital investment is fixed geographically for substantial amounts of time is of critical importance. It means that some markets are local—perhaps limited to a neighborhood or community—and that all have localized implications even as they seek sales afar. And from the outset, public policies shape the patterns of private investment by defining the ways in which land is transformed into a commodity that can be bought and sold—by creating real estate.[1] While investors can and do shift their investments to obtain higher profits and increased liquidity, and may do so in response to public policies that discourage investments in some locations and encourage them in others, they leave behind them landscapes of their own construction. These settings of dwellings and stores, of manufacturing plants and service centers, channel the course of future investment as well as economic, social, and political efforts to preserve, protect, and promote the investments that remain. The results are neighborhoods and communities, a city and its suburbs, whose futures are molded by their pasts.

Philadelphia's origins were as a part of a quasi-religious utopian experiment of William Penn, who successfully established the central area of Philadelphia in 1683, laying out a grid system of streets and properties that persists to the present day. The grid pattern chosen by Penn reflected not only his aesthetic preference for ordered, rectangular blocks but also his acumen as a real estate developer. Hoping to profit from the sale of land in the new colonial city, Penn chose a ground plan that allowed for quick and easy trading in land as a commodity. The grid, which Philadelphians extended outward in the eighteenth century as the urban economy grew, was an "ideal method, since it treated all land similarly, for a real estate market composed of hundreds of speculators and home builders and thousands of petty landlords and small home buyers."[2]

Although William Penn had intended, as a health measure, that Philadelphia would be a city of single-family houses on large lots, subsequent generations of builders and property owners thwarted his plans by drastically increasing the density of land coverage. As large landholders sold off their farms for residential development, speculative builders endeavored to multiply the number of streets available to them and the number of houses per street. One way they accomplished this was by maximizing their street frontage: eliminating diagonal streets that did not conform to the grid pattern and subdividing Penn's grid blocks by adding streets and alleys between the originally planned streets. Another way they increased density was by the introduction of the rowhouse.

The classic Philadelphia rowhouse, a variation on the London design, was built up against the sidewalk with a front footage of 12 to 22 feet and a service alley leading to a rear yard. By 1800, rowhouses had become the dominant form of residence in Philadelphia. They were attractive not only to speculators but also to homeowners, being cheap to buy and maintain, with their brick facades and attached party walls. Inexpensive and private, rowhouses provided ownership opportunities for many working-class families who would have lived in tenements in other cities. This architectural form in large part accounts for the relatively large proportion of owner-occupied housing in Philadelphia.[3]

Philadelphia's position in the larger world system of cities influenced its internal growth and development. As a port city in the British colony, Philadelphia rose to prominence as a national center of the agrarian United States. The largest city in the Colonies until the development of the Erie Canal, it was the gateway to Ohio, Illinois, and Indiana, the early American Northwest. The economy centered on trade and small-scale production. The port on the Delaware River was the center of the town's activities, even though Penn's planned street grid stretched many blocks off to the west. Outside the city's northern and southern boundaries of Vine and South streets, the suburban districts of Northern Liberties and Southwark housed those members of the poor and working class who could not afford to live in the more established city neighborhoods.

The city was small and densely populated. Although there was some clustering of types of industry and some residential differentiation by occupation and social class, the degree of segregation was limited by the fact that walking was the main mode of transportation. Independent artisans, a large category of the workforce, tended to work at home or in an adjacent structure, as did innkeepers. Even merchants and port workers lived only a few blocks from their work places.

Philadelphia's geographical growth in the nineteenth century was complicated by the fact that, in addition to a straightforward pattern of growth outward from the center, the city also built up around the nuclei of several smaller nearby villages. Some of these adjacent districts, such as Southwark, Northern Liberties, and Spring Garden, were primarily suburbs, but others, such as Germantown, Manayunk, and Frankford, were independent communities. In 1854 the city and county were consolidated, increasing the area of the city from 2 to 100 square miles (see Figure 1.1). Many city neighborhoods have retained their names from their preconsolidation existence.[4]

When the industrial revolution occurred in Philadelphia, most of the available land close to the center of urban activity was already occupied by political, commercial, or residential activity. Only the waterfront boasted any industry to speak of, and that was largely limited to shipbuilding and its associated activities (wood treatments, rope making, and the like). Most available land for intensive industrial development lay to the north and south of the central city areas, in the Kensington, Northern Liberties, and Southwark areas of the city. These lands were essentially agricultural or swamp lands and were quickly transformed to industrial use, with its concomitant workers' housing. Early industrial development in Philadelphia was thus forced both upriver and downriver from the early settlement clustered around the port—a shift that represented the first, but certainly not the last, time that existing economic uses helped determine the location and pattern of new development.

Nineteenth-century industrialization created an immense diversity of manufacturing firms. The city's boosters boasted about this variety when they appealed to entrepreneurs to locate in Philadelphia. One of the city's leading iron manufacturers and Republican leaders played on this theme to make the case that the nation's centennial celebration in 1876 should be held in the Quaker city: "If it is conceded that an industrial exhibition is to be made in the city where the industries are found in greatest variety and perfection, no further enumeration of Philadelphia's advantages or claims need be made."[5] In 1880 the leading industry was clothing and textiles, which employed more than 40 percent of the city's workforce. But the other 60 percent was scattered across a wide range of manufacturing: machine tools and hardware (7 percent), shoes and boots (5 percent), paper and printing (4 percent), iron and steel (2 percent), lumber and wood (3 percent), glass (2 percent), furniture (2 percent), chemicals (2 percent), shipbuilding (2 percent) and a host of other, smaller sectors.[6]

This remarkable industrial base was spread across the city, creating a variety of specialized districts: the leather and wool district expanding northeast from the center of town, the south-side garment sweatshops, the

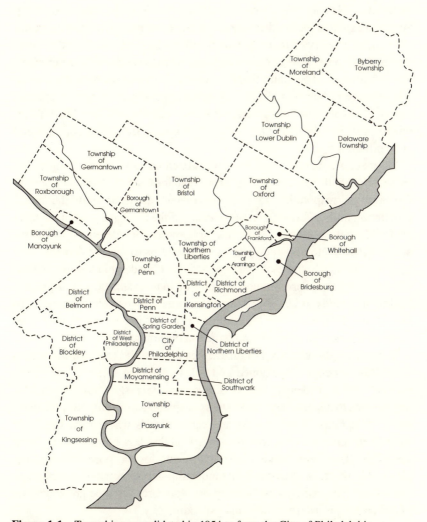

Figure 1.1 Townships consolidated in 1854 to form the City of Philadelphia
Source: Philadelphia City Planning Commission. *Philadelphia: A City of Neighborhoods* (Philadelphia, 1976).

furniture and woodworking in West Philadelphia, and the metalworking on the northwest side of town. Unlike some industrial centers, Philadelphia retained many small manufacturers throughout the industrial era and into the twentieth century.

Even the city's largest industry, textiles and apparel, was composed mainly of establishments that were small by the standards of Lowell (Massachusetts), Newark (New Jersey), and other textile towns. Historian Philip Scranton explains the smaller size of Philadelphia textile mills as the result of financial conservatism on the part of mill owners, who preferred to operate on a cash basis instead of borrowing to finance their plants, equipment, and inventories.[7] The claim that Philadelphia's capitalists have been more conservative in business affairs than other urban elites is one that appears repeatedly in accounts of this city's history. Sociologist Digby Baltzell and others have cited this stodginess as a factor limiting the city's economic and civic progress.[8]

Yet its consequences have not always been negative. For example, because nineteenth-century textile firms remained small, they had greater flexibility in responding to changing market demands than the mass-production mills of Lowell. At the opening of the Civil War, when the market for blankets, uniforms, and knitwear boomed, Philadelphia mill owners adapted their factories quickly to meet federal procurement demands and captured the lion's share of war production.[9] Philadelphia's industrialization suggests that our common reading of industrialization as a process leading inevitably to larger and larger factories may need to be revised. In fact, some of the reason for Philadelphia's success in the industrial era may hinge on its mixture of small and large establishments.[10]

Today's neighborhoods of Philadelphia contain the relics of the industrialization process. Abandoned and still functioning factories are cheek by jowl with high-density blocks of two- and three-story rowhouses. Old monuments to upper- and middle-class conspicuous consumption, the mansions of captains of industry, sit in neighborhoods where their large lots have been replaced with row housing. Middle-class homes dating from the 1920s have been divided into apartments for the poor and working classes. In short, investment in the industrial development of the city, and concurrent requirements for housing the workforce, created an integration of old communities into a new and expanding city.

Population and Settlement Patterns

With the onset of the industrial era, which reached its apogee between 1880 and 1930, Philadelphia's population increased dramatically, largely as a result of European migration. This was followed in turn by a substantial migration of southern blacks during World War I and immediately after. The combination of ethnic communities and racial segregation that characterized many neighborhoods of the city can be seen as the immediate

Table 1.1   The growth of the Philadelphia metropolitan area population, 1850–1950

	Total population		% black	% of population residing in central city		Black population as % of total	
	White	Black	% black	White	Black	City	Suburbs
1850	663,461	34,079	4.9	58.6	58.0	4.8	5.0
1860	869,644	37,768	4.2	62.5	58.7	3.9	4.6
1870	1,016,427	42,107	4.0	64.1	52.6	3.3	5.2
1880	1,239,893	56,095	4.3	65.8	56.5	3.7	5.4
1890	1,508,458	69,410	4.4	66.7	56.7	3.8	5.6
1900	1,787,991	102,226	5.4	68.8	61.2	4.8	6.6
1910	2,136,501	130,062	5.7	68.5	64.9	5.5	6.3
1920	2,521,310	191,222	7.0	67.0	70.2	7.4	6.4
1930	2,834,785	299,898	9.6	61.0	73.2	11.3	6.8
1940	2,862,794	334,543	10.5	58.6	75.0	13.0	6.6
1950	3,187,121	480,075	13.1	53.1	78.3	18.2	6.5

Sources: The Seventh Census of the United States, 1850 (Washington, D.C.: Robert Armstrong, Public Printer, 1853); *Population of the United States in 1860, Compiled from the Original Returns of the Eighth Census* (1864); *Ninth Census—Volume 1—The Statistics of the United States* (1872); *Statistics of the Population of the United States at the Tenth Census (June 1, 1880)* (1883); *Report on Population of the United States at the Eleventh Census: 1890—Part 1* (1895); *Census Reports Volume 1—Twelfth Census of the United States Taken in the Year 1900—Population, Part I* (1901); *Thirteenth Census of the United States Taken in the Year 1910—Population, Part I* (1913); *Fourteenth Census of the United States Taken in the Year 1920—Volume II—Population General Report and Analytical Tables* (1921); *Fifteenth Census of the United States: 1930. Volume III—Population— Reports by States* (1931); *U.S. Census of Population, 1940: Population and Housing Statistics for Census Tracts, Philadelphia, Pennsylvania* (1942); *U.S. Census of Population, 1950: Census Tract Statistics Vol. III, Chap. 42, (P-042) Philadelphia, Pennsylvania and Adjacent Area* (1952). All published in Washington, D.C., by the Government Printing Office unless specified otherwise.

precursor to modern Philadelphia. Table 1.1 summarizes information about the size and location of the black and white populations in the Philadelphia metropolitan area from 1850 to 1950. It shows that from the Civil War to World War I, Philadelphia's black population hovered between 4 percent and 6 percent of the total population, keeping pace with the growth of the white population resulting from the arrival of European immigrants.

Interestingly, the figures in Table 1.1 demonstrate that the pattern of black concentration in the central city and white domination of the suburbs has not always been characteristic of Philadelphia. Indeed, during the nineteenth century blacks in Philadelphia were more suburbanized than whites. Since 1870, when about 50 percent of the region's black population lived in Philadelphia, blacks have become increasingly concentrated in the central city. By contrast, since 1900 whites have become increasingly suburbanized.

Table 1.2   Index of segregation for ethnic and
racial groups in Philadelphia, 1850–1950

	1850	1880	1910	1920	1930	1940	1950
Great Britain			.21	.21	.24	.23	.22
Germany	.37	.32	.25	.27	.32	.35	.31
Ireland	.35	.28	.20	.20	.28	.32	.29
Italy			.61	.53	.59	.60	.54
Poland				.52	.54	.57	.54
Russia			.58	.50	.56	.57	.54
Black	.53	.61	.46	.45	.61	.68	.71

Source: Theodore Hershberg et al., "A Tale of Three Cities: Blacks and Immigrants in Philadelphia: 1850–1880, 1930 and 1970," *Annals of the American
Academy of Political and Social Science* 441 (1979): 55–81.

Note: The table reports "Foreign Born" for 1910, 1920, 1940, 1950, and "Foreign stock" for 1850, 1880, 1930, on the basis of 248 identical geographic areas for
1850, 1880, 1930, and on 47 wards for 1910 and 1920.

Within the city itself, the experience of black Philadelphians differed
dramatically from that of European immigrants. To a much higher extent, blacks have historically lived in segregated communities. Presented in
Table 1.2 are indices of segregation that measure the extent of residential
segregation for the city's racial and ethnic groups for each census year between 1850 and 1950. (See Appendix A for an explanation of the index of
dissimilarity.) Note that the level of segregation experienced by the Germans and Irish, who entered the city in the middle of the nineteenth century,
was substantially lower than the segregation of the Italians, Poles, and Russians, who arrived in Philadelphia around the turn of the century. At all
times except 1910 and 1920, blacks were more segregated than any other
group, and their separation increased significantly in the twentieth century.

We can explain these patterns of segregation largely in terms of the
basic structure of the city, the opportunities that it provided, as well as the
changing positions of particular groups in the urban opportunity structure.
For most of the nineteenth century Philadelphia continued its colonial pattern as a "walking city" characterized by considerable population density,
centralized economic activity, and few socioeconomic distinctions among
neighborhoods. The low levels of ethnic segregation found in the nineteenth
century reflected, as in the eighteenth, the density of settlement, centralized
industrial employment, and the need for almost everyone to walk to work.
The Irish, Germans, and blacks, though concentrated in a few neighborhoods, were, by today's standards, residentially integrated with the native
white population.

By the beginning of the twentieth century industrialization had changed the picture substantially. The electric streetcar had made it possible for white-collar workers to commute to work in the central city from the new bedroom communities in West and North Philadelphia. Historians refer to these communities as "streetcar suburbs," even though they were located inside the city's boundaries. More important for the development of ethnic communities, industrial employment had expanded and concentrated in the northeastern and southern sectors of the city.

Immigrants from different nations came with different skills. The passenger manifests of the immigrant ships document the informal social organization that characterized the "huddled masses" immigrating from Europe. Individuals and families followed migration chains—informal networks of friends and relatives. The results of different skills and networks was a "cultural division of labor," with ethnic and national groups being concentrated in different industries and occupations. Thus, in 1900 Germans and British were overrepresented as manufacturing workers. Russians were especially concentrated in tailoring and in leather products. Italians and Poles had substantial minorities who were laborers. The Poles were concentrated in iron, steel, and leather produce manufacture; the Italians, in tailoring.

As Golab has shown, the occupational concentrations of immigrants influenced their choice of neighborhoods.[11] Manufacturing and wholesale centers provided employment for the newly arriving immigrants who established "ethnic villages" in Kensington, Schuylkill, Manayunk, and South Philadelphia close to their work places. These were "ghettoes of opportunity" that provided the social and institutional supports for the emergence of American ethnic groups.

The growth of the black ghetto, however, cannot be explained by the proximity to work. In 1930 more than 80 percent of the black population lived in areas that were within one mile of five thousand or more industrial jobs, yet less than 13 percent of black workers were employed in manufacturing. Blacks were more likely to be employed as laborers, servants, and waiters. Unlike the white ethnic communities whose neighborhoods were "ghettoes of opportunity," black communities tended to be "ghettoes of last resort"—residential areas that had been rejected or abandoned by other ethnic groups.

Machine Politics in the Industrial Era

As it did in many nineteenth-century American cities, the political machine operated in Philadelphia as a buffer between investors whose capital built the city's factories, houses, and trolley lines, and the working people of all nationalities who crowded into the neighborhoods. Ethnic and racial cohesion within the city's neighborhoods facilitated ward organizations and made possible almost a hundred years of machine-style politics. From 1850 to 1950 a Republican machine controlled Philadelphia, challenged only intermittently and unsuccessfully by temporary coalitions of reformers.[12]

The literature on the municipal reform movement identifies bankers, businessmen, lawyers, and other upper-class individuals as leading proponents of reform. Oddly enough, Philadelphia's business community proved extremely tolerant toward a machine whose operation was in many respects detrimental to Philadelphia commerce and industry. For example, the politicians' ruinous neglect of the city's harbor facilities in the latter part of the nineteenth century brought the port by 1907 to the point at which "there is but one covered pier at which a steamship of any considerable draft with miscellaneous cargo can unload."[13] Other major community assets, like the gas works and the public transportation system, were similarly exploited by the machine, to the disadvantage of Philadelphia's businesses and citizens. Yet in the face of this mismanagement, Philadelphia remained "corrupt and contented."[14] The reformist wave that swept other American cities in the early twentieth century left Philadelphia's machine relatively undisturbed until after World War II. Why?

One oft-repeated explanation for the machine's survival in Philadelphia is the Quaker influence among the city's commercial and industrial elites. Quaker merchants and bankers, it has been said, avoided active involvement in politics rather than using their economic base to influence municipal government. Thus, the core of the city's commercial leadership declined to exercise its authority to promote civic betterment.[15]

There is another, equally plausible, explanation for the business community's tolerance for a corrupt and inefficient municipal administration well into the twentieth century. Philadelphia manufacturers tolerated the city's Republican machine because it produced a congressional delegation that consistently supported protective tariffs, shielding American industry from foreign competitors. Boies Penrose, a Philadelphia Republican and U.S. senator for twenty-four years (1897 to 1921), became a champion for protectionism in Washington. Philadelphia industrialists were not moved to throw the Republican rascals out because, in doing so, they might have lost powerful allies in Congress. According to one observer at the time, "the smug prosperity enjoyed by the manufacturers of Philadelphia, as the result of tariff favors, has lulled the conscience of the people and made them look upon corrupt and expensive government as a comparatively unimportant incident in a career of peaceful industry and the accumulation of wealth." [16]

What the machine supplied to Philadelphia industrialists was congressional support for protective tariffs. What it offered to the poor immigrants in the German, Irish, and Italian sections of the city was jobs. By the Republican party's own account in 1879, the total number of employees who owed their jobs to the party boss, "King" James McManes, was 5,630.[17] Although black voters, it appears, never shared proportionately in the machine's patronage, a certain number of key organizers in the so-called Negro wards did secure city positions (much to the dismay of W. E. B. DuBois, who chastised his fellow blacks for succumbing to the temptation to sell their votes for personal gain).[18]

What the machine did *not* provide for the citizens of Philadelphia was any consistent representation of the public interest in guiding the city's dramatic economic expansion during the era of industrialization. As Warner has so eloquently argued, rather than being shaped by public planning, Philadelphia grew upward and outward on the strength of private schemes.[19] Street railways, which played a crucial role in determining the patterns of residential and commercial growth, were operated by dozens of different private companies in the latter half of the nineteenth century. Even when the city moved in 1901 to create a single, integrated transit company for all public transportation, the company was held by private investors who were awarded a blanket fifty-year contract by the city government. Nor was the city's port—the key to its commercial vitality—under public supervision. In 1909 the municipality controlled barely 8 percent of the 7-mile-long Delaware River waterfront; all the rest was controlled by private owners, principally railroad companies.[20] Thus, major elements of the urban infrastructure that undergirded the city's development were beyond the reach of municipal government.

Politically, the legacy of the industrial era in Philadelphia, as in other American cities, was a politics based on the organization's ability to deliver jobs, services, and favors to constituents in the wards, and a politics that tolerated an antiquated municipal administration. In 1927 a Philadelphia novelist symbolized the city's municipal backwardness in its "City Hall, symbol of dishonesty and ugliness, squatting over the city's heart, its immense meaningless bulk blocking traffic where it was thickest, wasting space, shutting out sun and air from the gloomy ruins within." [21]

The Transition to Postindustrialism

The drastic economic shift that transformed Philadelphia from a port city providing access to a vast hinterland to an industrial and commercial center within a specialized and integrated national economy is not the last development point in this picture. Economists may view the Great Depression as a temporary aberration in the developmental curve of the nation's economy, but for Philadelphia it was a watershed. It signaled the beginning of the end of industrial production as the backbone of the city's economic base.

The forces of national and international expansion after the Depression deeply affected the traditional locations of industry. From a peak of 39 percent in 1920, the percentage of the nation's labor force employed in manufacturing dropped to only 21 percent by 1984. Explaining these national trends helps us to understand the changes that took place in Philadelphia. First, technological improvements permitted manufacturers to expand production with fewer workers. As automation increased the efficiency and volume of production, manufacturers devoted even greater efforts to marketing their products, thereby stimulating service employment. To reduce their costs, manufacturers reduced their workforces, increasingly purchasing engineering, advertising, accounting, legal, financial, and other support services from outside companies rather than trying to produce these service internally. Smaller firms were increasingly absorbed into giant conglomerates with the ability to shift production from one area to another. Finally, as other nations industrialized, competition by foreign firms also undercut American manufacturers on the grounds of cost, quality, or both.

It was partly a recognition of the increasing economic competition facing Philadelphia in the 1940s, and the need for an aggressive municipal response, that galvanized a group of civic and business leaders to challenge the Republican machine that had monopolized City Hall for so long. The challengers were emboldened by the general spirit of optimism that followed America's overseas triumph in World War II and convinced that the city could not prosper in the postwar economic climate with the obsolete structures that dotted its central area, the decaying transportation and education systems, and the city's moldering governmental machinery.

Beginning in the late 1940s a coalition of lawyers, bankers, business people, and representatives of various civic organizations joined forces to support a platform that, in many respects, duplicated the standard Progressive litany. They aspired to purge municipal government corruption, install a new professionalism in city departments, improve the efficiency of services, and minimize the influence of patronage in filling city jobs.

To replace the machine, the city's business and civic elite proposed a more rational, businesslike approach to municipal government. They rewrote the city's Home Rule Charter to enhance the power of the mayor, to reorganize the City Council, to strengthen the civil service system, and to expand the role of the city planning commission. Only months after the new charter was adopted in 1951, they succeeded in getting a leading reformer, Joseph Clark, elected as mayor and fifteen reform Democrats elected as members of the reorganized City Council. Clark was followed in office by another reform Democrat, Mayor Richardson Dilworth.

As in so many other American cities, reform politics in Philadelphia was closely linked to an emerging planning apparatus and a program for physical renewal. One account of this period written by an insider suggests that the reformers' interest in city planning was actually a cover for their interest in governmental reform.[22] Not long after his election, reform mayor Clark launched a series of projects to remove outdated structures from the downtown area and to replace them with office towers, luxury housing, university expansion, and specialized shops.

For reasons that we outline in Chapter 5, the reform spirit lasted only a decade in Philadelphia. Nevertheless, the reformers achieved far-reaching changes in the structures of municipal government and in the Philadelphia skyline. They fundamentally reorganized the city government's financial, planning, and record-keeping systems. And they initiated a plan for physical renewal that guided the city's redevelopment efforts in the downtown area all the way through the early 1980s.

If we can label the reformers' approach to transforming downtown Philadelphia a "success," we cannot be so generous in characterizing their efforts to revitalize the city's residential neighborhoods. In a "city of neighborhoods," the neighborhoods have been the main victims of gradual disinvestment that government policies have failed to stem. As in many American cities, the shift of production southward and westward in the United States, and later overseas, has reverberated throughout the city's residential neighborhoods. As we see in Chapter 3, problems of abandonment, gentrification, and homelessness resulted from the economic and population shifts accompanying the new postindustrial order. Further, the older problems persisted and interacted with the newer ones: segregation produced redlining, which produced further segregation and abandonment.

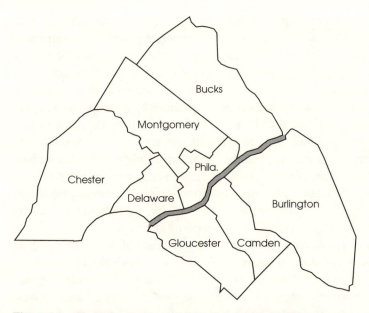

Figure 1.2   The eight-county area of the Philadelphia SMSA

Gentrification was demonstrably linked to the racial composition of neigh-borhoods. These unfortunate patterns reflected a city in flux—shedding its industrial framework and rebuilding on a service economy base, dealing with a substantially decentralized economic and social base that was largely beyond its political control.

The balance of population and economic activity began shifting toward the suburbs as early as the 1920s, but the city's dominance in the region was not seriously challenged until after World War II. (For a map of the region, see Figure 1.2.) In Table 1.3 we see that by 1960 the suburbs had gained more than half of the region's residents; by 1980 the suburban share had grown to almost two-thirds of the total population. Employment fol-lowed people to the suburbs, lagging a bit behind the shift in population. Yet by 1980 the office and industrial parks, shopping malls, and other sub-urban employers were providing close to two-thirds of the region's jobs. Of course, the positive suburban trends did not affect all townships evenly. In Montgomery County, for instance, two older centers, Norristown and Pottstown, suffered losses even while the nearby retail and industrial devel-opment at King of Prussia mushroomed.

The job opportunities and housing opportunities that the suburbs offered

Table 1.3   County population and employment shares, 1950–1980

County	Population				Employment			
	1950	1960	1970	1980	1951	1959	1970	1980
Philadelphia	56.4%	46.1%	40.4%	35.8%	67.5%	60.2%	51.2%	38.6%
Bucks	3.9	7.1	8.6	10.2	2.9	4.2	6.1	9.1
Chester	4.3	4.8	5.8	6.7	2.9	3.8	4.8	6.6
Delaware	11.3	12.7	12.5	11.8	7.7	8.5	9.0	9.8
Montgomery	9.6	11.9	12.9	13.6	9.0	11.2	15.6	19.4
Burlington	3.7	5.2	6.7	7.7	1.8	2.6	3.6	5.0
Camden	8.2	9.0	9.5	10.0	7.0	7.8	7.8	8.7
Gloucester	2.5	3.1	3.6	4.2	1.2	1.6	1.9	2.7

Sources: U.S. Census of Population, 1950: Characteristics of Population, Part 40 (1955); *U.S. Census of Population, 1960: Characteristics of Population*, Part 40 (1963); *U.S. Census of Population, 1970: Charac-teristics of Population*, Part 40, sec. 2 (1973); *U.S. Census of Population and Housing, 1980: 5% Microdata File*, prepared by the Bureau of the Census (machine-readable data file) (Washington, D.C., 1983); *County Business Patterns, 1951: United States Summary* (Part 1) (1955); *County Business Patterns, 1951: Middle Atlantic States* (Part 3) (1955); *County Business Patterns, 1959: United States Summary* (Part 1) (1963); *County Business Patterns, 1959: Middle Atlantic States* (Parts 3a and 3b) (1963); *County Business Patterns, 1970: United States Summary* (CBP-70-1) (1971); *County Business Patterns, 1970: New Jersey* (CBP-70-32) (1971); *County Business Patterns, 1970: Pennsylvania* (CBP-70-40) (1971); *County Business Patterns, 1980: United States Summary* (CBP-80-1) (1982); *County Business Patterns, 1980: New Jersey* (CBP-80-32) (1982); *County Business Patterns, 1980: Pennsylvania* (CBP-80-40) (1982). All published in Washington, D.C., by the Government Printing Office unless specified otherwise.

in the 1960s and 1970s drew a population that was younger, whiter, and better educated than city residents. Not all of the new suburbanites were refugees from Philadelphia itself. Many who moved into the new housing developments in Montgomery and Bucks counties, and into the small towns of southern New Jersey, were families from other metropolitan areas.

During these decades of suburban expansion, as Philadelphia's popula-tion was shrinking, those who remained in the city were disproportionately its minority residents (see Table 1.4).

Like the racial profile of city and suburban residents, the educational profiles have become more dissimilar since 1960 (see Table 1.5). In 1960, when only 5 percent of the city's population was college educated, the most highly educated suburban population, that of Montgomery County, had 13.5 percent college educated—a difference of only 8.5 percentage points. As of 1980, the city trailed the best-educated suburban county on this indicator by 15 percentage points. Nor can the city expect to narrow this gap, given its inability to spend as much on educating its youngsters as the suburban townships spend. In 1985 suburbs on the Pennsylvania side

Table 1.4 Nonwhite population as
percentage of whole, Philadelphia
area by counties, 1960 and 1980

County	1960	1980
Philadelphia	26.7%	41.5%
Bucks	1.9	3.6
Chester	8.4	9.0
Delaware	7.1	10.0
Montgomery	3.8	6.1
Burlington	6.9	15.4
Camden	9.2	18.6
Gloucester	9.2	9.6

Sources: U.S. Bureau of the Census, *City
and County Data Book* (Washington, D.C.:
Government Printing Office, 1962, 1983).

Table 1.5 College-educated population
as percentage of whole, Philadelphia
area by counties, 1960 and 1980

County	1960	1980	Percentage point change, 1960–1980
Philadelphia	5.0	11.0	6.0
Bucks	9.0	13.5	4.5
Chester	11.5	26.0	14.5
Delaware	11.5	19.0	7.5
Montgomery	13.5	25.0	11.5
Burlington	8.0	18.5	10.5
Camden	7.0	16.0	9.0
Gloucester	6.0	13.0	7.0

*Sources: U.S. Census of Population, 1960: Character-
istics of Population*, Part 40 (Washington, D.C.: Government Printing Office, 1963); *U.S. Census of Population and Housing, 1980: 5% Microdata File*, prepared
by the Bureau of the Census (machine-readable data file)
(Washington, D.C., 1983).

of the region spent an average of $4,058 per child, and the New Jersey
suburbs spent an average of $4,033, while the Philadelphia school district
spent only $3,727 per child.)[23]

Even more striking than the demographic disparities in the region are the
diverging economic indicators in the city and suburbs. The seven suburban
counties that surround Philadelphia divide generally into two categories.

Table 1.6 Per capita income (in 1967 dollars) in the Philadelphia SMSA, 1960–1980

County	1960	1980	Change 1960–1980
Philadelphia	$2,121	$2,496	17.7%
Bucks	2,267	3,319	46.4
Chester	2,398	3,614	50.7
Delaware	2,617	3,317	26.8
Montgomery	3,181	3,943	26.2
Burlington	2,256	3,163	40.2
Camden	2,364	3,001	26.9
Gloucester	2,133	2,861	35.4

Source: Anita Summers and Thomas Luce, *Economic Development within the Philadelphia Metropolitan Area* (Philadelphia: University of Pennsylvania Press, 1987), p. 22.

The high-growth counties of Bucks and Chester (in Pennsylvania) and Burlington and Gloucester (in New Jersey) have seen dramatic increases in both employment and population in the past two decades. Not surprisingly, per capita incomes in these counties (measured in constant dollars) also rose substantially between 1960 and 1980, at rates of increase on the order of 35 to 50 percent. In the three moderate-growth counties—Montgomery and Delaware (in Pennsylvania) and Camden (in New Jersey)—incomes rose by about 25 percent. Philadelphians, however, saw only an 18 percent gain in their incomes from 1960 to 1980 (see Table 1.6).

The 1980s brought an extraordinary economic boom to the region. From the end of the 1981–82 recession, employment has grown dramatically in the Philadelphia metropolitan area. Table 1.7 shows that in all eight counties of the metropolitan area, including Philadelphia, employment grew substantially between 1982 and 1987. That growth was especially strong in service employment, up 24 percent over the five-year period. At the same time, a building boom drove up construction employment by an astonishing 49 percent. Almost as impressive was the growth in jobs in finance, insurance, and real estate (see Figure 1.3). Some of the growth was the result of expansion by the city's largest employers, especially hospitals, colleges, and universities, and commercial and savings banks. But many more jobs were created in smaller firms, employing fewer than a hundred employees. The greater Philadelphia region now ranks among the most diversified economies in the country, with a mix of services and industries very similar to that of the United States as a whole.

Table 1.7 Total employment and unemployment
in the Philadelphia area, 1982 and 1987

	October 1982		October 1987	
County	Total employment	Unemploy- ment rate	Total employment	Unemploy- ment rate
Philadelphia	631,000	9.8%	712,300	6.5%
Bucks	237,100	8.7	281,700	3.9
Chester	156,200	7.6	184,000	3.3
Delaware	251,200	7.5	291,500	3.8
Montgomery	321,600	7.1	376,100	3.6
Burlington	157,400*	6.1	179,400	2.9
Camden	202,900*	8.1	226,500	3.8
Gloucester	86,700*	7.5	98,400	3.6

Sources: U.S. Bureau of Labor Statistics, *Local Area Unemployment Statistics*
(Washington, D.C.: U.S. Department of Labor, 1982; 1987).
*Not precisely comparable to 1987 figures because of changes in methodology.

Perhaps the most visible outward sign of the employment gains is a boom
in office construction that has dramatically altered Philadelphia's skyline in
only a few years. In the 1980s city businesses absorbed new office space at
an average rate of 1.4 million square feet per year. Investors had regained
confidence in downtown Philadelphia as a real estate market and seemed
eager to invest. Particularly striking was the flood of foreign investments
in real estate. Asahi Mutual Life Insurance Company of Japan paid $35
million for a half-interest in the thirty-two-story IVB Bank Building at 17th
and Market streets. Japanese banks were prominent investors in a $113
million hotel and retail complex, Two Liberty Place, at 17th and Chestnut streets. The government of Singapore bought Four Penn Center. And
a French bank, Banque de Paribas, became the lead lender on a fifty-four-
story tower, the Mellon Bank Center, as well as helping to finance the $80
million renovation of the 30th Street Railroad Station at the western edge
of the downtown.

Foreign investors also ventured into the suburbs during the 1980s.
Japan's largest life insurance company, Nippon Life Insurance Company,
refinanced the Court and Plaza at King of Prussia, a massive shopping
center in Montgomery County. Swiss interests bought Suburban Square in
Ardmore on the Main Line. And at the Great Valley Corporate Center, a
Chester County industrial and office park, five foreign-owned companies
began turning out products ranging from disposable diapers to brake lin-
ings for locomotives, industrial vacuum cleaners, bakery equipment, and
airplane instruments.

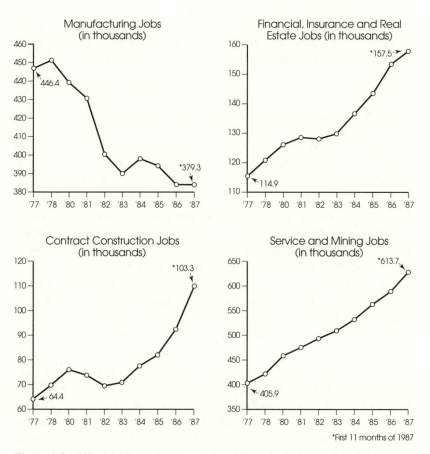

Figure 1.3   Philadelphia area employment: Number of jobs by sector in the eight-county area

Sources: U.S. Department of Labor, Bureau of Labor Statistics Monthly Civilian Labor Force Estimates. (Washington: D.C. Government Printing Office, 1977–1987 [annual]).

After several decades of steady decline Philadelphians are understandably buoyed by the good economic news of the 1980s. Yet to anyone who lives or works in the city, it is apparent that the good times have not reached into all of its neighborhoods. Indeed, some groups seem needier than ever before. Poverty, homelessness, illiteracy, and health problems continue to haunt some residents of Philadelphia, Camden, Chester, Norristown, Bristol, and many older communities in the region. Prosperity is skewed by the legacy of past patterns of employment, ownership, education, and residence, which continues to influence the distribution of opportunities today. Nowhere are the effects of this skewed opportunity structure more evident than in the city's race relations. The economic restructuring has increased competition between lower- and working-class blacks and whites in the city, fueling racial tension that erupts periodically into open conflict.

Declining Economic Opportunity and Racial Conflict

On October 31, 1985, a young black couple returned to their newly pur-chased home in Southwest Philadelphia to find a soft-drink bottle had been thrown through the window. Three weeks later a crowd of some four hun-dred white neighbors gathered in a "peaceful demonstration" outside their house. On December 12 the house was burned. Just seven months earlier vandals had driven another black couple from their newly purchased home nearby. Racial conflict was not new to the area: in April of 1980 a gang of twenty-five to thirty young blacks had beaten and stabbed a white teenager, apparently in retaliation for a stabbing that had taken place on a trolley a week earlier. In 1979 two white men had crawled onto the roof of a factory and shot the first black who came by.

All of these incidents took place in a single neighborhood in South-west Philadelphia. The area, Woodlawn, was originally built around the turn of the century as a streetcar suburb and became the home of second-generation white ethnics—Italians, Irish, Poles—who had "made it." Over the past forty years the neighborhood had undergone considerable change. Home ownership is high, but relatively few young people have chosen to move in, and thus the population has been declining and the number of vacant homes has increased. An all-white neighborhood, Woodlawn sits next to an area that underwent racial transition during the 1960s and 1970s. In a very real sense Woodlawn's residents may be viewed as "trapped." An increasingly elderly population of homeowners, they find themselves in a housing market where demand is so low that it is impossible to sell their houses for enough money to purchase other homes elsewhere. Unable to move, the residents of Woodlawn have chosen to resist the encroachment of blacks.

Woodlawn is not the only neighborhood in Philadelphia that is character-ized by racial tension and conflict. In one recent year (1986) more than three hundred interracial "incidents" were called to the attention of the city's human relations commission. Interracial tension and conflict are products of the changing social structure that accompanies the postindustrial trans-formation. When groups come into direct competition for scarce resources,

Table 1.8   Percentage of respondents who agreed with statements on racial attitudes

Statement	Percentage agreeing	
	White	Black
I would not want a member of my family to bring a black (white) friend home to dinner.	12.3%	1.4%
In order to maintain a nice neighborhood, blacks (whites) should be prevented from living in it.	16.0	na
White and black students should attend separate schools.	6.6	.9
If necessary, black and white children should be bussed to schools outside their neighborhood in order to achieve racial integration.	27.5	92.8

intergroup tension emerges, group boundaries become crystallized, and conflict is the likely result.

That competition extends to both the job market and the housing market. Whites and blacks who have less than a high school education are competing for fewer and fewer well-paying jobs that require only a limited education. Moreover, they are competing for neighborhoods. White working-class communities, geographically proximate to the city's old manufacturing centers, have been characterized by high rates of home ownership and residential stability. The closing of nearby manufacturing plants has meant the loss of the economic core upon which these communities were built and increasing poverty. There is little to attract the younger generation; thus the population is not being replaced, and the remaining population is aging. Housing values have not kept up with inflation, and more and more blocks are dotted with vacant and abandoned homes. The prices in some of these neighborhoods make them attractive to black buyers. And yet, despite the proximity of these neighborhoods to the growing black population, they have remained predominantly white.

In an attitude survey done in 1976 a representative sample of 1,492 Philadelphians was interviewed. The results are presented in Table 1.8. They show that whites are more likely to express prejudicial attitudes than blacks. This pattern is perhaps best illustrated in responses to one additional question on the survey that is not shown in Table 1.8: "Would you prefer to live in a neighborhood with: (1) all whites, (2) mostly whites, (3) mostly blacks, or (4) one that is mixed half and half?" Almost 80 percent of whites expressed a preference for neighborhoods that are all or mostly white. By contrast, only 10 percent of blacks preferred a predominantly black neighborhood. Four times as many blacks (83 percent) as whites (18 percent) preferred an integrated neighborhood.

In order to examine the characteristics of those who expressed the most racial prejudice, we combined the individual items on the 1976 questionnaire into a single scale of racial attitudes. We found that the whites who were likely to score the highest (most prejudiced) on this scale were those who lived in the city as opposed to the suburbs, had less than a high school education, and lived in predominantly white neighborhoods that were stable and close to predominantly black areas. The most liberal racial attitudes were observed among whites living in neighborhoods that were racially integrated—defined as those in which at least 5 percent of the local population was black.

How do we explain this relationship between neighborhood type and racial prejudice? The answer lies in the different social and economic characteristics that are associated with different types of neighborhoods. In general, the city's stable white neighborhoods have large numbers of residents over fifty years old, whether those neighborhoods lie close to black concentrations or not. Yet in neighborhoods close to black areas, we found, residents were less likely to have finished high school and more likely to be employed as craftsmen, operatives, or laborers. The highest levels of education and occupational status were found among whites living in racially integrated neighborhoods. We conclude that the neighborhoods whose residents are most likely to encounter competition with blacks are those where prejudice is greatest.

The same conclusion results from an analysis of 316 interracial incidents reported to the Philadelphia Human Relations Commission during 1986. When we tested the association between several neighborhood characteristics and the level of racial tension (defined as the number of incidents per 10,000 population reported within the neighborhood), we found that the most important factors associated with racial tension in a neighborhood are the racial composition of the area and the loss of manufacturing jobs. As might be imagined, the greatest loss of manufacturing jobs has occurred in the older manufacturing areas of the city. Tension events are also positively associated with neighborhood stability and age of housing, and negatively correlated with the level of family income. These factors—job loss, older housing, residential stability, and low income—form a cluster of characteristics that perfectly describe the white working-class "urban villages."

If we compare the independent effects of each of these factors upon the

Table 1.9   Relative importance of neighborhood
characteristics in predicting racial tension

Variable	Beta weight	Significance
1980 population	.220	.000
Percentage elderly population	−.129	.026
Percentage white population	.464	.000
Median family income	−.296	.000
Racial segregation	.162	.021
Loss of manufacturing	.134	.012
Multiple R	.468	
R square	.219	

rates of interracial tensions (see Table 1.9), we find that the single most powerful predictor of racial tension is the white predominance in the area in 1980. Second is the median family income. The other important factors were the size of the population, the degree of segregation, the loss of manufacturing jobs, and the age of the population. Taken together, the data indicate that racial conflicts are more likely to occur in poorer white neighborhoods that are still viable in terms of their size and demographic makeup, but that have suffered from the recent transformation of the city from a center of manufacturing to a service center. In areas whose sense of community was based upon the presence of manufacturing, the economic vertebrae have weakened. When these communities are invaded or threatened by the migration of other racial or ethnic groups, their weakened economic competitiveness is transformed into community solidarity and conflict.

The image that persists is of neighborhoods displacing their anger at the economic declines accompanying the growth of the service sector onto the shoulders of those groups that are nearest. The legacy of racial ideologies and conflict that characterizes so much of America's history is brought to bear once again in a situation of economic change. The fact that minority communities in the city are experiencing the same travails as whites—and in some situations worse troubles—serves as an ironic footnote to these events.

The Central Argument of the Book

It is clear in retrospect that Philadelphia's industrial decline was due to a fundamental transformation in the types of businesses and labor-finding success within the region. Whereas recent works on urban change have stressed the rise of the service sector and the impact of corporate control centers on national and local economic patterns, our interpretation of Philadelphia's transition to postindustrialism stresses the interplay among local, national, and international markets for labor, goods, and services, public policies affecting both private and public investments, and aging physical, social, and economic structures.

Philadelphia is a city of old industrial plants in loft buildings; of neighborhoods that, like the industrial villages they once were, emphasize local interaction rather than easy access to the outside world; of rowhouses that are not easily adapted or transformed to more contemporary detached dwellings; of populations still being educated as industrial immigrants; of communities still organized around traditional ethnic and racial lines, and still excluded, in the main, from the benefits of the new economic order; of a city government that is funded on an inadequate, industrially oriented tax base; and of a growing black community systematically excluded from a declining industrial job base, being first the object of public policy and then shaping public policy in an era of extraordinary fiscal privation.

Although Philadelphia's suburbs are more advantaged, these advantages have only slowed rather than reversed the effects of the long-term decline of manufacturing. Indeed, the very nature of suburbs is to create balkanized communities unable to cooperate or to deal with the congestion and increased demand for public services that their growth produces. The result is a reprise of many of the complaints leveled against the city itself.

Philadelphia's shift to postindustrialism has increased the divisions among classes, races, and neighborhoods in both the city and suburbs. This divisiveness is not necessarily because the region is more heterogeneous than in the past. It is a mistake to assume, as many present-day commentators do, that Philadelphia was once a harmonious community of citizens sharing a common vision of development. In fact, Sam Bass Warner has demonstrated persuasively that, from its founding, Philadelphia has been composed of a collection of disparate interests, all pursuing their own ends in a highly "privatist" fashion. Philadelphia was never united by a single political and civic agenda; it was always composed of separate communities (as in the famed "city of neighborhoods").

What overlaid this parochialism in previous eras, however, was a network of linkages created by the economy. The preindustrial and industrial economies operated as the "glue" that held the region together. According to Warner's analysis, the diverse communities that inhabited preindustrial Philadelphia were held together by a "remarkably inclusive network of business and economic relationships." [24] Those links persisted well into the industrial era, when large manufacturers bought equipment, materials, and components from local suppliers, sold much of what they produced in the regional market, and reinvested a large portion of their profits within the region. The vast web of economic interconnections between firms and sections of the city helped to establish social and political cohesion in a diverse citizenry.

As the succeeding chapters show, the new postindustrial economy does not serve that same unifying function because of the kinds of industries it supports, because of the kinds of jobs it generates, because of the substitution of national and international linkages for what were previously local linkages, and because of the lopsided development pattern that fuels downtown growth at the expense of many neighborhoods. In the new economy a large number of the city's neighborhoods have simply become disconnected from the structures of opportunity. One recent study of the increase in pockets of urban deprivation in the 1970s reports that of America's fifty largest cities, Philadelphia fared the worst. [25] The report documented the extent to which urban poverty became concentrated during the 1970s in census tracts having at least twice the level of male unemployment, school leaving, single-parent families, and welfare recipients as the surrounding metropolitan region. From 1970 to 1980 the number of such tracts in Philadelphia, Camden, and Chester City—the region's three urban centers— grew from eight to forty-four. In this region even more than in other metropolitan areas, disparities in the character and quality of people's living environments widened dramatically.

Along with these disparities came growing gaps in people's life chances. For example, job training experts in the region say that many of the unemployed live in such total isolation from the world of steady work that they have little understanding of how it operates and no way to imagine themselves as part of it. Some candidates for training programs in the city report to interviewers that they do not know a single working adult. [26]

In the face of these growing disparities among economic and racial groups, the region's political infrastructure is no longer able to mediate economic and social conflict, to make side payments to disadvantaged groups, and, in other ways, to overcome inherent divisions. In part, that is because there is less federal funding—a resource that was used to political advantage in the 1960s and early 1970s by mayors James Tate and Frank Rizzo. But more importantly, it is because the Democratic political coalition has disintegrated.

People living in the neighborhoods of the region correctly perceive that the current rising tide of economic expansion will not necessarily float all boats. They question whether the economic gains made by other sections of the region will have positive spillover effects for them. Even though jobs multiplied at an accelerating rate in this region in the 1980s (to the point where some observers predicted labor shortages), economic expansion did not produce social harmony. The tried-and-true political strategy for dealing with the disadvantaged in American politics—to expand the whole pie in order to improve the lot of the poorest—simply will not work under these circumstances.

We have organized our discussion to reflect the theoretical logic sketched out above. We move immediately to a consideration of the shifting economic base of the region, documenting both the decline of industrial employment and the growth of the new service sector. We are concerned with two main questions: (1) Which kinds of jobs have multiplied in the region and which have disappeared? and (2) Where are the growth and decline located?

As part of that chapter we consider the consequences of shifting employment patterns for household incomes. Philadelphia has a long history of racial and ethnic stratification of life chances. Today, this is reflected in the fundamental distinctions among white, black, and Hispanic communities across a wide variety of economic, political, and personal dimensions. The latter part of Chapter 2 details the social disparities among Philadelphia's major class, ethnic, and racial groups arising from the region's changing economic structure.

The effects of income and wealth differences are reflected particularly strongly in the operation of the housing market. Housing patterns are analyzed in Chapter 3 as an outcome of basic distributions of wealth and income, conditioned strongly by the traditional practices of realtors, lending institutions, appraisers, and insurers relative to specific racial and ethnic categories. Reacting to the impacts of both suburbanization of the population and the shifts in the nature of the workforce, the housing market in recent decades has been trifurcated into ghosttown, gold coast, and middle-income housing submarkets.

Following these two chapters, which set forth the large-scale market forces that have buffeted the region's industries, its residents, and its neighborhoods, we turn in Chapter 4 to consider how politics interacts with these market forces. As in other cities, governmental, business, and civic groups in Philadelphia have tried to intervene to battle the physical decay that accompanied economic decline. Chapter 4 focuses on the conflict in the city's urban renewal program between capital-friendly renewal projects and neighborhood needs. The central thrust of the argument is that the recent economic transition of Philadelphia has depended upon the active intervention by government, through the use of urban-renewal dollars, to subsidize the transition from an industrial to a service economy. City leaders' determination to transform the central business district has led to a concentration of resources downtown, at the expense of neighborhood renewal programs.

Chapter 5 sketches out the changing political context of postwar Philadelphia, which reflects the growing economic divisions between its neighborhoods, and between racial and ethnic groups. This chapter examines the changing face of Philadelphia politics, from the do-good era of Richardson Dilworth to the recent disputes between a black mayor and a substantially black council. The consequences for current policy making, as well as for the future of the city, are considered. One constant theme of governmental reformers in Philadelphia, as in other metropolitan centers, has been the need for regional political solutions to problems that spill over the boundaries of city and suburbs. Chapter 6 offers our evaluation of the realistic prospects for regional solutions to some of the problems facing Philadelphia and its suburbs. It appears that the city's political disunity is its greatest handicap in the effort to lure suburban politicians into cooperative arrangements. Finally, in Chapter 7 we speculate briefly about the future of this deeply divided region, considering alternative scenarios and their implications for economic and social inequality.

2

Economic Erosion and the Growth of Inequality

Philadelphia's economic base has undergone a wrenching change in the years since World War II, from a major source of manufactured goods to an economy dominated by business and consumer services. While the nature of work has changed, the location has as well, increasingly shifting the locus of newer jobs away from the older industrial neighborhoods and into the suburbs. The personal and spatial dislocations implicit in this dramatic change in Philadelphia's economy have further ramifications, as jobs have increased in both the low-wage and high-wage sectors, but not in the moderate-wage range. This restriction of middle-income job opportunities has had a tremendous impact across the region, and particularly seems to have fueled the neighborhood and political conflicts explored in later chapters.

This economic shift is not unique to Philadelphia—but it has dominated the social relationships of the city's recent past, as well as those of the present. Explaining what has happened here does not require us to focus only on Philadelphia's history as an industrial city. This is not the story of a one-industry town, collapsing under the strain of sudden competition from another source. Nor can recent events be explained by the venality, greed, or stupidity of the city's industrialists. The roots of change in Philadelphia lie in a national shift in the nature and location of work—from manufacturing to service industries, from Frostbelt to Sunbelt, and from central city to suburbs and beyond.

Built as a railroad center, a shipping center, and a manufacturing center, Philadelphia was the industrial hub of a region that contained prosperous farms as well as numerous smaller commercial centers and factory towns. The story of its transition since World War II from a manufacturing center to a service center is similar in broad outlines to that of many older American cities, yet distinctive in important respects. The city's factories fell victim to broad national forces affecting all urban industrial centers—

economic expansion, changing patterns of corporate organization that accelerated the movement of capital, and spatial decentralization of economic activity. Philadelphia's economy proved particularly vulnerable to these broad trends because of its industrial structure.

No sector of the economy better illustrates the postwar fate of Philadelphia manufacturers than textiles and apparel, which accounted for one-quarter of the city's total manufacturing employment in 1947. So susceptible were these two industries to competition that by 1986 these two industries had lost more than 91,000 jobs, or 74 percent of their 1947 total. To put these losses into perspective, manufacturing as a whole had lost 115,000 jobs between 1947 and 1986. In gross terms, the job losses in textiles and apparel represent 79 percent of the total losses.

The roots of textiles' decline can be traced back to the 1920s, when new manufacturing capacity began shifting from the mid-Atlantic and New England regions to southern and western states that attracted investment with lower wages, free or subsidized sites and plants, cheaper utility costs, subsidized worker training, and forgone taxation. After the war the trend simply accelerated. Philadelphia's textile firms, like those in other mid-Atlantic and New England textile centers, lost ground quickly to their new Sunbelt competitors. And by the end of the 1950s they faced foreign competitors whose workers often were paid only a tenth what American labor was paid.[1] The domestic textile industry was assaulted as hard by foreign competition in the 1960s as the automobile and computer chip industries were in the 1980s.

But there were local causes as well for textile's decline. Many Philadelphia textile firms produced silk hosiery, which was quickly supplanted by nylons—"the soldier's friend"—after World War II. Most of these firms could not convert to new products and simply closed.[2] Other Philadelphia area firms were leaders in the production of wool carpet yarns and wool carpeting, viable industries until the invention of tufted carpeting in 1950, which used nylon and other synthetics and took the market away from the far more expensive woven carpets.[3] The technology for making both the new yarns and the new carpeting was completely different, and few firms made the transition successfully.

Philadelphia's deteriorating labor climate also inhibited new investment in the local textile industry. A long and bitter strike against the Apex Hosiery Company in 1937 poisoned labor-management relationships in the textile industry for years afterward and opened a decade of rising labor militancy across the local economy. Reaching a crescendo with strikes against Baldwin Locomotive, Westinghouse, and General Electric in 1945–46, the workers' militancy clearly contributed to the shift of capital to the non-unionized South in the 1950s and 1960s.[4]

To be sure, these local strikes echoed national trends in labor militancy, but their effects on Philadelphia's postwar textile industry were particularly significant because of the rapid changes in technology and products. In the late 1940s and early 1950s the industry was at a critical transition point: new products had to be produced from new materials in new ways in new plants. The question for factory owners was whether to build new textile plants in the Philadelphia metropolitan area or elsewhere. Their answer was to move elsewhere.

Even when Philadelphia manufacturers successfully adapted to changing technologies and markets, low-cost foreign competition often took a toll. The knitwear industry is a case in point. Because it has always used machines more intensively in its production than other apparel manufacturers, it withstood competition from lower-wage sites until the 1970s. By switching to synthetic yarns, specializing in highly styled women's wear, integrating into one organization what had been a series of subcontracting operations, investing in new plant and equipment, and selling directly to retailers, the knitwear industry actually expanded employment in Philadelphia from 4,649 in 1948 to 10,000 in 1965.[5] Eventually, however, Asian producers, using the profits from the low-margin knitwear ceded to them by domestic manufacturers (for example, tee-shirts), moved to compete directly with domestic producers at the high end of the market as well. Starting in the 1970s Philadelphia's knitwear manufacturers began disappearing.[6]

The decline of other apparel manufacturing followed a similar timetable. Throughout the 1950s and most of the 1960s apparel employment remained relatively stable in the face of rising competition from southern, western, and offshore producers. Philadelphia's concentration on the production of men's and boys' clothing appears to have helped protect the industry, since it was the larger and more competitive market for women's clothing that was most vulnerable to southern and foreign competition. Because of the greater standardization of men's and boys' clothing, machines could be employed more extensively in its production, making it somewhat less sensitive to labor costs. By the 1960s, however, it was clear that the industry was in trouble. Producers complained of being unable to find needed room to expand within the city at rentals they could afford, and they worried about a critical shortage of skilled labor.[7] Despite some city and state programs to aid the industry, the 1970s and 1980s have seen almost universal decline in the manufacture of clothing. The only exception to this overall trend is the appearance in the 1980s of some firms that rely on immigrant labor. In particular, the recent immigration of Koreans to Philadelphia appears to have permitted manufacturers to find workers willing to accept wages at levels competitive with Far Eastern production. Interestingly, this small-scale revival of apparel is not based on a new source of labor for old-line American firms; traditionally these firms were begun by immigrant Jews who initially employed Jews, followed by Hispanics and blacks. In contrast, these new firms have been established by immigrant Korean entrepreneurs who employ Koreans.

Analysts of Philadelphia's postwar economy invariably note that the loss of manufacturing has been accompanied by a rise in service industries in both the city and suburbs. Yet it would be a mistake to assume, as so many popular commentaries do, that the region has traded its dependence on manufacturing for dependence on a new economic base. For, in fact, much of this service employment remains closely tied to manufacturing. With increasing automation, fewer and fewer workers are required for production and more are needed for marketing. For the individual firm, buying a new plant and equipment means cutting back on the number of production workers but incurring larger fixed costs.[8] Hence, the firm must sell more of whatever it produces to make a profit. In order to do this, firms typically hire more sales and other nonproduction workers. In other words, as manufacturers upgrade production processes, the share of their labor force actually engaged in manufacturing tends to shrink while the share engaged, directly or indirectly, in the marketing of their product grows. *Thus, the transition from manufacturing to service employment occurs within manufacturing as well as outside of it.*

The growth of service employment within the manufacturing sector is documented in Table 2.1, which shows the percentage of manufacturing employment engaged in "nonproduction" occupations from 1950 to 1987. The first column shows that the percentage of nonproduction workers increased from 25 to 44 percent. The second column gives similar data for advanced-technology industries—industries distinguished by unusually high spending on research and development and a high percentage of their labor force in engineering and other technical occupations.[9] We would expect that advanced-technology industries—many of which exist only because of recent discoveries in physics, biochemistry, chemistry, and biology—would be more heavily invested in capital equipment than manufacturing as a whole. From the preceding argument, they should therefore have higher fixed costs and a greater fraction of their labor force in nonproduction work. Column 2 confirms that they do, and that the fraction

Table 2.1 Nonproduction occupations as a
percentage of manufacturing employment in the
United States and Philadelphia, 1950–1988

	United States		Philadelphia	
Year	All industries	Advanced technology	All industries	Advanced technology
1950	25.3	na	na	na
1960	30.5	na	na	na
1970	32.4	37.2	37.6	51.3
1980	34.9	42.5	38.3	49.5
1988	44.4	53.9	50.3	61.2

Sources: U.S. Census of Population: 1950, *Special Report, Industrial Characteristics*, vol. IV, part I, chap. D (1955); 1960: *Subject Reports, Occupation by Industry*, Final Report PC(2)-7C (1963); 1970: *Subject Reports, Occupation by Industry*, Final Report PC(2)-7C (1973); and tabulations from the 1970 and 1980 Public Use Sample and the March 1987 Current Population Survey. All published in Washington, D.C., by the Government Printing Office.

has increased dramatically. In 1980, 43 percent of their employment was nonproduction, and only eight years later the figure was 54 percent. Note as well that the percentage spread between all industries and advanced-technology industries increased with time, suggesting that capital investment and reinvestment occurred at a higher rate in the latter group of firms. Columns 3 and 4 give comparable data for the Philadelphia SMSA from 1970 to 1988 and are generally consistent with U.S. figures. However, reflecting the area's status as a relatively high-wage labor market that tends to discourage labor-intensive industries, the percentages in nonproduction labor are substantially higher. For example, whereas 54 percent of advanced-technology jobs in the United States are nonproduction, 61 percent of these jobs are nonproduction in Philadelphia.

Among the fastest growing segments in the region's economy are those that support manufacturing activities. These include business services such as finance, insurance, real estate, law, accounting, engineering, advertising, equipment leasing, data processing, and the like. They also incorporate a substantial amount of the wholesale trade and transportation/communications/utilities industries, although economies of scale have limited their share of the growth. In the case of transportation/communications/utilities, for example, economies of scale have reduced their share, even though the actual number of jobs grew 23 percent in the Philadelphia area and 92 percent in the United States. In part, the shift to services can be understood

Table 2.2   Manufacturing-related services as
a percentage of all jobs in Philadelphia, its
suburbs, and the United States, 1947 and 1986

	Finance, insurance, and real estate	Business services	Wholesale
City of Philadelphia			
1947	6.2	2.2	4.1
1986	10.9	10.9	3.8
Suburbs			
1947	3.3	.8	1.8
1986	7.0	9.5	6.8
United States			
1947	4.9	1.8	7.9
1986	7.9	8.4	8.0

Sources: *County Business Patterns, 1947: United States Summary*, Part 1 (1949); *County Business Patterns, 1947: Middle Atlantic States*, Part 3 (1949); *County Business Patterns, 1986: United States Summary* (CBP-86-1) (1989); *County Business Patterns, 1986: New Jersey* (CBP-86-32) (1989); *County Business Patterns, 1986: Pennsylvania* (CBP-86-40) (1989). All published in Washington, D.C., by the Government Printing Office.

as specialized firms undertaking functions relating to the manufacturing process that manufacturers once did for themselves. Because of their connection to manufacturing, they have shared in its profits (see Table 2.2).

Economic shifts as broad and deep as those occurring in the Philadelphia region since World War II are produced by multiple and complex forces. Our account of the change focuses on two principal explanations, which are elaborated in the sections that follow. First we review the national trends and policies that undermined Philadelphia's economic base. We then turn to a discussion of the particular characteristics of the city's industrial infrastructure that accelerated its transformation.

The National Context

To a substantial degree, Philadelphia's economic history since the end of World War II was part of a larger economic transformation experienced by the nation as a whole. From 1946 to 1968 the percentage of nonagricultural jobs in manufacturing dropped in half—from 35 to 19 percent.[10] Markets for goods and services that were regional became national and national markets became international. The United States declined from a position as *the* technological leader in the world to *a* technological leader. To understand the reasons for these changes is to understand a good part of why so many of American manufacturing cities—like Philadelphia—have seen their economic foundations erode during most of this period.

Why did it happen? There were five principal reasons. The first two, as noted earlier, involved technological improvements that permitted manufacturers to increase production with fewer workers but demanded that they devote ever greater efforts to the marketing of their products. Third, manufacturers undertook organizational changes in order to reduce costs and to improve quality by increasingly purchasing engineering, advertising, accounting, legal, financial, and other support services from outside companies rather than trying to produce all of these services internally. Fourth, manufacturers shifted production to the South and West, and particularly in the last two decades, to other nations in which costs are substantially lower. Finally, since the 1950s, foreign competition increasingly undercut American manufacturers on the grounds of cost, or quality, or both.

Taken together, these factors meant that plants in southern and western cities were going to take business from their eastern and midwestern competition. Not only would a steel producer in Philadelphia find it difficult to compete against a steel producer in Los Angeles, but it would find it difficult to compete against the Los Angeles plant in selling to customers in Denver and Omaha.

These new plants also provided an industrial base to attract both new populations and other new industries. For example, steel companies attracted metal fabricating companies that attracted metal finishing companies; chemical companies attracted pharmaceutical companies that attracted medical instrument companies; and so on. As the populations of these southern and western cities grew in response to the economic opportunities, they attracted new and unrelated industries to serve both those populations and markets more distant. And these new industries created further competition for the older cities like Philadelphia.

The emerging competition proved particularly difficult for Philadelphia because the industrial structure of both the city and its suburbs long centered on manufacturing. As Figure 2.1 shows, during the postwar period the Philadelphia metropolitan area has, until quite recently, had about 4 or 5 percent more of its privately employed labor force in manufacturing than the United States. Thus, as manufacturing competition increased in

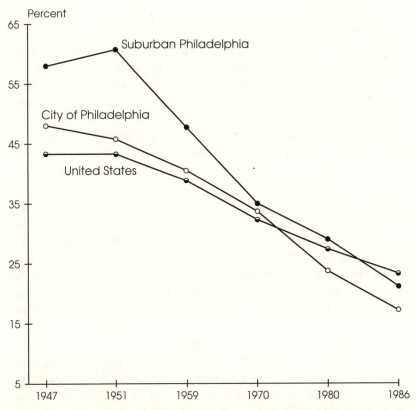

Figure 2.1   Proportion of private labor force in manufacturing in Philadelphia, its suburbs, and the United States, 1947–1986

Sources:County Business Patterns, 1947: United States Summary, Part 1 (1949); *County Business Patterns, 1947: Middle Atlantic States*, Part 3 (1949); *County Business Patterns, 1951: United States Summary*, Part 1 (1955); *County Business Patterns 1951: Middle Atlantic States*, Part 3 (1955); *County Business Patterns, 1959: United States Summary*, Part 1 (1963); *County Business Patterns, 1959: Middle Atlantic States*, Parts 3a and 3b (1963); *County Business Patterns, 1970: United States Summary* (CBP-70-1) (1971); *County Business Patterns, 1970: New Jersey* (CBP-70-32) (1971); *County Business Patterns, 1970: Pennsylvania* (CBP-70-40) (1971); *County Business Patterns, 1980: United States Summary* (CBP-80-1) (1982); *County Business Patterns, 1980: New Jersey* (CBP-80-32) (1982); *County Business Patterns, 1980: Pennsylvania* (CBP-80-40) (1982); *County Business Patterns, 1986: United States Summary* (CBP-86-1) (1989); *County Business Patters, 1986: New Jersey* (CBP-86-32) (1989); *County Business Patterns, 1986: Pennsylvania* (CBP-86-40) (1989). All published in Washington, D.C., by the Government Printing Office.

the South and West, Philadelphia's employment base was more subject to adverse effects than the nation as a whole.

Federal procurement policies beginning during World War II also helped to create new and competing manufacturing firms in the South and West. These new plants in the Sunbelt had three important advantages over existing plants in the East and Midwest: (1) they represented the most modern technology and therefore could produce at a lower unit cost, (2) they had lower transportation costs to part of the markets traditionally served by the manufacturers in the East and Midwest, and (3) their construction costs were substantially borne by the taxpayer rather than by the firms themselves.[11]

The Korean War in the early 1950s combined with a major strategic shift in national defense policy to exacerbate the problems of eastern and midwestern cities. Even as it fought the war, the United States traded a reliance on conventional armed forces for dependence on aerospace, electronics, and nuclear weaponry.[12] With a few notable exceptions, the beneficiaries were the same rising cities of the South and West targeted by federal capital investment just a few years earlier. And as conventional forces were reduced, their traditional suppliers in eastern and midwestern cities either had to find new markets or reduce operations.

The benefits were both direct and indirect. The direct benefits arose from federal expenditures for the goods and services of these rising cities. But their economies also gained indirectly from the spillover into civilian applications of federally financed military technology.

In addition to federal procurement policies, federal tax policies accelerated the shift of manufacturing to the Sunbelt, by allowing firms to depreciate industrial plants over a twenty-year period. As long as these plants have value to depreciate, firms are unlikely to close them, but after the plants are fully depreciated they are substantially freer to reallocate their assets. As an executive of the Budd Company, a major transportation equipment manufacturer located in Philadelphia, commented to the vice president of Philadelphia's Chamber of Commerce a few years ago: "Our [Northeast Philadelphia] plant is written off. Every year we remain here is a gift to the city."[13]

The 1970s was a watershed decade for both United States and Philadelphia manufacturers. Until roughly 1970, they competed with foreign manufacturers, as Thurow put it, "on the basis of superior technology rather than lower production costs."[14] But during the 1970s it became clear that foreign competitors equaled or exceeded U.S. technology in products ranging from automobiles to steel to VCRs. Both locally and nationally, manufacturers had failed to invest in the research and development and new plant and equipment that is required to maintain an effective competitive status in emerging world markets. The erosion of the U.S. technological advantage meant that production costs—largely labor costs—came to dominate the competitive process. The relatively high labor costs in U.S. cities, compared with overseas competitors, exacerbated the problems faced by domestic manufacturing. So did the inflationary trend of the late 1960s and 1970s, which was fueled by the U.S. government's Vietnam build-up (without a supporting tax increase), by the decision in 1971 to free the dollar from the gold standard, by the drastic rise in energy costs caused by the 1973 oil embargo and the 1979 OPEC price increases, and by the Federal Reserve's hike in interest rates from 1977 through mid-1981. These trends created a net price advantage for foreign-produced goods over U.S. goods.[15] Taken together with the growing technological sophistication of foreign producers, these trends kept the number of U.S. jobs in durable manufacturing constant between 1970 and 1986, even as total private employment grew 47 percent.

Philadelphia's Special Vulnerability to National Trends

Although virtually every aging industrial eastern and midwestern industrial metropolis suffered a loss of manufacturing since World War II, Philadelphia's decline was particularly aggravated by the disproportionate role played by the manufacture of nondurable goods in the region's economic base. Compared with the production of durable goods (such as machinery, automobiles, washers, and construction), the manufacture of nondurable goods (for example, clothing, magazines, cigarettes, or shoe polish) is likely to take place in smaller establishments, to require less capital investment, and to pay lower wages. Less dependent on a large investment in plant and equipment, plants that manufacture nondurable goods are therefore more easily moved than plants that are more capital intensive. Nondurable firms also have a lower wage structure, which encourages them to seek locations where labor is cheap. Nondurable producers are, therefore, particularly sensitive to changes in their economic environment. In 1947 about 30 percent of Philadelphia's privately employed labor force was in nondurable manufactures; in contrast, the percentage for the entire United States was only 19 (see Figure 2.2).

In both the city and suburbs the percentage in nondurable manufacture

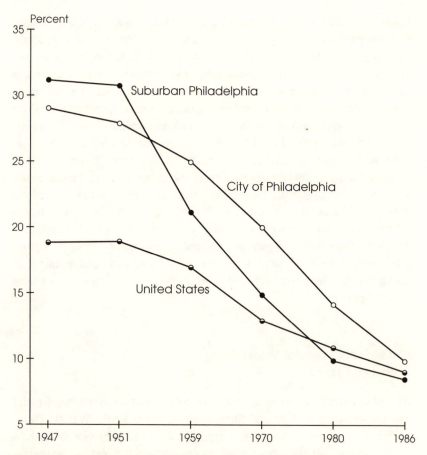

Figure 2.2   Proportion of private labor force in nondurable manufacturing in Philadelphia, its suburbs, and the United States, 1947–1986
Sources: See sources for Figure 2.1.

ran roughly 50 percent higher than in the national economy. By 1959, as the overall percentage employed in manufacturing declined, the economic paths of Philadelphia and its suburbs began to diverge. Nondurable goods continued to dominate manufactures in the city, but durable goods assumed primacy in the suburbs (see Figure 2.3). In 1984 nondurable goods manufacturing in the city continued to employ 69 percent more workers than durable, while in the suburbs only half as many worked in nondurable manufacture as in durable. As we have already noted, nondurable goods manufacturers are more mobile than durable goods manufacturers. Thus, the city's disproportionate reliance on nondurable goods was a weakness that the surrounding suburbs did not share.

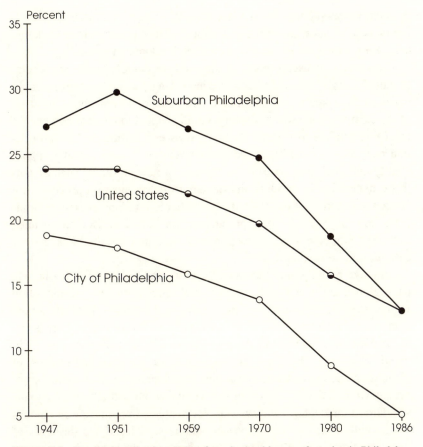

Figure 2.3   Proportion of private labor force in durable manufacturing in Philadelphia, its suburbs, and the United States, 1947–1986
Sources: See sources for Figure 2.1.

Why did durable goods manufacture assume primacy in the suburbs? The
answer to that question lies in the developmental status of the metropolitan
area at the end of World War II. In 1947 the suburbs were as yet largely undeveloped. They contained only 27 percent of metropolitan employment,
a third of the business establishments, and approximately 43 percent of
the population. Agriculture was still a viable enterprise in many suburban
communities.

The decades of rapid suburban growth in the 1950s and 1960s coincided
with a period when durable-goods industries were expanding, while the
prospects for growth in most of the divisions of nondurable manufacture
were dim. Kain has persuasively argued that the dispersal of durable-goods

production was significantly stimulated by the government through its funding of new plants to meet the war effort.[16] These plants helped to define areas for postwar industrial and residential development.

The suburbs answered many of the needs of durable-goods producers. Manufacturers located in Philadelphia increasingly found that the city could not meet their space, transportation, and labor requirements. Almost all of the existing space was multistory and ill adapted to the requirements of emerging continuous-flow production processes. Continuous-flow production processes offered higher volume, lower costs, and generally, higher quality than their predecessors. In the case of new products, such as synthetic materials, the product and the automated production process were conceived together; it was not simply a matter of building an existing product a new way. But for new products or for old, manufacturers wanted to build continuous-flow production lines, and they required single-story structures to house them.

Although roughly one-quarter of the city—the Northeast—was largely undeveloped at the end of the war and met some of the need, competition with residential developers for space drove up the price of land and forced many manufacturers to seek sites outside of the city. In Philadelphia's traditional districts for manufacturing—Center City, Kensington, Port Richmond, Northern Liberties—there was little vacant land, and the cost of demolition and reconstruction was generally prohibitive. These sections of the city were also handicapped by the age of their infrastructure. Built to the standard of nineteenth-century technology, streets were narrow and blocks were small, creating congestion and adding significantly to the costs of transportation. Only in the late 1950s and afterward were public programs created to subsidize the costs of demolition and infrastructure development, and they were often too little and too late.

Labor was also less expensive in the suburbs, though not because a company could avoid unionization by establishing or moving its operations to the suburbs. Generally, the same union represented both city and suburban workers in an industry. The means to keep down labor costs were rather more subtle and sometimes unintended. Because suburban plants were typically more automated than urban plants, they required fewer skilled workers, thereby lowering labor costs. In some instances suburban manufacturers replaced skilled male workers with semi- or unskilled female workers at wage levels below comparably skilled males. In addition, if a plant moved from city to suburb, it often experienced considerable turnover in its workers because some would choose not to commute. The result was that the plant would lose experienced workers at the high end of the pay scale and gain inexperienced ones at the low end.

The Changing Distribution of Jobs in the Postindustrial Economy

Pressure on the domestic economy has resulted in the replacement of full-time, full-year manufacturing jobs by service jobs that are part-time, part-year or that require fewer skills and pay lower wages. Even in manufacturing—long considered the foundation of the middle class because of its high production of unionized, full-time, full-year employment—jobs are increasingly part-time, part-year and consequently pay less.[17]

These trends have implications for the distribution of earnings for both the nation and Philadelphia. In their 1986 report, "The Great American Job Machine," Bluestone and Harrison found that between 1979 and 1984, 58 percent of all new jobs in the United States paid less than half the median wage, while the fraction of new jobs paying more than twice the median wage declined 5.5 percent.[18] The clear implication of these findings is a growing inequality of earnings in the United States.

Broadly speaking, Philadelphia reflects this pattern—and, contrary to popular images, it extends to both city and suburban job opportunities. The data in Table 2.3 indicate that the suburbs have at least as large a low-wage component for their jobs as does the city—in fact, a greater proportion of their jobs fall into the low-wage category in both 1980 and 1987.[19] In contrast, throughout the decade the city saw its high-wage jobs receive a greater share of earnings than high-wage jobs in the suburbs. And both city and suburbs experienced losses in the fraction of middle-income jobs.

This increase in both high- and low-income jobs at the expense of middle-income jobs does not directly tell us about the relative rates of growth underlying these trends. Figure 2.4 depicts those growth rates by portraying the percentage change in jobs between 1980 and 1987 in each earnings category. In the city jobs paying less than half the median grew 15 percent while 13 percent of the jobs with moderate pay disappeared, but high-paying jobs rose 108 percent. As expected, the middle group lost jobs; notably, however, the high group gained three times as many jobs as the low.

We can view these results in two ways. On one hand, the ratio of high- to low-income jobs is an impressive sign of the attractiveness of the city to the kinds of firms that create high-quality employment. On the other hand,

Table 2.3 Proportion of jobs and proportion of earnings by job categories in the city and suburbs of Philadelphia, 1980–1987

	Percentage of Jobs		Percentage of Earnings	
Category of Job	1980	1987	1980	1987
City of Philadelphia				
Paying less than half of median	12.1	14.3	3.8	4.1
Paying half to twice median	82.9	74.8	84.1	69.6
Paying more than twice median	5.0	10.9	12.1	26.3
(*N*)	(670,250)	(648,987)	($2,490M)	($3,694M)
Suburban Philadelphia				
Paying less than half of median	14.8	16.6	5.8	5.9
Paying half to twice median	79.9	72.8	82.2	70.5
Paying more than twice median	5.3	12.0	10.6	23.6
(*N*)	(1,046,536)	(1,245,889)	($3,663M)	($6,547M)

Source: Computed from data tapes from the New Jersey Department of Labor and Pennsylvania Department of Labor and Industry.

the number of high-paying jobs generated during the 1980s amounted only to 52 percent of the middle-income jobs lost. If these trends continue, the employment base of the city will continue to shrink. And it will create a distribution of earnings that will increasingly divide the city into the rich and the poor. The number of jobs that support the city's middle class is diminishing.

Even the rapid growth of high-income jobs in the city is likely to bring few direct benefits to city residents because high-paying jobs go disproportionately to suburban residents. In 1980, the latest year for which data on place of work and place of residence are available, 64 percent of all persons whose private-sector jobs were in Philadelphia and who were paid more than twice the median earnings actually lived in the suburbs.[20]

For the suburbs, Figure 2.4 shows a somewhat different situation. Although the absolute number of jobs grew in all three earnings categories and middle- and high-income jobs grew somewhat more than the low,[21] high-paying jobs grew by 134 percent—far larger than the 9 percent growth in middle-income jobs or the 33-percent growth in low-income jobs. Thus, the employment base for a middle-class lifestyle remains strong in the suburbs. (For more detail on employment shifts in Philadelphia and its suburbs, see Appendix B.)

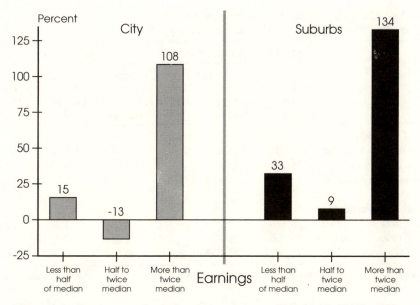

Figure 2.4 Employment change by earnings category, Philadelphia SMSA, 1980–1987

The Changing Earnings Profile

Looking at jobs provides only part of the picture. We also need to know how the changing regional economy is affecting earnings. Table 2.4 provides one answer by displaying average annual earnings for workers in each earnings category in 1980 and 1987, and the absolute growth or loss of real income—that is, controlling for inflation—during the eight years. It is striking that in the city real average earnings for full-time workers hardly changed over the eight-year period in the low and moderate earnings categories—the low-income group lost $5 and the moderate category gained $7. In contrast, real earnings increased by $5,205 in the highest category. To put it another way, only the highest earners—those who on average earned *eight* times more than those in the lowest group—were better off in 1987 than they were in 1980!

The suburbs fared little better, *despite evidence of a more even distribution of job growth depicted in Appendix B*. Jobs in the low-wage group lost $178, and the moderate category gained only $74. But those in the highest paid establishments gained $3,403.

What role did the growth of part-time employment play in these changes? The last three columns of Table 2.4 answer this question by showing what

Table 2.4   Change in real earnings by level of earnings, city
and suburbs of Philadelphia, 1980–1987 (in 1987 dollars)

	Full-time equivalent workers			All workers		
	Annualized 1980 average earnings	Annualized 1987 average earnings	Diff. 1980– 1987	Annualized 1980 average earnings	Annualized 1987 average earnings	Diff. 1980– 1987
City of Philadelphia						
Less than half of median	$ 6,537	$ 6,532	$ −5	$ 8,766	$ 8,700	$ −66
Half to twice median	21,170	21,177	7	24,356	24,666	310
More than twice median	49,947	55,152	5,205	57,812	58,707	895
Suburban Philadelphia						
Less than half of median	6,576	6,394	−178	8,671	8,503	−168
Half to twice median	20,756	20,829	74	22,815	23,231	315
More than twice median	48,647	52,050	3,403	50,519	53,522	3,003

Source: Computed from data tapes from the New Jersey Department of Labor and the Pennsylvania Department of Labor and Industry.

would have been the average earnings, if all workers had worked a 40-hour week.[22] Where part-time employment is high, this number will be significantly larger than the average earnings per worker, given on the left-hand side of the table. We would expect that discrepancy to be the widest in the low-wage category of jobs—such as the oft-mentioned fast-food stores—because part-time employment is so prevalent there. But Table 2.4 demonstrates that the effect of the adjustment actually increases with earnings in both the city and the suburbs. Apparently, there are part-time workers at all levels of earnings. In addition, the effects of the adjustment are larger in the city than in the suburbs, because the mix of industries in the city relies more heavily on part-time employment or has a conventional work week of less than 40 hours. Of the seventy-two industries for which average weekly hours are available for 1987, 70 percent have work weeks under 40 hours and 63 percent have work weeks under 35 hours (a common dividing point between full and part-time work). Eighty-nine percent of the city's workforce is in industries with less than a 40-hour week and 55 percent is in industries averaging less than 35; the corresponding figures for the suburbs are 79 and 49 percent.[23] But the fact that the adjustment increases with level of earnings also suggests that the stereotype of part-time workers as retail clerks and fast-food counterpersons needs reexamination.

A recent *Wall Street Journal* reported that, in an effort to reduce costs, a growing number of firms are discharging professional and middle-management workers and then often hiring them as consultants to do the same work they did as employees![24] The benefit to the companies is two-fold: first, they have converted a salaried employee into a "piece-work" employee; he or she gets paid only for the amount of work done. Second, they are no longer responsible for the costs of their former employees' fringe benefits.

The practice has led to the rapid growth of temporary help and employment agencies. Within the last few years specialized temporary-help firms have arisen to provide certified public accountants, attorneys, nurses, and other professional and technical personnel. Between 1980 and 1987 employment agencies grew 129 percent, the fastest of any type of business service in the city of Philadelphia. Temporary-help agencies expanded 37 percent, the fourth fastest of the business services. Clearly, we need to know a good deal more about part-time employment in such rapidly growing industries as business services.

What is particularly arresting about the concentration of lower work-week jobs in Philadelphia is their association with higher average earnings. City jobs, at all pay levels, have higher average earnings than suburban jobs. We suspect that this is the result of some combination of the following reasons. First, in a number of industries marked by firms that do business in several locations, it is common for the headquarters to be located in the city; since the headquarters staff is likely to be better paid than branch employees, the city's average wage is raised. Examples range from manufacturing to finance to retail to business services. SmithKline Beecham, a major pharmaceutical manufacturer, is headquartered in the city, with production and support facilities in the suburbs. Core States Financial Corporation, the major locally headquartered bank, has its central offices downtown, but branches and support facilities are located throughout the region. Strawbridge and Clothier, the largest department store chain, has its flagship store and executive offices in Center City. Large law and big-eight accounting firms have established branch offices to cater to the burgeoning economic activities in the suburbs; the major partners remain downtown. Second, unions have traditionally been stronger in the city than in the suburbs. Although union strength—even in the city—is a faint shadow of what it was in the 1940s and 1950s, the city-suburb difference persists. Third, Philadelphia's wage tax may have the effect of raising city wages and salaries because employers feel the need to compensate for the negative effects it would otherwise have on earnings and on their ability to attract employees.

However, the information presented in Table 2.4 suggests caution in interpreting the suburbs' situation too positively. Earlier we observed that

during the 1980s the benefits of economic growth in the city of Philadelphia
went disproportionately to those with high earnings working in the center
of the city, a phenomenon that primarily benefited suburban residents. In
the suburbs the distribution of jobs was more equal. But these data also suggest that the suburban middle-wage jobs, while growing in number, often
do not pay well enough to stay much ahead of inflation. Thus, even in the
suburbs the benefits of growth went predominantly to those already most
advantaged—those earning more than twice the median level for the area.

Who Gains? Who Loses?

To reiterate a point raised earlier, jobs are not people. Whatever we have
learned about the kinds of jobs the changing economy provides does not directly speak to how these changes affect the life chances of individuals and
their families. Like other metropolitan areas, Philadelphia is profoundly
divided, both economically and racially. The changes to the economic structure of the region have taken place against the mosaic of its communities
separated by space and, most profoundly, race. What this means is that the
economic changes described earlier in this chapter—in which high- and
low-income jobs have grown while moderate-income jobs declined—must
be understood against the background of the region's spatial and social
divisions. The changes in the nature and amount of work are manifested in
a growing disparity between the incomes of white and black families.[25]

As a part of these shifts, many of the new jobs carry higher educational
qualifications than was true in the past, which has damaged black employment prospects more than white. As shall be seen, although racial differentials in educational attainment have diminished significantly, blacks' educational gains have not kept up with rising requirements, a situation that has
contributed significantly to a decline in black labor-force participation. Past
patterns of discrimination are thereby reinforced and institutionalized in the
changed skill requirements of the postindustrialized Philadelphia economy.

In Philadelphia, as elsewhere, the distribution of family incomes between
whites and blacks favors whites. In 1988 about 4 percent of white and 23
percent of black families in the Philadelphia metropolitan area had total
incomes below the poverty line, and the difference has grown over time.
Figure 2.5 presents the income distributions of black and white families for
the years 1970 and 1988 expressed in 1988 dollars. It is a picture of rapidly
increasing inequality.

The two-tiered labor market with middle-income jobs giving way to high-

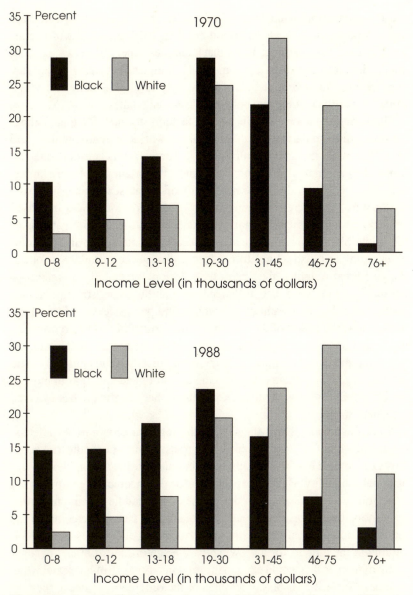

Figure 2.5 Total family income by race, Philadelphia metropolitan area, 1970 and 1988 (in 1988 dollars)

Sources: U.S. Census of Population, 1970: Public Use Samples of Basic Records from the 1970 Census. 15% Sample, prepared by the Bureau of the Census (machine-readable data file) (Washington, D.C., 1977); *Current Population Survey, 1988, Annual Demographic File (March)*, prepared by the Bureau of the Census (machine-readable data file) (Washington, D.C.: Bureau of the Census, 1989).

and low-wage employment described earlier has not equally affected the region's population. Over the period between 1970 and 1988 white families improved their earnings while black families experienced two different trends. Incomes increased for some black families, but many others saw their incomes remain at or below the poverty level. The net effect was a worsening of the income gap between blacks and whites.

Three major factors, or clusters of factors, account for this finding: (1) racial discrimination; (2) differentials in workforce participation; and (3) differentials in family composition.[26] These factors are not independent—they are mutually reinforcing. Equally important, if not more important, however, are shifts in the nature of work (that is, its increasing part-time nature, the increased feminization of the workforce, and increased educational requirements), which resonate very strongly with patterns of life in the black community (that is, educational attainment and opportunities, and family structure) to produce a divergence in family incomes. We give great weight to the first of these factors—racial discrimination—but this is a complex concept, depending upon the social structure at particular times for the meaning, magnitude, and pervasiveness of its effect. In our view, the lesson of the industrial transformation and its accompanying reduction of the American standard of living is that the size of the economic pie is diminishing, with the economically disadvantaged diners getting the smallest share of a shrinking pie. In Philadelphia, as in most of the United States, it is the black community that historically has received the smallest slice.

What this means is that the shift in the regional economy has affected black and white families differently. The transition to a postindustrial economy exacerbated black-white differentials and intensified a complex system of racial inequality. But the explanation for the income differential is not to be found in the assumption that a loss of the middle-income manufacturing jobs disproportionately affected blacks. In fact, if we compare the industrial and occupational distributions of blacks and whites since 1950, we find scant support for a growing divergence of industrial and occupational outcomes that would explain the growing disparity of black and white incomes. Table 2.5 displays measures of the differences between the percentage of blacks and whites in industries and occupations from 1950 to 1988. The measures—indices of dissimilarity—take on a maximum value of 0 when they are identical.[27] The table shows that the black and white occupational dissimilarities declined from 1950 to 1970 and moved up since 1980. However, the increase in dissimilarity between 1980 and 1988 is not due to an increasing exclusion of blacks from manufacturing—as might be

Table 2.5   Index of dissimilarity between
blacks and whites for industry and occupation
in the Philadelphia metropolitan area

	1950	1960	1970	1980	1988
Industry	.24	.19	.14	.15	.20
Occupation	.38	.39	.30	.19	.15

Sources: U.S. Census of Population, Occupation by Industry, Special Reports, P-E, No. IC (1954); *U.S. Census of Population, 1960: Occupation by Industry*, Subject Report Final Report PC(2)-7C (1963); *U.S. Census of Population, 1970: Characteristics of Population*, Part 40, Sec. 2 (1973) —all published in Washington by the Government Printing Office; *U.S. Census of Population and Housing, 1980: 5% Microdata File*, prepared by the Bureau of the Census (machine-readable data file) (Washington, D.C., 1983); *Current Population Survey, 1988: Annual Demographic File (March)*, prepared by the Bureau of the Census (machine-readable data file) (Washington, D.C.: Bureau of the Census, 1989).

expected from the industrial transformation—but rather from a substantial growth of blacks in professional services (for example, law and health).[28]

The reason blacks have not been hurt by the loss of manufacturing jobs is simple: for more than a century blacks have largely been excluded from these jobs in Philadelphia.[29] In fact, the percentage of blacks in manufacturing has actually increased during the postwar period. But the manufacturing jobs blacks hold are seldom comparable to those held by whites.

As Table 2.6 documents, as recently as 1988 the median earnings of blacks employed in manufacturing in the Philadelphia metropolitan area were only 45 percent of their white counterparts. Those blacks employed in manufacturing found and find themselves in jobs at the bottom of the pay scale. In contrast, blacks employed in local services (serving markets largely within the metropolitan area) averaged 88 percent of the white median, and blacks in export services (markets outside the metropolitan area) averaged 81 percent. Thus it can be argued that blacks have benefited by the shift to services inasmuch as the income gap is diminished by it. Yet to make this argument is to fail to recognize that the overall gap increased, despite increases in the number of jobs in which blacks earn a higher fraction of white income.

Table 2.7 displays the continuing significance of job segregation in city and suburb.[30] The upper part (A) gives the industrial distributions and shows blacks overrepresented in transportation/communication/utilities,

Table 2.6 Median earnings by industrial sector
and race, Philadelphia metropolitan area, 1988

Industrial sector	Total	White	Black	Black as percentage of white
Local services	$15,000	$16,000	$14,000	88
Manufacturing	$20,000	$22,880	$10,400	45
Export services	$20,000	$21,000	$17,000	81

Note: Local and export services are distinguished from one another by whether the markets they serve are primarily local or outside the metropolitan area.

consumer services, nonprofits, and government, and underrepresented in other manufacturing, wholesale, retail, and advanced technology services.

Occupational segregation is depicted in part B, which shows that in both city and suburbs blacks are overrepresented in the lowest paid occupations: clerical, operative, labor, and service. These are also the occupational groups that predominate in the industries where blacks are the most heavily represented; for example, more than half of the employees in transportation/communications/utilities, consumer services, and government fall into these groups. The clustering of blacks in nonprofits has two sources: the success of blacks in entering teaching and nursing—both professional/technical occupations—and their substantial presence in the service occupations in hospitals. The high fraction of blacks in suburban finance/insurance/real estate arises from the "back office" clerical jobs that are located in the suburbs.

It is not difficult to explain why blacks are underrepresented in manufacturing, wholesale, retail, and advanced-technology services. Since manufacturing typically pays better than other industries, it is not surprising that blacks, who face discrimination in obtaining higher paying positions, should be less represented in regular manufacturing than whites. Nor are the figures for advanced-technology service firms surprising, given that these firms employ a high fraction of managerial and professional/technical workers—63 percent. These are occupations with histories of substantial barriers to black entry, reflected in the fact that 96 percent of all workers are white.[31] In the case of wholesale and retail industries, the most likely explanation is in employers' historic discriminatory hiring policies that exclude blacks from "people" positions.[32]

Clearly, the issue is not simple. It is complicated by the decades of decentralization of economic activity and population, which has placed 69

Table 2.7 Industrial and occupational distributions
by race, city, and suburbs of Philadelphia, 1988

	City		Suburbs	
	White	Black	White	Black
A. Industry				
Agriculture/mining/construction	4.6%	1.6%	5.6%	5.7%
Adv.-technology manufacturing	4.0	4.1	8.4	11.7
Regular manufacturing	9.6	8.2	11.4	3.7
Transportation/communications/utilities	8.1	9.0	6.7	12.9
Wholesale	5.0	1.9	4.5	0.0
Retail	14.5	10.3	16.4	9.7
Finance/insurance/real estate	7.2	4.1	8.5	10.2
Adv.-technology services	3.8	0.0	4.6	0.0
Producer services	5.2	5.2	5.2	3.6
Consumer services	8.8	17.9	11.1	12.7
Nonprofits	22.8	25.2	14.0	18.5
Government	6.5	12.5	3.8	11.3
(N)*	(393)	(223)	(1,490)	(102)
B. Occupation				
Managerial	20.7	17.8	16.0	14.6
Professional/technical	19.6	19.3	21.4	12.5
Sales	9.3	1.4	10.1	3.8
Clerical	16.6	22.4	19.6	21.8
Crafts	10.2	5.3	11.5	13.8
Operative	7.8	12.7	7.8	8.5
Labor	4.4	5.3	3.7	4.5
Service	11.4	15.9	9.9	20.5
(N)*	(393)	(221)	(1,482)	(102)

Source: Current Population Survey, 1988: Annual Demographic File (March), prepared by the Bureau of the Census (machine-readable data file) (Washington, D.C.: Bureau of the Census, 1989).
*Numbers are given in thousands.

percent of the region's jobs and two-thirds of its population in the suburbs. It is further complicated by the fact that by 1988, 77 percent of the region's white population lived in the suburbs whereas 75 percent of its black population lived in the city. Despite the improvement in segregation across industries and occupations shown in Table 2.5, black-white disparities remain very evident and are intensified by residential segregation. Residential segregation reduces access to the growing jobs base in the suburbs, making the finding and keeping of a job more difficult for blacks.

What this means is that industrial and occupational segregation, taken

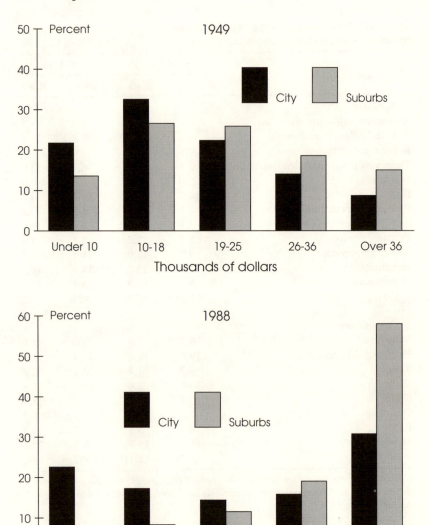

Figure 2.6 Distribution of family incomes by income level, Philadelphia and suburbs, 1949 and 1988

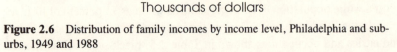

Sources: U.S. Census of Population, 1950: Characteristics of Population, Part 3, No. 42 (Washington, D.C.: Government Printing Office, 1955); *Current Population Survey, 1988: Annual Demographic File (March),* prepared by the Bureau of the Census (machine-readable data file) (Washington, D.C.: Bureau of the Census, 1989).

together with the steadily growing disparity of job opportunities between the city and suburbs, can and does play a part in the increasing divergence of family incomes even as levels of segregation diminish. Figure 2.6 portrays this mounting disparity over the past forty years. In 1949 there was a roughly similar distribution of incomes in the city and suburbs, with lower income families constituting a somewhat higher proportion of suburban households. By 1988, however, the two income profiles differed dramatically. Low-income families made up a far larger share of the city's than of the suburbs' population, while high-income families constituted a disproportionately large share of suburban households.[33]

The industrial shift in Philadelphia has thus played itself out across both race and location. As jobs have decentralized, the better paying positions concentrated in the suburbs, and the minority population, spatially concentrated in Philadelphia itself, increasingly has faced poorer paying opportunities. The consequence is to leave the black population doubly disadvantaged; in the city, they face lower wages than they would in the suburbs in both manufacturing and export services, and if they commute to the suburbs, their wages are effectively lowered because of the substantial commuting expenses they incur.

Workforce Participation

A second major factor in explaining earnings differentials is workforce participation. Put simply, a major precondition to earnings equity is participation in the labor market—without parity in the latter, the former is virtually impossible. When data on persons not in the workforce is compared over time and examined for gender differences (see Table 2.8), we note the following. In general, Philadelphians are much more likely to be out of the workforce in recent years than in 1970. In 1988 white men were 50 percent as likely to be out of the labor force as black males, more than half of whom were likely to be outside the labor force.

The labor-force participation of women roughly paralleled that of men. White women moved out of the labor force during the 1970s and began to move back in during the 1980s. But black women who in 1970 were more likely to be *in* the labor force than white women were, in 1988, 40 percent more likely to be *out* of the labor force; this change also runs counter to national data, which show black women continuing to enter the labor force.

If we focus on those persons actually employed, as Table 2.9 does, we find that employment rates (the proportion of those in the workforce who

Table 2.8   Proportion of adults not in workforce
by sex and race, Philadelphia SMSA, 1970–1988

	White		Black	
Year	Male	Female	Male	Female
1970	15.1	36.3	16.1	28.6
1980	23.7	51.8	36.5	51.9
1988	23.0	41.6	53.6	58.4

*Sources: U.S. Census of Population, 1970: Public Use Samples
of Basic Records from the 1970 Census. 15% Sample*, prepared
by the Bureau of the Census (machine-readable data file) (Washington, D.C., 1977); *U.S. Census of Population and Housing,
1980: 5% Microdata File*, prepared by the Bureau of the Census
(machine-readable data file) (Washington, D.C., 1983); *Current
Population Survey, 1988: Annual Demographic File (March)*,
prepared by the Bureau of the Census (machine-readable data
file) (Washington, D.C.: Bureau of the Census, 1989).

Table 2.9   Adult employment rates by sex and race,
Philadelphia metropolitan area, 1960–1988*

	Whites		Blacks	
Year	Male	Female	Male	Female
1960	82.7%	33.3%	73.9%	45.9%
1970	75.6	37.1	65.1	43.3
1980	79.7	52.4	62.3	48.4
1988	69.6	48.9	47.8	48.7

*Sources: U.S. Census of Population, 1960: Characteris-
tics of Population*, Part 40 (Washington, D.C.: Government
Printing Office, 1963); *Current Population Survey, 1988: An-
nual Demographic File (March)*, prepared by the Bureau of
the Census (machine-readable data file) (Washington, D.C.:
Bureau of the Census, 1989); data for 1970 and 1980, see
Table 2.8.
*Persons aged twenty or more.

were employed) declined for both white and black males, but the black decline of 26 percent was twice that of whites. For whites, lower employment
rates are primarily a product of the 1980s, but for blacks, the decline dates
at least since 1960.[34]

The table also shows that the increase in employed women is, in Philadelphia, an increase in employed *white* women. White women showed a
50-percent increase in employment, while the workforce participation of

Table 2.10   The rate of full-time and part-time employment
by sex and race, Philadelphia metropolitan area, 1970–1988

	1970		1988	
	White	Black	White	Black
Full-time male	62.4%	55.5%	47.8%	36.2%
Part-time male	4.7	3.8	7.1	7.4
Full-time female	24.1	32.0	29.8	42.2
Part-time female	8.7	8.7	15.4	14.2
(N)	(1,338,937)	(269,900)	(1,826,515)	(309,225)

Sources: *Current Population Survey, 1970: Annual Demographic File (March)*, prepared by
the Bureau of the Census (machine-readable data file) (Washington, D.C.: Bureau of the Census, 1981); *Current Population Survey, 1988: Annual Demographic File (March)*, prepared by
the Bureau of the Census (machine-readable data file). (Washington, D.C.: Bureau of the Census, 1989).

black females has hardly changed at all. In 1960 white males had the highest employment rate, followed, in order, by black males, black females, and white females. However, in 1988 the white male rate was still highest, but there was little difference among the latter three groups.

As male labor-force participation and employment declined, so has male full-time work as a fraction of all work. Table 2.10 shows the declines in full-time employment as a proportion of the labor force, for both males and females by race. For both whites and blacks, the relative role of full-time male employment dropped substantially over the period. But the percentage drop was much greater for blacks than for whites and impacted on a population already marginalized with respect to full-time employment.

Although the concomitant growth in female labor participation since 1970 increased both full- and part-time female work among all women, it was far more significant for blacks than whites. Of blacks who hold jobs, women constitute a rapidly growing share. Indeed, the decline of employment among black men and growth of full-time employment among black women produced a black employment corps in the metropolitan area that was more than 56 percent female in 1988.

How can we explain the changes in the patterns of labor-force participation and employment? Two important factors are united under what have been termed the "mismatch" hypotheses.[35] The first of the hypotheses, which is supported by the data on jobs presented earlier, argues that most blacks live in the city, which has been losing jobs, while most of the job growth has occurred in the suburbs. Thus, blacks find it more difficult

Table 2.11   Proportion of workers aged 25–54 in selected
educational categories, by industrial sector, 1970 and 1988

	Local service	Manufacturing	Export service	Total
1970				
Less than high school	30.4%	39.7%	14.5%	31.6%
High school graduate	42.4	40.2	50.4	42.8
Some college	8.9	8.4	15.3	9.7
BA or more	18.4	11.7	19.8	15.9
1988				
Less than high school	7.0	8.8	4.3	13.8
High school graduate	44.9	50.3	39.6	42.4
Some college	19.7	18.3	21.2	23.2
BA or more	28.4	22.6	34.9	23.3

Sources: See Table 2.10.

and expensive to find employment. When they have been laid off from firms closing or contracting in the city, they often face the twin burdens of distance and age.

The second mismatch hypothesis asserts that blacks lack the education demanded by the contemporary urban economy. Although it is true that black levels of education have long lagged behind that of whites, comparisons of census data from 1950 to 1988 show that these differences rapidly diminished during the postwar period. Indeed, since 1960 the level of education among Philadelphia's black adults actually improved at a faster rate than among whites. On this evidence, then, it would seem that the differentials could not explain the patterns of labor-force participation and employment.

However, this evidence fails to consider how the educational attainment demanded by the labor market has changed over time. If the demands of the labor market have escalated faster than black educational attainment has improved, blacks could find their position deteriorating rather than improving.

Table 2.11 displays the educational levels of prime-aged workers—those aged 25–54—in three industrial sectors in 1970 and 1988.[36] The patterns are clear. First, in both years, the level of education in the growing export service sector was substantially higher than the level of education found among local service and manufacturing workers. Second, between 1970 and 1988, overall levels of education substantially increased. The percentage of college graduates in manufacturing and local service doubled and increased by more than 76 percent in export services and 54 percent in local

Table 2.12   Employment rates by educational level,
Philadelphia metropolitan area, 1970 and 1988

Year	<9	10–11	12	13–15	16+
		Years of Schooling			
1970	67.5	76.2	78.7	71.4	83.2
1988	18.4	35.3	66.7	65.6	79.6

Sources: U.S. Census of Population, 1970: Public Use Sample of Basic Records from the 1970 Census, 15% Sample, prepared by the Bureau of the Census (machine-readable data file) (Washington, D.C.: Bureau of the Census, 1983); Current Population Survey, 1988: Annual Demographic File (March), prepared by the Bureau of the Census (machine-readable data file) (Washington, D.C.: Bureau of the Census, 1989).

services. Regardless of industrial sector, the percentage of workers with less than a high school education in 1988 was a third or less of its value in 1970. Clearly, workers entering the labor force with less than a high school diploma are severely disadvantaged.

But the real meaning of education for employment in the region is demonstrated in Table 2.12, which gives rates of employment among adults by level of education from 1970 to 1988. In 1970 there was only a relatively weak relationship between levels of education and employment. Sixty-seven percent of those who did not complete high school, compared with 83 percent of those who graduated from college, were employed. In 1988 only 18 percent of adults who had not completed high school were employed, whereas those who attended or completed college remained employed at almost the same level as 1970. In short, it appears that graduation from high school is becoming a prerequisite for employment in the contemporary urban economy.

What these figures mean is that even though black educational attainment is increasingly similar to that of whites, whatever difference remains can damage black employment prospects. And about 35 percent of adult blacks, compared with 20 percent of adult whites, have less than a high school education. For these blacks, their lack of education is a clear barrier to employment.

The combination of a legacy of racial discrimination, differential access to employment, and differential workforce participation (including changed educational minima for jobs in the region's postindustrial economy) all contribute to the striking differentials in family incomes between whites and blacks.

Table 2.13   Average family income by number
of earners and race, Philadelphia SMSA, 1987

Number of earners	White	Black	Black as a percentage of white
None	$10,157	$ 6,912	68
One	$24,045	$17,000	71
Two	$35,750	$26,650	75
Three or more	$40,975	$40,000	98

*Source: Current Population Survey, 1988: Annual Demographic
File (March)*, prepared by the Bureau of the Census (machine-
readable data file) (Washington, D.C.: Bureau of the Census, 1989).

Family Wage Earners

The third major factor that must be examined relative to family income
differentials by race is the structure of families and the earning power of
family members. Not surprisingly, there is a strong relationship between
number of wage earners and family income. Table 2.13, which compares
black and white families with the same number of wage earners, indicates
that white families have higher incomes regardless of the number of wage
earners present—reflecting the facts of the preceding discussion.

Overall, the differentials between black and white family incomes decline as the number of wage earners increases. The growth of two-earner
families overall is related to the changing mix of part-time and full-time
employment in the region; part-time jobs typically pay less than full-time
and seldom offer the fringe benefits (for example, health insurance, retire-
ment plan) of the latter. Table 2.11 demonstrates that part-time work has
increased and full-time work has declined for males. Both have increased
for females.[37]

Thus, family incomes for both blacks and whites are directly dependent
upon the number of earners and the number of jobs they hold. It has already
been noted that Philadelphia's workforce is moving toward a pattern of
part-time work. It is also evident that Philadelphia's families are made up
of multiple earners and that the number of multiple job holders has also
increased. Thus we must conclude that although the income distribution for
families has remained relatively constant over time, it has done so only because more family members are working more jobs for the same net pay. By
implication, the fewer the wage earners, real or potential, within a family
unit, the lower is the expected income level.

Do Philadelphia black and white families exhibit significant differences

Table 2.14   Average number of earners by
family type and race, Philadelphia SMSA, 1988

		Family type		
Race	All	Married couple	Single female	Single male
White	1.72	1.78	1.42	1.35
Black	1.28	1.55	1.11	.82
Total	1.62	1.75	1.24	1.21

Source: Current Population Survey, 1988: Annual Demographic File (March),
prepared by the Bureau of the Census (machine-readable data file) (Washington,
D.C.: Bureau of the Census, 1989).

in the average number of earners or potential earners within the family?
Table 2.14 documents the differences by family type and race for 1988. In
both races families headed by a married couple have the most wage earners;
but notice, too, that the number of wage earners is higher among white
families regardless of whether they are headed by single or married adults.
Given the higher rates of employment among whites, these differences are
not unexpected.

If we push the analysis further, we can see that major differences exist
between white and black family structures, limiting black family earnings
even more. Over time the proportion of families headed by single women
has grown among both blacks and whites. But that proportion has increased
far more rapidly among blacks in recent years, so that by 1988 about 45
percent of black families in the region were female-headed, compared with
only 13 percent of white families (see Figure 2.7). Given what we now have
already demonstrated about the lower earning power of one-parent families, we must conclude that family configuration contributes significantly to
blacks' income disadvantage.

Family earnings differentials can thus be seen as the outcomes of several different and substantially reinforcing features of racial stratification
and family dynamics. Whatever legacy of racism persists—and a regression
analysis contained in Appendix C provides substantial evidence of just such
persistence—is reinforced by shifts in the city's economic structure and
differential access to those changes by black workers, by shifts in workforce
participation, and by changes in the number of wage earners present in the
family. As the proportion of Philadelphia's black population has increased,
its earnings potential has been deeply affected.

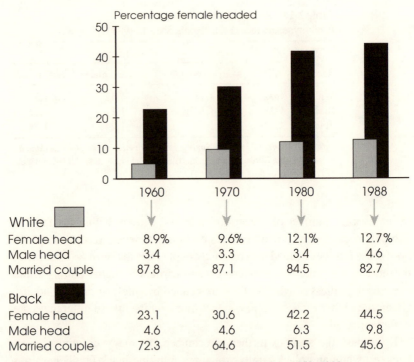

Percentage female headed

	1960	1970	1980	1988
White				
Female head	8.9%	9.6%	12.1%	12.7%
Male head	3.4	3.3	3.4	4.6
Married couple	87.8	87.1	84.5	82.7
Black				
Female head	23.1	30.6	42.2	44.5
Male head	4.6	4.6	6.3	9.8
Married couple	72.3	64.6	51.5	45.6

Figure 2.7   Family structure by race, Philadelphia SMSA, 1960–1988

Sources: U.S. Census of Population, 1960 Public Use Sample: One-in-One-Thousand Sample, pre-pared by the Bureau of the Census (machine-readable data file) (Washington, D.C.: Bureau of the Census, 1963); *U.S. Census of Population, 1970: Public Use Sample of Basic Records from the 1970 Census, 15% Sample*, prepared by the Bureau of the Census (machine-readable data file) (Washington, D.C.: Bureau of the Census, 1973); *U.S. Census of Population, 1980: 5% Microdata File*, prepared by the Bureau of the Census (machine-readable data file) (Washington, D.C.: Bu-reau of the Census, 1983); *Current Population Survey, 1988, Annual Demographic File (March)*, prepared by the Bureau of the Census (machine-readable data file) (Washington, D.C.: Bureau of the Census, 1989).

Conclusion

There can be little doubt that the loss of manufacturing jobs has hurt the city both directly and indirectly. The direct impact has been felt when plants closed or relocated and workers who lost their jobs were unable to find new ones that paid as much as the ones they had lost. While some accepted jobs at lower wages, others were forced out of the labor market, and still others had to leave the area in order to find work. Nor is it likely that the city can find new manufacturers to replace the ones they have lost because of the negative aspects of its physical infrastructure—the congestion, poor access to superhighways, cost of space, and inadequacy of space that caused manufacturers to seek other locations. If the city is to recover, it must seek ways to foster the creation of nonmanufacturing jobs.

The city is also hurt indirectly in a variety of ways. First, it is hurt because manufacturing jobs stimulate more employment than jobs in other industries (they have what economists called a higher "employment multiplier"). For example, in 1966 Philadelphia's apparel industry, which then had 50,000 jobs, supported at least 2,000 jobs in the carton and corrugated box industry alone.[38] Jobs in other related industries add at least 8,000 more to the total, not counting the many jobs that depend upon the expenditures of the more than 60,000 workers. One recent estimate for the Philadelphia metropolitan area fixed the employment multiplier at 1.9 for manufacturing and 1.5 for nonmanufacturing;[39] in other words, each new manufacturing job creates 1.9 more jobs, whereas each nonmanufacturing job only produces 1.5. Thus, the loss of manufacturing jobs had a domino effect, and this effect is larger for manufacturing than for other industries. Second, as part of this domino effect, the closure of one manufacturing plant may cause the closure of another firm dependent on it; even if the dependent firm does not close, it may be forced to scale back its operations, which may make survival more difficult for still other firms dependent on the contracting firm. An advertising firm, faced with the loss of a major client, may be required to drop staff, which, in turn, makes it less competitive in seeking new accounts. A neighborhood retailer catering to the employees and their families may suffer. A neighborhood bank, which may be creditor to all of the above, may have to reduce the availability of funds or even close, making recovery all the more difficult.

The city's injuries are compounded when some of the discharged workers leave in search of employment elsewhere. Typically, these are the individuals with the most skills, who are the most employable. As a result, the quality of the labor force and the city's attractiveness to new employers declines. Whenever a city is losing part of its employment base, it becomes less attractive to new firms, who may fear that needed goods and services will be increasingly unavailable and that taxes and other costs of doing business may increase. The city loses tax revenues from the closed firm, other dependent firms, and the discharged employees while simultaneously experiencing a demand for greater expenditures for social, educational, and other supportive services. Moreover, in an effort to attract new business, a city may develop a program that subsidizes new business in the hope of gaining a long-term benefit in terms of increased tax revenues. The evidence supporting the effectiveness of such efforts is, at best, mixed.

Finally, the housing stock of the city suffers as the workers' hardships cause them to defer needed maintenance. Similarly, reduced tax revenues often force the city to choose between needed social services and maintenance of its physical infrastructure. In Philadelphia, as in a number of other eastern and midwestern cities, maintenance has been deferred so long that the issue is often not maintenance, but replacement.

The situation is quite different in the suburbs because they have only begun to lose manufacturing since 1980, and the growth of nonmanufacturing jobs (roughly 236,000 jobs between 1980 and 1987) compensated for the loss.[40] However, particular suburban communities may experience problems quite similar to those of the city. When U.S. Steel shut down most of its steel mills in suburban Bucks County in 1983, the impact on nearby communities was substantial. As in the city, growth of service-industry jobs offers no guarantees that laid-off steelworkers will be able to find employment at comparable earnings. Indeed, the better paying service jobs are likely to require skills that production workers do not have.

At the individual level, the consequences of these changing conditions are distinctly unfavorable for those who live within the city. The jobs being created in Philadelphia in the 1980s have been either high paying or low paying, with few new opportunities in the middle.

In contrast, the employment changes occurring in the suburbs have been far more evenly balanced with respect to pay: roughly equal shares of new jobs were created in each of the three earnings groups. Yet, although the suburban labor market continues to offer jobs that can sustain a middle-class lifestyle, there are disquieting signs of future problems. The loss of suburban manufacturing jobs since 1980 and the absence of significant growth in real income for the 95 percent of the workers who earned less than twice the median wage in 1980 suggests there may be difficulties ahead.

The economic transformation of the region has changed the nature of work but is also pivotal in shaping individual's lives and the relationships of their communities to one another across the region.

A fundamental change in the nature of work and its relationship to the families of the region has taken place. Families are dependent on more workers and more jobs per family to keep parity in income levels over time. Thus, the change in the nature of jobs has yielded a change in the nature of the workforce and of work itself. It is clear that the economic base of the region is imposing fundamental divisions upon its communities, especially between city and suburbs and between whites and blacks.

Nowhere are these trends seen more vividly than in the continued discrepancy between white and black family incomes in the region. Past patterns of wage discrimination and lack of access to jobs are reinforced by the changing nature of work and wages. The increased reliance of households on dual income sources leaves single-earner households at a distinct economic disadvantage. It is in this mix of workplace and domestic structures that the discrepancy between white and black incomes is rooted.

What the Philadelphia region thus confronts is a growing division between significant components of the region. The City of Philadelphia itself has watched its population, its jobs, and its tax base erode, especially over the past five decades. The suburbs have become the location of job opportunities in a metropolitan economy lagging behind the nation. As we examine the political and social tensions between Philadelphia and its suburban committees, this fundamental economic disparity must always be recognized as the root of these conflicts. The intersection of economic dynamics with the differential demographic and family structures of black and white communities suggests that the persistent racial divisions in the Philadelphia region will worsen before they will improve. The spatial isolation of the black community, discussed in further detail in the next chapter, exacerbates the problem and makes concerted social or political responses to these persistent inequities difficult, if not impossible.

In short, Philadelphia remains a metropolitan area strongly divided by race, class, and economic opportunity. These divisions are the fundamental theme of the remainder of this volume.

3

Housing and Neighborhoods

In preceding chapters we have focused on the dramatic shift in the economic base of the city and the degree of racial and ethnic conflict that has taken place against this backdrop. The new service economy that dominates the region has benefited some of the region's communities and bypassed others. Nowhere is the uneven character of Philadelphia's economic transformation more evident than in its housing stock.

To even the most casual of observers, the charm of refurbished row-houses in gentrified and historically certified neighborhoods pales next to the wholesale abandonment found in many of the neighborhoods inhabited by black, Hispanic, and white as well. The quiet splendor of central city high-rise apartments and condominiums gives way to the noise and crowding of the vertical ghettoes of public housing. Homebound suburbanites push and crowd by the sprawled, often incoherent figures of women and men without homes, whose address is a steam vent and whose roof may well be cardboard, if that.

The economic changes that have swept the city since World War II have transformed the residential landscape of the city, but hardly with the uniformly beneficial effects generally assumed by the ideologies of progress and planning. The decentralization of economic and residential locations over the past forty years has created, in Philadelphia's case, graphic examples of the paradox of poverty and plenty, virtually side by side. The contemporary picture of housing in the city itself is one of gentrified splendor next to public housing, of abandoned houses and homeless people, and of a black population expanding into many of the city's neighborhoods, yet more segregated now than at any time over the past four decades.

These contrasts, extreme though they may be, reflect fundamental inequalities in the city's new economy, expressed in that most visible of indicators of social standing—the house. When we talk of the housing of the city of Philadelphia, in one sense we are simply indicating that the city has rich as well as poor neighborhoods, black, Hispanic, and white communities, gentrified as well as abandoned areas. If the only purpose of this chapter were to affirm that fact, we could be content with a simple two-dimensional description of the city's housing issues—a tabular display, some maps, and a discussion of possible scenarios for the future.

However, a discussion of housing offers much more of an opportunity than simply a reflection on current inequalities of income and wealth. Housing, especially in its neighborhood context, represents an image of the city's past patterns of development and opportunity. It bears the imprint of households and their incomes and customs, stages of rapid growth and speculative expansion, and most often today, the differential effects of neighborhoods revitalized as against those forgotten. It is, in short, a dynamic sculpture of the city's historical patterns of growth, capturing moments of change in the destruction, the creation, and the adaptation of housing to social and economic shifts across the urban landscape.

In a city with as long a history as Philadelphia's, this is a remarkably complex sculpture. If we limit ourselves to only the most recent changes in the neighborhoods and housing of the city, the image is still being shaped in some areas and for some of the people of the city, while it is fairly complete in others. It presents a picture of a city making a break with its past—trying to recast the built environment of the past into different forms using the energy of a new set of developmental forces, corresponding to the emerging postindustrial, service-oriented industries of the 1980s.

The housing of contemporary Philadelphia thus reflects the set of economic, social, and political forces that divide the city. In its newer forms it is setting a physical character to the city with which future generations will wrestle. It is both centralizing and decentralizing, expanding and abandoning, creating new opportunities as well as reinforcing old barriers. The housing of the city is thus a paradoxical representation of a community caught on the cusp of social and economic change. At the conclusion of this chapter the roots of these paradoxes in both recent history and the social structure of the city should be much more visible.

This chapter outlines the structural roots of Philadelphia's current housing crisis—the operation of a housing market that directly produces neighborhood displacement (via gentrification), reinforcement for racial and ethnic segregation, abandoned dwellings, and homeless people. Our interpretation should not be misread as an attempt to account for inadequate housing solely by the unscrupulous actions of individual property holders, realtors, bankers, and the like. Instead, we argue that class and racial bias in the distribution of jobs, wages, and other resources at one time has been reproduced at a later time in housing and other commodities. Thus, housing patterns essentially reflect and help reinforce the larger system of inequality.

This basic structural reality is present within historically specific circumstances. Ghettoization, redlining, suburbanization, and infrastructural insufficiencies, for example, are problems emerging from economic growth and consequent migration trends. We have already seen in Chapter 2 that the economic base of the city went through a wrenching deindustrialization after World War II—an experience similar to many other older, industrially based northeastern and midwestern cities. Philadelphia's wartime recovery had proved to be illusory, after it had fueled both suburbanization and new immigrant migrations to the city. The subsequent decline and collapse of the city's manufacturing jobs base produced selective migration from the city, the decline of the volume of the housing stock, and the eventual abandonment of some neighborhoods. The subsequent "revitalization" of part of the city represents a new form of city economic base, with new requirements for its labor force and with new neighborhood investment patterns. The simultaneous emergence of gentrification and displacement, speculative activity, and large-scale abandonment provides a schizophrenic image of a city half-phoenix and half-ashes. In the midst of the ashes stand not only empty houses but unhoused people, truly a paradox of the new order.

Housing in Philadelphia: An Overview

Table 3.1 provides various housing indicators for the city, the metropolitan area and the nation as a whole, to serve as a backdrop for this chapter's discussions. As might be expected, there are the usual differences between city and suburb, reflected particularly in the higher housing values across the metropolitan area than in the city itself. Further evidence of the significant income differences and the growth of that disparity over time is also evident, as the median income for the region has increased at a faster rate than for the city, among both owners and renters. More significant for the city is the fact that the suburban housing stock has clearly increased (indicated by the constant growth of the occupied housing stock), while the city suffered a dramatic loss of its stock during the 1970–78 period. It has shown a resurgence more recently in the net number of its housing units, but its occupied housing stock still lags behind the 1970 levels. It is somewhat paradoxical to note an increase in overall housing stock without a market to support such an increase. Two processes seem to be suggested. On the one hand, the demand for higher cost housing drives an increase in new housing stock, while on the other, growing abandonment at the low end of the market increases the vacancy level.

Table 3.1 Selected housing characteristics of Philadelphia, the Philadelphia SMSA, and the United States, 1970–1985

	1970			1978			1982			1985		
	City	SMSA	U.S.	City	SMSA	U.S.	City	SMSA	U.S.	City	SMSA	U.S.
Total units (in 000s)	673.5	1536.7	67699	663.2	1724.0	82833	688.3	1780.7	91675	706.5	1874.8	99931
Occupied (in 000s)	642.1	1480.2	63445	610.8	1609.8	77167	624.6	1655.4	84638	632.6	1736.4	88425
% owner occupied	58.7%	67.1%	62.9%	61.0%	68.2%	65.2%	60.7%	68.5%	64.7%	62.9%	68.3%	63.5%
Median value	$10.6	$14.9	$17.1	$24.3	$39.2	$41.5	$31.4	$51.6	$59.7	$37.0	$61.0	$62.1
Median monthly rent	$80	$90	$108	$151	$183	$200	$211	$247	$315	$334	$392	$364
Median income (owner occupied)	$9.4	$11.0	$9.7	$15.2	$19.3	$16.8	$18.1	$25.9	$24.4	$21.3	$30.4	$27.8
Median income (renter occupied)	$5.5	$6.4	$6.3	$7.9	$10.1	$9.3	$9.5	$12.0	$12.4	$11.6	$17.5	$15.5

Sources: U.S. Census of Population and Housing, 1970: Census Tracts: Philadelphia, PA-NJ Standard Metropolitan Statistical Area (PHC 1-159) (Washington, D.C.: Government Printing Office, 1972); *Annual Housing Survey, 1978: Philadelphia SMSA Data File*, prepared by the Bureau of the Census and Abt Associates (machine-readable data file) (Cambridge, Mass.: Abt Associates, 1981); *Annual Housing Survey, 1982: Philadelphia SMSA Data File*, prepared by the Bureau of the Census (machine-readable data file) (Ann Arbor: Interuniversity Consortium for Political and Social Research [ICPSR], 1986); *American Housing Survey, 1983: National Core Sample*, prepared by the Bureau of the Census (machine-readable data file) (Ann Arbor: Interuniversity Consortium for Political and Social Research [ICPSR], 1986); *American Housing Survey, 1985: Philadelphia SMSA Data File*, prepared by the Bureau of the Census (machine-readable data file) (Ann Arbor: Interuniversity Consortium for Political and Social Research [ICPSR], 1989).

A comparison of Philadelphia's with national housing patterns over the same period reveals a remarkable pattern. In 1970 the city of Philadelphia was remarkably close to its suburbs in terms of housing values and rent levels, and markedly closer to the national averages for income levels of owners and renters alike. By 1985 a marked divergence between city and region is apparent along housing lines, and the region, not the city, is close to the national income averages. At one level, this is further evidence of a growing disparity between city and suburb that forms the basis of much of our analysis in this and other chapters. The growing discontinuity between the core and the remainder of the region heightens political tensions, for instance, and exacerbates the trend toward uneven economic development.

We begin to see the dilemma facing would-be consumers in a housing market that puts out conflicting messages. Philadelphia offers tremendous value for the housing dollar of the consumer, as average housing costs remain somewhat less expensive to the consumer than either in the region or nationally (see Figure 3.1). The dilemma consists of the more limited investment climate suggested by these lower values, at least by comparison with regional and national housing markets. Put simply, although the housing values would seem to entice persons to remain in the city, will they be able to obtain a mortgage? Will renters be able to find landlords who are treating housing as a long-term investment rather than as a short-term tax shelter or speculative venture?

These questions are particularly evident when we examine more closely the phenomenon of home ownership. Philadelphia, long said to be a "city of homes," has a 61 percent home ownership rate (66 percent for the entire metropolitan area), ranking fourth among major American cities. As of 1982, however, some 50 percent of the homeowners had no mortgages on their properties—they owned them free and clear. As the goal of most individuals, this level of home ownership might be applauded. In terms of housing dynamics, however, it probably means that the sale of many of these homes is complicated by the age of the residents as well as that of their properties. People who want to move on (either because children have grown or the neighborhood has changed) find themselves trapped in a house and a neighborhood that holds no charm for the "new wave" of home buyers.

New housing in Philadelphia was brought into the housing stock at a substantial rate in the 1980s, considering the already densely constructed nature of the city. Indeed, after suffering two decades of losses in its housing stock, Philadelphia in the early 1980s (according to the 1982 Annual Housing Survey by the U.S. Census Bureau) was estimated to be

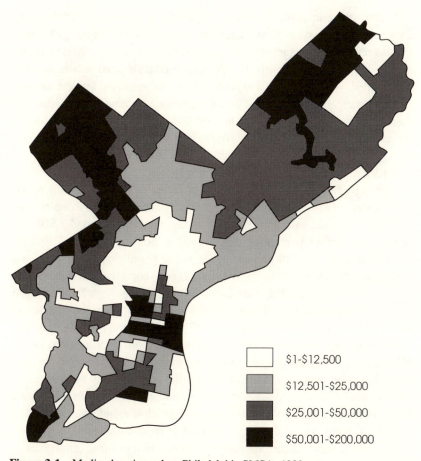

Figure 3.1   Median housing value, Philadelphia SMSA, 1980

Source: U.S. Census of Population and Housing, 1980: Summary Tape File 3A, prepared by the Bureau of the Census (machine-readable data file) (Washington, D.C.: Bureau of the Census, 1982).

expanding its stock at between two and three thousand units per year, even while the population continued to decline. This anomaly is easily explained by the presence of more single-person and single-headed households in the population, which increases the number of housing units needed for the city. New housing, however, was targeted at a limited market: the average purchase price of these new units was between $100,000 and $125,000, and the median rental price was above $550 per month (1982 estimate). By contrast, the citywide median purchase price for housing in 1980 was $23,500, with a median rent of $168 per month.

At the other end of the housing scale, while we have seen much housing constructed, the estimated number of properties abandoned but still standing has remained constant over the past decade: roughly 22,000 structures. During that same time nearly 10,000 additional residential structures were demolished. When these figures for buildings are translated into the number of housing units involved (most of the buildings were multifamily), the estimated loss is in the range of 50,000 to 60,000 units, nearly 10 percent of the current housing stock in the city. At least as significantly, Annual Housing Survey (AHS) interviewers reported in 1977 that one in three residents in the city had boarded-up dwellings on their block.[1]

Although the city has seen an upsurge in upper-income dwellings, the current state of lower-income households provides a substantial contrast. In 1980, for instance, half of the people with an annual income under $10,000 paid more than 47 percent of that income in housing costs. In 1982 we know that more than 40 percent of the entire population of the city paid more than 45 percent of their income in housing costs (based on AHS estimates). The worst hardships are borne by the city's poorest families, who must seek shelter in an increasingly tight market. Although the number of available low-rent units in the city in 1970 was considerably higher than the number of very low income renters (defined as those with incomes under $7,500), by 1982 there were more than twice as many very low income renters as there were affordable units. Needless to say, many low-rent units are seriously substandard.[2] It is clear that a remarkable division of housing cost and housing equality is emerging in Philadelphia. Indeed, as stated at the outset, this is a city of extreme differences in its housing.

One of the basic factors affecting the distribution of these differences is the neighborhood. The condition, costs, and character of housing reflect not just the social standing of the individuals and households of a neighborhood but the place of that neighborhood in the distribution of housing investment dollars (capital) across the city and the region—even nationally. Neighborhoods are social networks but are also investment sites as well.[3] As only one instance, housing, because of its great cost, usually reflects an allocation of credit at the time when the building is constructed as well as when it changes hands. Credit institutions evaluate not only the economic standing of the individuals seeking a mortgage but the market potential of the residence in question, that is, the economic position of the neighborhood as reflected in its proximity to work, its position in a class-based system of residence, and its access to capital. The neighborhood's investment potential is affected as well by the ethnic and racial separations that emerge from that framework, governmental development and redevelopment efforts, and the extent to which the neighborhood can mobilize to develop itself as an investment site.

Housing Conditions at the End of World War II

At the close of the war Philadelphia had a well-established pattern of neighborhoods, linked directly to the industrial economic base of the city. The spatial separation of residential areas centered on access to work, creating four distinct types of neighborhoods. It is important to appreciate the patterns that were set in the 1940s, because the housing existing then constitutes the bulk of the contemporary stock and creates both the opportunities and the costs associated with the uneven nature of the development we now witness. In 1980, 58.5 percent of Philadelphia's housing was built prior to 1939; only Boston and St. Louis had higher concentrations of older stock.

In the urban core much of the residential character of the city was set by the Tenderloin and slum areas. Largely renter occupied, the dwellings dated to the early industries of the city (especially the garment trades), some of which were still functioning as late as the onset of the Depression. Multifamily walk-ups and boarding houses interspersed themselves with the retail and wholesale buildings of the downtown.

Beyond the downtown areas lay the industrial neighborhoods of North, West, and South Philadelphia, clustered along the major freight routes, and the river communities of Fishtown, Kensington, Bridesburg, and Grays Ferry. These neighborhoods had some of the oldest and least commodious forms of housing available in the city. The traditional form of the housing was the "trinity" house, so-called because it consisted of three levels (father-son-holy ghost), typically with one or two rooms to a level, with low ceilings. This small space was often shared by multiple households, sometimes being run as a rooming house.

Even in the better-off industrial neighborhods the housing style was that ubiquitous form of Philadelphia housing, the rowhouse. Whole blocks of homes were built at one time, sharing the external walls with neighbors on either side. A clear indication of the income base of the neighborhood was the number of levels in the house—ranging from two to four, and the width of the properties (from 12 to 22 feet). This form of housing dominates the neighborhoods of Philadelphia and raises very difficult issues when neighborhoods decline in population and livability. To revitalize not one house, but a row; to tear down one house in the middle of a row; to face the image of the contemporary suburban detached home as a model of consumer preference—all these issues combine to make revitalization a complex question for policy makers.

Beyond the working-class neighborhoods lay a set of neighborhoods known as "streetcar suburbs." They were either built on lands held by the early- and mid-nineteenth-century wealthy of the city that were developed as suburban housing, or they were communities that had developed contemporaneously with the city and became integrated into the city by road and rail networks. Before the introduction of the automobile to the metropolitan landscape, large areas of relatively distant housing became accessible to the city by the introduction of first horse-drawn and then electrically powered streetcars. The establishment of an extensive transportation grid linked the newly suburbanized homeowners, mostly drawn from the management sectors of the industrial plants and the financial and retail businesses downtown, to their place of work. At the same time, it facilitated the distinct separation of these communities from the noise, dirt, and generally noxious nature of the neighborhoods immediately contingent to either place of work.

These streetcar suburbs consisted of a mix of large row homes (with extensive porches and small front and back yards), duplexes, and some single, large homes, typically on corner lots. Much of West Philadelphia, Overbrook, Wynnefield, Germantown, Oak Lane, Olney, Frankford, and the Oxford Circle areas had this type of mix. These suburbs in the city were occupied by a solid middle class that had emerged from the expansionist 1920s, held on, and further expanded during the wartime years.

There also existed a fairly privileged class of wealthy families who had long ago either chosen a fashionable downtown (Rittenhouse Square) address, or left the central city. The growth of the "Main Line" suburbs, along the main western rail line of the Pennsylvania Railroad, was fueled by the upper class, particularly those who had obtained wealth through industry and commerce. The alternative community for families of wealth and power who wished to remain in the city was the far northwestern area of Chestnut Hill.

As late as 1940 there was no evidence of massive concentrations of either black or Hispanic neighborhoods in the city; the relatively small black population lived in a few spatially delineated areas, with the exception of those in quarters attached to the more affluent housing in the streetcar suburbs. (Indeed, the Hispanic presence in Philadelphia was not a significant part of the neighborhood scheme until the 1960s.) From 1930 to 1950, despite substantial growth in their numbers, black Philadelphians remained in the neighborhoods immediately south, west, and north of Center City. Indeed, for more than twenty years large sections of West and North Philadelphia were racially integrated. The Depression and World War II limited the expansion of the city's housing supply and, consequently, limited residential mobility. The growing black population settled in areas that already contained substantial numbers of blacks. Thus, although population density increased in these neighborhoods, there was little neighborhood change.[4]

Postwar Reorganization

The process of housing development in the immediate aftermath of World War II had two important effects. On the one hand, home ownership and acquisition boomed, under the explosion of demand and the facilitating mortgage-financing arrangements. On the other, a new black community emerged in Philadelphia, spatially constrained and with access limited largely to a newly created, absentee-owned rental stock. Figure 3.2 documents the relationship between increased minority presence and owner occupancy rates in the neighborhoods undergoing the greatest ghettoization during this period. West Philadelphia and Lower North Philadelphia had relatively greater proportions of the city's black population at an earlier stage, which was reflected in a lower than city average home-ownership rate in 1940. After the war, expanding home-ownership opportunities drove the citywide average from 35 percent to nearly 60 percent in one decade. Yet in each neighborhood, the decade of most rapid growth in black population was matched by a corresponding decline in home ownership. Increases in the proportion of owner occupancy in 1980 are actually offset by significant decreases in the occupied housing stock, as abandonment disproportionately shrank available rental housing.

To many observers this seemed to be a process of whites fleeing blacks. In actuality, at least in the years immediately after the end of World War II, the correlation between the growth of black communities and flight to the suburbs was neither empirically nor attitudinally expressed as cause and effect.

Early suburbanization was driven by large-scale changes whose effects had been masked by World War II. Chief among these were the increased role of the highway system in defining industrial and residential locations, spatial extension of the entire productive system in the United States, dramatic changes in capital liquidity—especially with respect to home purchases—and the unleashing of new housing demand that had been dammed up under wartime production planning.

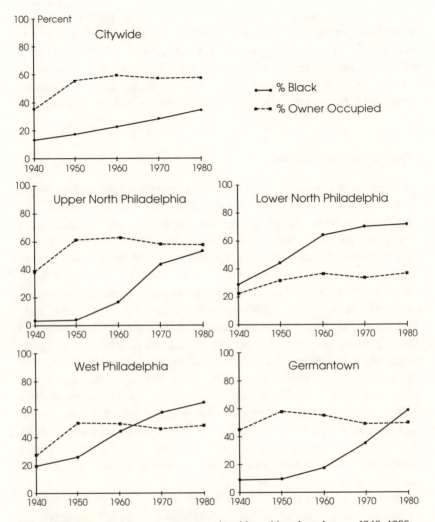

Figure 3.2   Race and owner occupancy, citywide and in selected areas, 1940–1980

Sources: Social Science Data Library Philadelphia Historical Data File, 1929–1985 (machine-readable data file) (Philadelphia: Temple University Social Science Data Library, 1989). Data reported in this figure are based on: *U.S. Census of Population and Housing, 1940: Statistics for Census Tracts, Philadelphia. PA* (Washington, D.C.: Government Printing Office, 1942); *U.S. Census of Population and Housing, 1950: Census Tract Statistics, Philadelphia, Pennsylvania and Adjacent Area* (vol. 3, chap. 42) (Washington, D.C.: Government Printing Office, 1952); *U.S. Census of Population and Housing, 1960: Census Tracts, Philadelphia, PA-NJ Standard Metropolitan Statistical Area* (vol. 1, no. 116) (Washington, D.C.: Government Printing Office, 1962); *U.S. Census of Population and Housing, 1970: Census Tracts, Philadelphia, PA-NJ Standard Metropolitan Statistical Area* (PHC 1-116) (Washington, D.C.: Government Printing Office, 1972); *U.S. Census of Population and Housing, 1980: Summary Tape File 3A*, prepared by the Bureau of the Census (machine-readable data file) (Washington, D.C.: Bureau of the Census, 1982).

Facilitating this centrifugal movement was the redefinition of home-ownership possibilities that had begun during the Depression but exploded after the war. Several federal "alphabet soup" agencies—the Home Owners' Loan Corporation (HOLC), the Federal Housing Administration (FHA), and the Veterans' Administration (VA)—developed forms of mortgage insurance that guaranteed the payment of the mortgage to the bank, savings and loan, or building and loan society that extended a loan to qualified applicants buying qualified homes.[5]

With the increased flow of mortgage capital at the end of the war, housing boomed. Between 1940 and 1950 housing increased in Philadelphia from 550,000 to 600,000 units. Suburban growth was substantial, too, especially after the development of the Levitt-type approach to construction. However, both FHA and VA mortgage programs allowed mortgage insurance only on newly constructed homes. Arguing that the length (20–30 years) of the mortgage meant that they should back only the best of the housing stock, these agencies largely limited the availability of mortgage loans to the new housing stock and thus to the suburbs.[6]

Two areas within the region were directly affected. The Far Northeast section of the city, isolated until a Work Projects Administration (WPA) road-building project linked it more directly to the city, was transformed from essentially farm land to an automobile suburb within the city. Similarly, early suburban communities just over the city boundary became immediately accessible by way of roads, streetcars, or railways to those jobs within the city. The years immediately after the war, before substantial economic decline, thus witnessed an explosive growth in the region's population, in households, and in the transformation of exurban and rural areas into suburban communities.

For the neighborhoods that remained, it seemed as if nothing much had happened, at least at first. Children got married and moved away; parents might move also as the nest emptied, but the neighborhoods remained the same—or did they? As Figure 3.3 shows, the period between 1940 and 1960 witnessed population downturns in the older, more centrally located neighborhoods, such as South Philadelphia, Lower North Philadelphia, and Kensington. Even West and Southwest Philadelphia, as well as Upper North Philadelphia (largely streetcar suburbs) saw some declines. At the same time the population increased in the more distant neighborhoods of the city, particularly in the Northeast.

Taken together, Philadelphia's population remained, in the aggregate, relatively constant, at approximately two million. But clear indications of a population redistribution were visible. The data on population changes

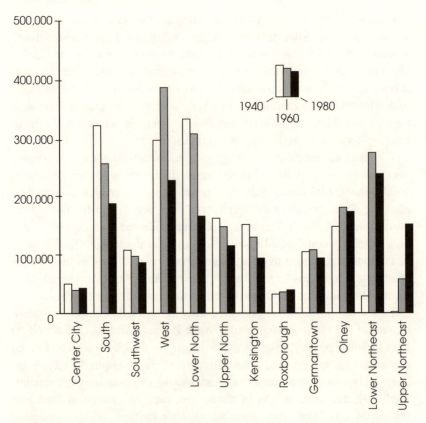

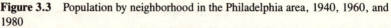

Figure 3.3   Population by neighborhood in the Philadelphia area, 1940, 1960, and 1980

Sources: Social Science Data Library Philadelphia: Historical Data File, 1929–1985 (machine-readable data file) (Philadelphia: Temple University Social Science Data Library, 1989). Data reported in this figure are based on: *U.S. Census of Population and Housing, 1940: Statistics for Census Tracts, Philadelphia, PA* (Washington, D.C.: Government Printing Office, 1942); *U.S. Census of Population and Housing, 1960: Census Tracts, Philadelphia, PA-NJ Standard Metropolitan Statistical Area* (vol. 1, no. 116) (Washington, D.C.: Government Printing Office, 1962); *U.S. Census of Population and Housing, 1980: Summary Tape File 3A*, prepared by the Bureau of the Census (machine readable data file) (Washington, D.C.: Bureau of the Census, 1982).

between 1960 and 1980 confirmed this shift in the distribution of the inner Philadelphia neighborhoods. Only Center City, undergoing a substantial gentrification process, evidenced a population growth over this period. This movement outward of the locus of the population is deeply entwined in the housing problems and political conflicts facing the city, as shall be seen. Given the suburbanization of economic opportunity, this pattern is not surprising.

The Philadelphia metropolitan area was experiencing a tremendous growth in population, which some naively attributed to a "baby boom." Baby boom there was, but the war had also set in motion tremendcus migration streams that brought significant changes to the neighborhoods of the city. The war had brought about a second great migration of black families from the southern United States, in a stream that continued throughout much of the 1950s. This black migration into spatially restricted housing opportunities came at a time when many Philadelphians were looking outside of the city for both their housing and their employment.

What we had, then, was a large population of newcomers looking for housing and employment in a city whose most mobile residents were leaving the city proper in pursuit of these same essentials in the suburbs. As long as the entire economy of the metropolitan area was growing, and as long as sufficient housing was made available through out-migration, no problem should have occurred—save the problems of any new migrant population to the city. Yet the restriction of housing opportunities meant that the black population of Philadelphia became spatially concentrated. Figure 3.4 shows that a number of white streetcar suburbs gave way to the sudden conversion of multiple communities into a spatially consolidated ghetto.

To a considerable extent, this seems to have been the result of the filtering down of housing opportunities in a very volatile housing market. Put slightly differently, the streetcar suburbs offered blacks more housing opportunities than the industrial blue-collar neighborhoods for several related reasons. Streetcar suburbs were inherently less stable because the residents did not have close ties to work place. The streetcar suburbs also contained a higher proportion of white-collar and professional workers who, with greater resources and earning power, were more mobile than factory workers. These communities were abandoned by families seeking new housing in the automobile suburbs. The result was rapid racial transition in many neighborhoods in West Philadelphia and North Philadelphia.

In particular, the housing market collapsed in the older streetcar suburbs such as Mantua and Strawberry Mansion when residents joined in the outward suburban movement from the city. Credit was not readily available for the sale of the houses for two reasons. First, as the lure of suburban space weeded out the more affluent home buyers, less affluent would-be purchasers did not qualify for loans on personal finance grounds. Additionally, the federal Home Owners' Loan Corporation had conducted an appraisal of the neighborhoods of the city in 1937 and had created maps of neighborhood mortgageability (maps that seem to have been transferred

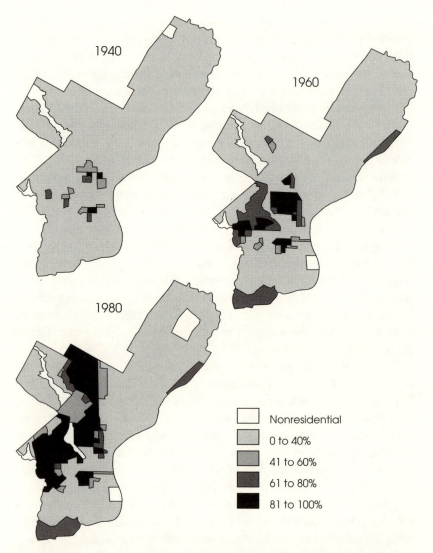

Figure 3.4   The proportion of blacks in Philadelphia neighborhoods, 1940, 1960, and 1980

Sources: Social Science Data Library Philadelphia Historical Data File, 1929–1985 (machine readable data file) (Philadelphia: Temple University Social Science Data Library, 1989). Data reported in this figure are based on: *U.S. Census of Population and Housing, 1940: Statistics for Census tracts, Philadelphia. PA* (Washington, D.C.: Government Printing Office, 1942); *U.S. Census of Population and Housing, 1960: Census Tracts, Philadelphia, PA-NJ Standard Metropolitan Statistical Area* (vol. 1, no. 116) (Washington, D.C.: Government Printing Office, 1962); *U.S. Census of Population and Housing, 1980: Summary Tape File 3A*, prepared by the Bureau of the Census (machine readable data file) (Washington, D.C.: Bureau of the Census, 1982).

directly to the FHA after the war) that identified the older industrial and streetcar suburb neighborhoods close in to the city as very risky areas for mortgage loans.

The assessment files accompanying these maps made explicit the previously implicit antiblack and anti-ethnic nature of the credit allocation process. References to hardworking Germanic stock in one area were contrasted with the "threat of Jewish encroachment"; areas of new housing were downgraded because they existed next to a 150-year-old black community that has yet to expand significantly above its 1940 level of 500 households; Italian, Slovak, and eastern European communities shared the disdain offered to most black neighborhoods. By denying credit in such neighborhoods, federal agencies fueled the process of neighborhood change.

The Decline of the City: Despair and Exodus, 1955–1975

Recall that we have described the industrial structure of the city as driving the housing and neighborhood structure; recall that the process of simultaneous exodus and influx characterized the years after World War II; and further recall that the national economy was undergoing a tremendous spatial shift. Now try to imagine what would happen to Philadelphia's neighborhoods if three out of every four industrial jobs were lost over a twenty-year span. That is precisely what happened between 1955 and 1975. And it is that economic decline that shaped the housing problems that emerged from the mid-1950s to mid-1970s, and that remain a part of the city's contemporary housing legacy.

In the 1950s the eventual depth of Philadelphia's postwar decline was only glimpsed. Estimates prepared during the late 1950s for the city planning commission suggested that a city of three million people was a real possibility, and that Philadelphia would need to grapple with problems of growth rather than decline.[7] In actuality, of course, the decline of stable employment was accelerating during these years. Textile mills had been closing and moving out of town. Associated industries began to be hit as well. The first danger signals were felt in the shipbuilding and shipping industries, as the Port of Philadelphia shrank in absolute and relative terms. Warehouses and factories alike emptied out; shipping became mechanized and dispersed, rather than labor intensive and concentrated. Jobs emptied out of the industrial neighborhoods, creating pressures on streetcar suburbs as well.

Although many residents moved away from the city, many others remained. Especially in the industrial neighborhoods of the city, residents seemed bound to the neighborhood by their house and by the institutions that had nurtured them during other periods of decline—the churches, the schools, the merchants, and the community and ethnic fraternal and sororal organizations. Within that network of social ties, and with little if any chance to attract new residents that were not perceived as threats, the housing market often became immobilized. Houses were capital investments that were locked into place, unable to attract significant new investment. As a result, the city's industrial neighborhoods became the locus of an aging population in an aging housing stock, and the arena for the kind of escalating conflicts described in Chapter 1.

Major and middle-range banking institutions reinforced the decline by their practice of disinvestment. Although exact data from this period are not available, the absence of home mortgages in large sections of the city, especially in black and working-class communities, made it appear that bankers had adopted a conscious policy of pulling money out of the city. To the investor, of course, disinvestment was simply the result of the search for the best return. Disinvestment in those terms is not necessarily purposeful; it is merely the automatic result of investment everywhere else *except* the older, industrial, and black communities of the city.

What data do exist (from community struggles with lending institutions, and from mortgage data obtained in 1977) reveal a mixed pattern. Ethnically structured industrial communities did have small lending institutions that would provide mortgages, despite the evident reluctance of major banks to lend in those same neighborhoods. The neighborhoods most deprived of housing credit were the older streetcar suburbs, particularly those that had become a part of the large ghetto that had formed in the late 1940s and early 1950s. Ownership had converted to rental housing, and low-income families crowded into some parts of West and North Philadelphia. But as the movement to the suburbs became more widespread, the overcrowding that had characterized many of these neighborhoods through the 1960s dramatically subsided. The publication of the 1970 census of population made plain to all that the extent of population loss was significant. Fully 15 percent of the city's population was lost between 1960 and 1970, much of it from the neighborhoods closest to the center of Philadelphia—the older low-income or transient neighborhoods (continuing a pattern noticed a decade earlier) and many of the earliest streetcar suburbs.

Some neighborhoods lost upwards of one-fourth of their population. By comparison, the losses in industrial communities were less severe, but still greater than in other city neighborhoods (see Figure 3.3).

The wholesale exodus from the city, and particularly the emptying of the inner-ring neighborhoods, continued through much of the 1970s. Despite the turn-around of some Central City neighborhoods starting in the mid-1970s, the revitalization of the city is spotty at best. As of 1980, for instance, the neighborhoods of North Philadelphia had lost an average of nearly 40 percent of their 1960 population—and some had lost over half of their residents. Overall, the city declined from 2.1 million people to 1.7 million in the years between 1960 and 1980. (Current estimates of continuing population loss between 1980 to 1990 range from 3 percent to 7 percent.)

Much of this loss occurred against an explicitly racial backdrop. What had been celebrated as the new affluence of the suburbs attracting people from an overcrowded city became viewed as white flight. Three events from the early 1960s seem, in retrospect, to typify that period. First, a black family was driven from a home they had purchased in the working-class suburb of Folcroft. Tactics associated with the South—burning crosses, vocal intimidation and epithets, broken windows—all came into play. Second, Mount Airy, an upper-middle-class community, gained much publicity as the only neighborhood to organize itself in order to integrate. What made this unusual was that many neighborhoods in Upper North Philadelphia and West Philadelphia, later developing streetcar suburbs, showed dramatic racial turn-arounds between the 1960 and 1980 census, making Mount Airy virtually the only exception to the pell-mell flight from the city.

The third event, and certainly the most important symbolically, was the riot that occurred in the summer of 1964. For three nights and two days the North Philadelphia neighborhood that had experienced some of the worst overcrowding, highest unemployment, and most intensive policing was the site of substantial violence and physical destruction. Newspapers reported the destruction as racially polarized; they emphasized the selective nature of property destruction, that is, against white merchants rather than the black barber shop. Additionally, when officials sealed off the neighborhood, they chose boundaries that seemed to assume a conspiracy of virtually all of the North Philadelphia black community against the city.

The public rhetoric after the riot was expressed in a variety of contexts (for instance, crime, safety, insurance, education, and so forth) but with a simple bottom line: if you are white, get out of the city if you can. Heightened racial paranoia marked the context within which people made decisions to move. More significantly for the politics of the city, racial

fears broke the back of whatever reform impetus was left. Public opin-
ions became polarized. City government was looked to as either a provider
of better services for excluded neighborhoods (the liberal public welfare
agenda, support by the national war on poverty, with strong civil rights
overtones), or as the last defense of neighborhoods threatened by unwanted
changes, whose residents could not leave (the conservative, law-and-order
agenda, played out against national images of riot and protest).

It is still not clear to what degree the movement of whites from the city
was actually grounded in explicit racism. Indeed, during the 1960s and
1970s the collapse of the manufacturing economy of the city and the shift
of jobs to the suburbs might just as easily explain whites' migration to
the suburbs. Nonetheless, the racially divided nature of the outmigration
is clear. From 1960 to 1977 more than 200,000 whites but only 20,000
blacks are estimated to have left the city of Philadelphia.[8] In public dis-
course and political symbols, "white flight" became the metaphor for the
emptying out of the city. It is at least as plausible to argue that this was a
flight *toward* economic opportunity as it is to argue that it was a flight *from*
racial conflict.[9]

Indeed, descriptions of neighborhoods undergoing racial transition were
often laced with military metaphors about "whites retreating in the face of
the black invasion." Although there is little question that racial prejudice
contributed to the rapid transition in many neighborhoods, one must also
recognize that many of these same areas had been racially integrated for
some twenty years, and that their rapid transition to black dominance occurred only after newer suburban housing was made available after World
War II. Consider also the kind of population that inhabited the neighborhoods in transition. Studies of racial prejudice indicate that younger,
more educated, and higher status whites are less prejudiced than older
blue-collar workers. Yet the neighborhoods that were dominated by white-
collar workers, presumably less prejudiced, were the very neighborhoods
that underwent rapid racial transition. Blue-collar communities, although
frequently located near large concentrations of blacks, remained predominantly white. We suggest that a factor more important than racial prejudice
in determining whether a neighborhood became black was the extent to
which it was being abandoned by suburbanizing white-collar populations.
By contrast, in those communities that were directly linked to the city's
manufacturing economy and that experienced less out-migration to the suburbs, blacks made few inroads.

In fact, of course, suburbanization had been a characteristic of much of
Philadelphia's history, and of most American cities, virtually from their

outset. In the late eighteenth and early nineteenth centuries, for instance, William Powel established a suburban community, removed from the original plan of the city and accessible only by ferry. Many other such communities formed the developmental backbone of the city, often linked to the establishment of new transit lines. Suburbanization—the development of new residential communities on the fringes of established neighborhoods—has been a constant pattern in Philadelphia's history. What has been striking about the recent period are two related characteristics: (1) the dominance of suburban populations and job markets over the core of the city; and (2) the expansion beyond the city itself into politically distinct areas of the region, namely, the seven contiguous counties, in two states, that form the metropolitan area.

Figure 3.5 presents the cumulative postwar growth in the population of Philadelphia and its surrounding counties. Philadelphia itself grew some 7 percent during the period of World War II and its aftermath but by 1980 had suffered a cumulative 13 percent loss of population. The older suburbs of Delaware and Camden counties showed modest overall gains, a nearly 70 percent increase in population (but note Delaware's declining growth pattern during the most recent decade). Camden city had been a major wholesaling, shipping, and industrial center throughout the war but has lost upwards of 40 percent of its population (from more than 150,000 in 1950 to some 85,000 in 1980). The bulk of the population expansion has been in suburban Camden county and has occurred at a greater rate than the overall curve for the county. Nonetheless, in aggregate terms, it has not emerged as the major recent growth area of the region. Burlington and Bucks counties have shown the greatest recent cumulative growth fueled by the emergence of major interstate road links through previously undeveloped agricultural land. Similarly, Chester and Gloucester counties have shown a less explosive but unrelenting growth pattern, which, given recent road networks, is expected to show a more drastic upward slope by the time 1990 data are entered into the graph.

The clear message that emerges is that the suburban growth pattern is constrained only by the fate of the region as a whole and that the city of Philadelphia has become less significant than it once was for the region as an employment and residential base. Beginning in the late 1960s Philadelphia could no longer claim that more than 50 percent of the region's residents lived within its boundaries. Today the figure is estimated to be between 35 percent and 40 percent, and it is continuing to decline.

The suburbanization of the Philadelphia metropolitan area was accomplished by people's leaving the city (for the suburbs as well as other metro-

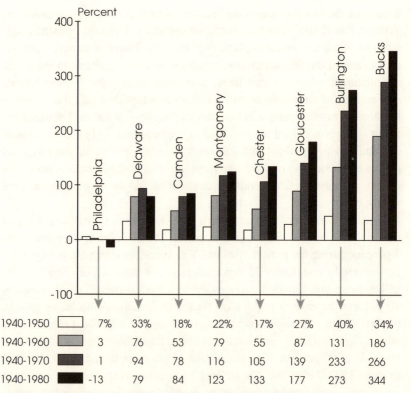

Figure 3.5 Change in population by county, Philadelphia SMSA, 1940–1980

Sources: U.S. Census of Population, 1950: Volume II, Characteristics of the Population, Part 30 (New Jersey) (1952); U.S. Census of Population, 1950: Volume II, Characteristics of the Population, Part 38 (Pennsylvania) (1952); U.S. Census of Population, 1960: Volume 1, Characteristics of the Population, Part 32 (New Jersey) (1963); U.S. Census of Population, 1960: Volume 1, Characteristics of the Population, Part 40 (Pennsylvania) (1963); U.S. Census of Population, 1970: Volume 1, Characteristics of the Population, Part 32 (New Jersey) (1973); U.S. Census of Population, 1970: Volume 1, Characteristics of the Population, Part 40 (Pennsylvania) (1973); U.S. Census of the Population, 1980: Characteristics of the Population (PC80-1-B32, New Jersey) (1982); U.S. Census of Population, 1980: Characteristics of the Population (PC80-1-B40, Pennsylvania) (1982), all published in Washington, D.C., by the Government Printing Office.

politan areas), and by a pattern of in-migrants choosing the suburbs in greater numbers than they chose in the city. Postwar suburbanization has thus partially reversed the traditional image of new migrants settling in the core of the city and moving out with success. Our focus at this point must turn to the effects of this process on the city's neighborhoods.

As neighborhoods selectively emptied out, Philadelphia experienced two major housing problems that were to continue to the present day. Beginning in the late 1960s and becoming increasingly obvious with each passing year was a problem of excess housing—housing that could not be sold or rented, and that was left to deteriorate by owners who saw no viable means of maintaining it. This disinvestment by individual owners was accompanied by a systematic process of disinvestment by institutions. Whole neighborhoods were redlined because of their economic, racial and ethnic, or building age, and they were denied mortgages through most conventional sources of lending.

This process often led to a vicious cycle within neighborhoods. As a neighborhood was redlined, the possibility of successfully selling properties diminished and the probability of their abandonment increased. As the probability of abandonment increased, the restrictions on credit grew even greater. Though each of these steps was related to the common factor of the neighborhood's position in the city's spatial economy and may have arisen independently, their linkage became real for many communities.

The Paradox of Revitalization and Decay, 1975–1985

The state of the city's housing in 1975 was a desperate one. Massive outflows of population, decreased investment from both private and public sectors, a vicious cycle of disinvestment and abandonment, and pressure to provide city services to newly developing neighborhoods had created housing scenarios that paralleled the more infamous scenes from the South Bronx in New York. The abandonment and redlining that characterized this time were concentrated in the neighborhoods of the early streetcar suburbs and in the old industrial areas.[10] Yet, in the midst of a bleak housing market came an indication in the mid-1970s that revitalization was being led in some areas by a group of urban "pioneers," who seemed to be reversing citywide trends in the Rittenhouse Square, Queen Village, and Fairmount neighborhoods. How do we explain this sudden reversal in the fortunes of a few select districts when so much of the city's housing stock was in an advanced stage of decay? Not surprisingly, the answer we offer is based on economic trends.

As we point out in Chapter 2, the current economy is marked by a growing division in the job opportunities present within the downtown economy—between businesses' high-level technical and administrative positions and the orderlies, janitors, clerks, and typists who carry out orders in the offices and labs. The discrepancy between the different pay levels of the top and bottom postindustrial jobs seems great and is growing greater, while the number of jobs, in absolute terms, is declining.

For the region's housing market, these economic trends generate a two-tier market. First, the new workforce is likely to demand accessible housing and has, at this point, been able to provide a ready cash market for housing units targeted at the demographic profile of this workforce: single or married with no children, receiving a professional salary, young, with a consumption profile stressing "urban" amenities and commodities. The gentrification of many neighborhoods is the result—a result that has been welcomed by housing offices running short on community renewal funds.[11]

At the same time that new housing is being constructed and refurbished for this new labor force, the low wages paid by many lower level service-sector jobs provide little support for the neighborhoods dependent on this employment sector, or on the declining industrial ones. The areas inhabited by low-wage workers are less likely to qualify as "investment sites" for housing capital. To understand the impacts of an uneven economy on the housing market, let us consider the following two profiles, of gentrification and housing credit allocation.

Gentrification, by now a well-known process in American cities, is the movement of middle- and upper-middle-income households into areas that were previously inhabited by low-income people. Affluent "urban pioneers" buy dilapidated buildings, usually in areas close to the central business district, and remodel them as comfortable middle-class dwellings—a process that not only increases the value of the renovated property but all of the properties around it.

The literature on gentrification that has appeared in the past decade describes in great detail the populations that move into and out of gentrified neighborhoods. Researchers generally agree on who the gentrifiers are: (1) white, (2) of higher education, occupational status, and income than the population they replace; (3) younger, single, or married with few, if any, children; (4) apt to settle in close proximity to the central business district.[12] Why do such people want to settle in the city after decades of flight to the suburbs? Several theories have been proposed, ranging from demographic and lifestyle shifts to changes in the supply and demand for housing to geographic and structural shifts in employment.[13]

Our own interpretation of gentrification is relatively straightforward and economically based. We believe that the structure of the local economy, in relation to the national and international flow of goods, services, and labor, determines which populations come into the city, what their purchasing power will be for housing, and what areas of the city their dollars will buy. Following this basic logic, we see gentrification as a stage in the process whereby urban land fluctuates between being valued and devalued by investors in relation to the economic structure of the city. The factors that make a given location more valuable at particular times include the history and technology of production and transportation of goods and alternate forms of and means to finance investments. The extent to which land in particular areas of the city becomes "increasingly prized and therefore more highly priced" [14] determines the existence, location, and nature of urban gentrification.

Why did land in inner-city neighborhoods become more valuable in the 1970s, drawing higher income populations? We have already seen that over the past fifty years the economy of Philadelphia has undergone a virtually complete metamorphosis from a site of production to one of service-sector, postindustrial activities. And we have also described the type of labor necessitated by this shift and the income distribution of these new workers. Resulting from these economic changes was an increased demand for housing for the white-collar professionals who constituted the new workforce of the service city. That demand was reflected in the gentrification that took place in areas of Philadelphia (as in other cities) where land and improvements had become relatively inexpensive (for instance, old and deteriorating lofts, multifamily structures, and abandoned dwellings that stand in the shadows of the abandoned factories that once served as the economic foundation of the area), and where reinvestment had become a "rational" response.

The conditions conducive to gentrification did not happen in a vacuum. Government played a vital role in promoting urban investment by creating an environment in which that investment became an attractive alternative. [15] One such governmental action was the passage of historic-preservation tax credits by the federal Congress in 1976, to encourage investors to rehabilitate historic buildings. Another federal intervention likely to spur gentrification was Congress's move in the 1986 Tax Reform Act to reduce all interest deductions except on loans secured by the home (that is to say, home mortgages and home equity loans). Governmental actions alone do not explain renewed private investment in gentrifying areas, but in combination with the economic shifts that generated more white-collar jobs in the city, the government provided the added incentive to make the process take hold.

An examination of gentrification in Philadelphia between 1981 and 1985 yields some interesting insights into what the neighborhoods looked like before gentrification. First, the areas that gentrified over this period were much more likely to be ones that had higher-than-average black concentrations. Many such areas had historically low housing values but also magnificent, albeit deteriorated housing stocks. Second, gentrification took place in areas below the city average for owner occupancy rates, probably because investors found it easier to displace or relocate renters than home-owners. Third, every area that gentrified over this period was under 150 percent of the median family income for Philadelphia in 1979; 92 percent of the gentrifying areas had over one and a half times the average share of families in poverty in the city. Fourth, gentrification was most likely to have occurred in areas below 150 percent of the city's median housing value. Points three and four above suggest the inability of the poor to oppose the more powerful forces characteristic of an invigorated interest by speculators and investors.

Gentrification is seen by many as the great and perhaps final hope for the declining inner-city core. Yet the nature of uneven development is such that one person's hope is another's dread. Gentrification, while serving to revitalize deteriorating neighborhoods, exacts a heavy cost. Every year, nearly half a million people nationally are displaced by urban redevelop-ment.[16] And displacement means not only that people are forced to move from their homes but that the neighborhoods themselves—the social and economic nucleus for many of Philadelphia's working-class families—are torn asunder.

The consequences of these forces for Philadelphia's black communities have been significant. Blacks were displaced from Center City neighbor-hoods and became increasingly concentrated in the oldest automobile sub-urbs in the northern and western sectors of the city. These areas had first been developed immediately following World War II, and, like the streetcar suburbs of the turn of the century, they contained relatively few manu-facturing employment opportunities. The redevelopment of such Central City neighborhoods as Society Hill, Queen Village, Schuylkill, and West Philadelphia forced black families out of these increasingly valued neigh-borhoods and into sections of the city that were located farther from the center. While the basis of the economy had changed from manufacturing to professional services, the pattern governing black residential choices re-mained the same as in earlier decades: blacks were to be excluded from those parts of the city that were the center of growth and thus of opportunity.

In stark contrast to the sudden influx of new investment capital into gen-trifying areas is the slow capital starvation suffered by other communities when they are redlined by banks. Admittedly, banks are now explicitly forbidden to develop maps similar to those of the Home Owners' Loan Corporation, identifying the boundaries of approved lending territories or

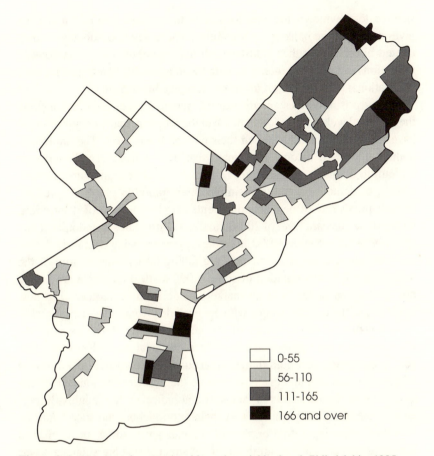

Figure 3.6 Number of conventional loans by neighborhood, Philadelphia, 1985–1986

Sources: Home Mortgage Disclosure Act Data Tapes, 1985, prepared by the Federal Financial Intermediaries Examination Council (machine readable data file) (Washington, D.C.: Federal Financial Intermediaries Examination Council, 1986); *Home Mortgage Disclosure Act Data Tapes, 1986*, prepared by the Federal Financial Intermediaries Examination Council (machine readable data file) (Washington, D.C.: Federal Financial Intermediaries Council, 1987).

neighborhoods. However, several studies indicate that redlining was an informal process at least during the 1970s.[17]

One recent examination of bank mortgage data from 1982 through 1985 demonstrated that mortgage availability and amount were directly affected by an area's income and racial composition.[18] Figure 3.6 demonstrates graphically how the dual effects of an uneven residential economy are played out. Those neighborhoods with the greatest access to suburban job sites or to downtown job locations have the greatest level of mortgage investments by the banking communities. Those neighborhoods with protracted histories of either industrial job loss or population decline due to migration (and not coincidentally, with the most sizable black and Hispanic populations) have the lowest levels of mortgage investments.

Not surprisingly, these credit-starved neighborhoods also demonstrate the greatest levels of abandonment. Over the long run, many neighborhoods have emptied out and have seen their income levels drop. The unpredictability of welfare income has meant that even a basic rental market is difficult to maintain. In these areas, then, the level of abandonment soars, leading to demolition and or a simple deterioration in place. At present, Philadelphia's rate of new abandonments matches the rate of demolition, so there is a constant level of 20,000 to 22,000 structures abandoned at any one time, while roughly 1,000 structures a year are being demolished.[19]

At the same time that structures are falling through the bottom of the housing market, a population of some 6,000 to 10,000 people are falling out the bottom of the housing market in one form or another. The new homeless of the city are people who are excluded from the housing stock.

Although traditional images of the homeless focus on those who are homeless by virtue of mental illness or a chemical dependency of some sort, recent research would indicate that such people constitute a minority of the homeless population. A census of the homeless conducted by the Coalition for the Homeless in Pennsylvania indicated that roughly 30 percent of the homeless population in shelters throughout the state could be classified as having a drug or alcohol dependency or some sort of mental illness or retardation that put them on the street. Far more significant was the high proportion of people who were out of work, were on welfare, or who worked in low-paying jobs that excluded them from the housing available in the communities of Pennsylvania. Given the disproportionately high number of Philadelphia respondents in the survey, this pattern can be presumed to apply across the city and region.[20] Dolbeare, in a complementary study, indicated that there were more than 100,000 households in the city (out of some 600,000) who could not afford housing at the 30 percent of income level of rent or housing costs.[21] Taken together, these suggest that a substantial threat of increased homelessness exists.

Race and the Regional Housing Market

These specific housing issues take on an even more serious tone when placed against the backdrop of racial change affecting the city and the region. As previously noted, a significant proportion of the region's abandoned housing units are found in black and Hispanic neighborhoods in Philadelphia. Similarly, the largest category of Philadelphia's homeless population are single black men between the ages of eighteen and forty-five (42.5 percent). The abandonment of their neighborhoods, fueled by the collapse of work places and housing credit, and their exclusion in large numbers from the labor market, the housing market, and the welfare rolls reflects the deadly simple combination of racial divisions and metropolitan change.

In the final analysis, the most significant characteristic of Philadelphia's housing market is its racial segregation, both within the city and the region. Blacks represent an increasing proportion of the city's population (39 percent in 1980), while the percentage of the suburban population that is black has remained relatively constant. Hovering between 4 and 6 percent until 1960, the suburban black population subsequently grew rapidly, yet still remained only 8.3 percent of the suburban minority population in 1980. (For county-by-county figures on the suburban minority population, see Table 1.4.) The Delaware Valley Regional Planning Commission projects that by the year 2000 minorities will have a considerably larger presence in the suburbs—about 14 percent of the total suburban population. The most impressive increases, they predict, will occur in the New Jersey counties of Camden and Burlington (see Table 3.2).

Just as racial separation marks the pattern of migration between the counties of the region, so, too, it characterizes the residential patterns within the counties making up the metropolitan area. Indeed, in 1980 almost three-quarters of the region's white population lived in census tracts that were more than 95 percent white. At the same time, almost two-thirds of the region's black population lived in census tracts that were more than 65 percent black. Only 3 percent of the region's white population and 15 percent of the black population lived in census tracts that could be considered racially integrated, that is, containing between 35 and 65 percent blacks.

One way to measure racial segregation is to compute the percentage of each census tract's population that is black, and to compare the average tract levels against the proportion of blacks and whites in the metropolitan region as a whole. If the Philadelphia area were racially integrated and blacks were evenly distributed across all census tracts, we would find that the percentage that was black for each census tract would be the same as the

Table 3.2 Nonwhite population of Philadelphia
region by counties, 1980 and 2000 (projected)

	1980		2000	
	Number	Percentage of total	Number	Percentage of total
Philadelphia	666,502	39.5	674,576	44.5
Bucks County	16,309	3.4	30,460	5.1
Chester County	25,573	8.0	36,775	9.3
Delaware County	55,028	9.9	73,229	13.8
Montgomery County	39,245	6.1	69,339	9.9
Burlington County	51,258	14.1	113,200	24.2
Camden County	74,924	15.9	159,800	27.7
Gloucester County	18,416	9.2	24,400	9.8

Source: Delaware Valley Regional Planning Commission, *Year 2010 Regional and County Population and Employment Forecasts* (Philadelphia: DVRPC, 1987).

Table 3.3 Racial composition of Philadelphia
SMSA, Philadelphia, and suburbs, 1980

	SMSA	Philadelphia	Suburbs
Average percentage black in all tracts	19.2%	39.3%	8.2%
Average percentage black in tracts containing black households	69.8	81.3	38.7
Average percentage black in tracts containing white households	6.4	9.9	5.1

Source: U.S. Census of Population and Housing, 1980: Summary Tape File 3A, prepared by the Bureau of the Census (machine-readable data file) (Washington, D.C.: Bureau of the Census, 1983).

percentage that was black for the region as a whole. Thus, every neighborhood would be about 20 percent black and 80 percent white. The degree to which the neighborhoods depart from this ideal balance of blacks and whites reflects the extent of separation into racially segregated areas. We have computed such a measure of racial segregation for the entire metropolitan area, the city of Philadelphia, and the suburbs.[22] The results are presented in Table 3.3.

Although blacks constituted about 20 percent of the region's total population in 1980, the average black person lived in a census tract that was about 70 percent black. The average white person lived in a census tract that was only 6 percent black. The most pronounced imbalances within the region lay within the city limits. Philadelphia was 39 percent black in 1980,

Table 3.4 Patterns of racial segregation
in the Philadelphia region, 1980

Areas	Percentage black	Index of dissimilarity
Total SMSA	19.2	78.3
Philadelphia	39.3	83.2
Suburbs	8.2	65.5
Bucks County	2.5	55.0
Chester County	7.5	52.0
Delaware County	9.1	76.8
Montgomery County	4.8	61.6
Burlington County	13.0	55.0
Camden County	11.0	71.0
Gloucester County	8.5	36.8

Source: Data calculated from *U.S. Census of Population and Housing, 1980: Summary Tape File 3A*, prepared by the Bureau of the Census (machine-readable data file) (Washington, D.C.: Bureau of the Census, 1982).

but the average black Philadelphian lived in a census tract that was 82 percent black. By contrast, the average white Philadelphian lived in an area that was more than 90 percent white. In the suburbs, although blacks constituted only 8 percent of the total population, the average suburban black lived in a neighborhood that was 39 percent black. On average, suburban whites lived in areas that were 95 percent white. Taken together, what these numbers portray is a white population that, despite the presence of a sizable black population in its midst, has managed to maintain its neighborhoods as predominantly white enclaves in both city and suburbs. Blacks within the city live in racially isolated areas that contain few whites. Admittedly, in the suburbs, where blacks make up only 8 percent of the population, they are much more likely to live in neighborhoods that are racially integrated—but even these integrated areas have an overrepresentation of blacks, relative to the suburban population as a whole.

The "contact" measure of racial segregation that we present in Table 3.3 provides an indication of the degree of racial isolation that members of a particular group experience. Unfortunately, its values depend heavily on the relative size of the two populations. Thus comparing the level of racial segregation in the suburbs to that in the city is difficult. So we present in Table 3.4 a second measure of racial segregation—the "index of dissimilarity"—which is less dependent upon the relative size of groups.[23] The index of dissimilarity reflects the percentage of a group that would have to be moved from areas where they are overrepresented to areas where they are underrepresented in order to achieve integration (defined as a uniform balance of the races throughout the geographical area under consideration). Table 3.4 confirms our earlier observation that the Philadelphia metropolitan area is heavily segregated by race. Almost 80 percent of the region's black population would have to move to a different census tract in order to achieve racial integration.

The table also confirms that levels of segregation in the suburban counties are lower than in the City of Philadelphia. However, considerable differences exist in the levels of segregation in the suburban counties. Gloucester, Burlington, Chester, and Bucks have relatively low levels of segregation, whereas in Camden and Delaware segregation is relatively high. Interestingly, there appears to be little or no relationship between the percentage of a county's population that is black and the level of racial segregation.

This changing distribution of black and white populations in the region has been shaped by both the flow of population into (and out of) the metropolitan area, and the flow between the city and suburbs. These two factors—movement to the suburbs from the Central City and migration from outside the metropolitan area—combined to produce an expansion of the white population in Philadelphia's suburbs and an increased concentration of the black population inside the city.

We can use the censuses of 1960, 1970, and 1980 to discover not only where white and black households were living at the time when the count was taken but also where they had lived five years earlier. For example, census counts show that during each of the five-year periods preceding the 1960, 1970, and 1980 censuses, Philadelphia had lost approximately 10 percent of its residents to the suburbs, while less than 2 percent of suburbanites had chosen to move into the city. Furthermore, the census data make it clear that not all migrants to the Philadelphia suburbs came from the Central City; many came from other parts of the country. More than two-thirds of migrants arriving in the Philadelphia metropolitan area during these three periods chose to live in suburbs. Although the data are not completely systematic, it appears that mobility between regions was at least as important as the city-suburban mobility in accounting for the shifting racial balance of the metropolitan area's population.

Table 3.5 shows clear racial differences in the destination of migrants. More than 70 percent of the white migrants into the region moved into the suburbs, whereas blacks showed a far greater tendency to settle in the city. For example, between 1955 and 1960 more than 70 percent of black newcomers settled within Philadelphia. In the 1960s and 1970s, although

Table 3.5 Proportion of migrants to the Philadelphia region choosing a suburban location, 1955–1980

	1955–1960	1965–1970	1975–1980
Total	66.7%	76.9%	77.7%
Whites	73.4	81.4	80.6
Blacks	28.1	40.1	56.0

Sources: U.S. Census of Population, 1960: Characteristics of Population, Part 40 (1963); *U.S. Census of Population, 1970: Characteristics of Population,* Part 40 (1973); *U.S. Census of Population, 1980: Characteristics of the Population* (PC80-1-B40, Pennsylvania) (1982), all published in Washington, D.C., by the Government Printing Office.

Table 3.6 City-suburban mobility of residential population of Philadelphia region by race, 1955–1980

	1955–1960	1965–1970	1975–1980
Percentage of city's population moving to suburbs			
Whites	11.8	10.9	10.5
Blacks	2.1	1.3	3.3
Percentage of suburban population moving to city			
Whites	1.5	1.4	1.4
Blacks	3.4	3.6	2.2

Sources: See Table 3.5.

an increasing proportion of black migrants settled in suburban areas, their proportions remained lower than those of whites.

Not surprisingly, whites have shown a greater tendency than blacks to move from Philadelphia out to the suburbs (Table 3.6). Between 1955 and 1960 almost 12 percent of the city's white population, contrasted with less than 2 percent of its black population, moved to the suburbs. Over these twenty-five years the exodus to the suburbs by whites declined slightly—to 10.5 percent between 1975 and 1980—but it remained substantially larger than the proportion of blacks who were moving to the suburbs.

Many commentators have observed that the consequence of racial segregation in cities has been to relegate blacks and other minorities to neighborhoods with lower quality housing and inferior public services. What is less appreciated is the extent to which black concentrations in the suburbs suffer similar disadvantages relative to white suburbanites. Racial steering in suburban real estate markets created black enclaves like the borough of Yeadon in Delaware County. In 1978 a suburban fair housing council undertook a study to determine the extent of such steering by real estate agents, using a well-established methodology. They sent into the local housing market black and white couples who were instructed to describe their incomes, occupations, families, and housing preferences similarly, to see whether real estate agents would show them the same prospective homes. The agents did not. In three out of four cases, the white couple saw no homes in Yeadon, while the black couple saw no homes outside of Yeadon.[24]

The development of black suburban enclaves recreates many of the disadvantages that accompany segregation within the city's borders. John Logan's study of black suburbs surrounding Philadelphia concludes that they are systematically different from white suburbs. They have more low-income families, a higher proportion of renters (as opposed to homeowners), more social problems like violent crime, and fewer resources. Logan's sample of black suburbs had an average per capita tax base that was 30 percent lower in 1980 than white suburbs, and they carried an average municipal debt that was double the debt of white suburbs. In short, they had less money to cope with more substantial public problems.[25]

Housing the City—Conclusion and Prospects

Depending on their circumstances, Philadelphians face three different housing futures: one of opportunities, one of defenses, and one of despair. Developers still reevaluate the neighborhoods of the city looking for the newest conversion possibilities for lofts and factories, for rowhouses and even prisons to convert. The only barriers to the continued development of newly gentrified areas appear to be limits on the expansion of the postindustrial workforce and limits to the cupidity of the consumer. At this point, there is some indication that gentrification demand has slowed somewhat, but it remains and will remain a significant part of the city's housing market.

Defensive reactions also abound, as middle-class neighborhoods struggle to maintain themselves in the face of an uncertain economic base. Several neighborhoods outside of downtown seem to be witnessing the first signs of gentrification, particularly in traditional middle-class enclaves. The impacts of this are several, but most striking is the potential for displacement inherent in such a process, accompanied by tales of people being displaced by upwardly moving house prices and tax appraisals.

A defensive posture is also being taken by other, substantially white neighborhoods, whose residents are fearful of either the social implications of integration or the tax implications of supporting a substantial local budget from real estate taxes. The most obvious example is in Northeast Philadelphia, where disgruntled residents recently organized a formal petition to secede from the city and form a new county. A less organized, more spontaneous kind of defensive reaction has been the increase in racial incidents that have occurred along racial boundaries of the city (see Chapter 1).

Finally, there is the city of despair. There is no other way to speak of the core areas of the city surrounding the gentrified center of Philadelphia. To give some examples of the scale of the problems involved there, we note that the City of Philadelphia estimates that it will cost $40,000 per structure for minimal rehabilitation on an average dwelling in the city. In any one year the city has only about $40 million that will be allocated to housing rehabilitation, cleaning and sealing, partial rehabilitation, and demolition. Housing officials face 1,000 units to be demolished at a cost of between $5,000 and $10,000 per structure; they face another 1,000 entering the abandonment stream every year and 22,000 already abandoned units. Among housing consumers, they face an increased inability to pay, and a growing homeless population over the past several years. In short, there is nowhere near the revenue needed to ameliorate housing problems on the scale that faces the city. That much of this despair is centered in black and poor neighborhoods simply reflects the patterns we have addressed earlier.

The city, quite plainly, continues to face a substantial housing problem, the solutions to which range from "wait until the new economy is mature" to "let's squat" to throwing one's hands up in despair. Our analysis suggests that before housing officials can realistically hope to alter basic trends, a sufficient job and tax base must be accessible to the city. Inherited problems of housing age and deterioration, as well as racial isolation and ethnic differentials in housing opportunities across neighborhoods, must also be addressed.

If one were to offer a concluding comment on the city's likely future, one would be forced to recall that Charles Dickens, in the middle of the past century, lamented Philadelphia's grid development because of its "distracting regularity." [26] One supposes that Dickens today would probably reverse his course, talk of the juxtaposition of plenty and poverty that was so near to his literary heart, and address the unevenness of its development in far more eloquent terms than we. Perhaps: "It was the best of times, it was the worst of times . . . ."

4

Philadelphia's Redevelopment Process

Up to this point our discussion has focused on the transformation of the regional economy since World War II, and its impact on neighborhood change, racial relations, and housing conditions. We have argued that the effect of economic change over the past forty years has been to widen the gaps between the haves and have-nots, measured in terms of incomes, housing, and educational opportunities, and the quality of life in different neighborhoods. Our quantitative analysis of these trends has stressed the structure of the economy—regional, national, and even international—as the primary force behind such changes.

Yet it would be a mistake to imagine that the region's postwar transformation has been entirely the result of large-scale, uncontrollable economic forces such as the decline in manufacturing jobs nationwide. Rather, the region's business and political leaders have responded to national and international economic forces by making decisions that have channeled investment and growth toward certain types of projects and certain geographical areas. Although many policy areas influence this spatial allocation of resources, redevelopment programs are one of the most important.

Thus, our examination of Philadelphia's transformation must turn from the quantitative analysis of economic trends and their consequences for individuals' employment, incomes, and social inequality to a more qualitative analysis of policy choices and their consequences for different economic and political factions, for different neighborhoods, and for the continued uneven development of different geographical areas of the metropolitan region. We will examine local leadership groups, both public and private, and their decisions within the context provided by the global economy and federal policy initiatives.

Continuous Redevelopment

The phrase "redevelopment in Philadelphia" conjures up visions of the city's famous urban renewal projects of the 1960s, projects such as Independence Mall, Society Hill, and Penn Center. Residents may also think of some less famous projects of the 1970s and 1980s, Market East, Penn's Landing, and Franklintown. But projects built since the 1960s represent only the most recent episode of redevelopment. Philadelphia has reconstructed its buildings, roads, and public facilities—the city's "built environment"—over and over again during its history. Each rebuilding has been an attempt to overcome the past, remove obsolete structures, and stimulate economic growth.

In the earliest wave of redevelopment in the eighteenth century, property owners and municipal officials overrode William Penn's carefully designated system of street grids by adding one, two, or even three alleys between the main streets on the grid. This modification of the street plan allowed the city to accommodate a larger population without greatly increasing its geographical size. It transformed Philadelphia from Penn's "green country Towne" to a dense urban center mirroring the European cities of the time. It also allowed homeowners to participate in the city's first real estate boom by turning their back yards into profitable house lots.[1]

Another episode in the history of Philadelphia's redevelopment process was the emergence of the new downtown after the Civil War. Although Penn's plan had called for the city center to be at Broad (14th) Street, the functional center of the city at that time was close to the Delaware River at 5th Street. In 1870 the city government proposed (and the citizens approved) the construction of a new City Hall at Broad and Market streets, on the fringe of the downtown. Large private companies such as the Pennsylvania Railroad and John Wanamaker & Company soon followed the city's lead. They positioned their new railroad station, department store, and other buildings around City Hall, thus solidifying the site as the new center of the business district.[2]

Another wave of redevelopment occurred early in the twentieth century. In 1909 the city decided to build a parkway from City Hall to Fairmount Park on the banks of the Schuylkill River. Eventually named for Benjamin Franklin, this enormous boulevard lined with monumental public buildings was the city's attempt to compete with the visions of urban grandeur being produced elsewhere by the City Beautiful movement. Its construction required some $25 million of public money and the demolition of more than a thousand buildings, most of them working people's homes.[3]

Since the late 1940s Philadelphia's downtown has undergone one more-or-less continuous wave of redevelopment. A significant difference separates the earlier projects, however, from those undertaken since 1945. Replotting the streets, moving the City Hall, and building the Parkway were projects driven by the growth and industrialization of the city. As the population grew in the late nineteenth and early twentieth century, the geographic boundaries and the nature of the built environment had to be changed to accommodate that growth.[4] Since World War II, however, redevelopment projects have been built in response to the absence of growth. They have, in fact, been attempts to stimulate growth and channel it into certain areas of the city. As we shall see, the recent history of redevelopment has sprung from the economic transformation of the city already discussed in the preceding chapters.

Philadelphia's redevelopment plans have borne a striking resemblance to those of other large cities. Part (but only part) of the reason for that resemblance has been that cities' redevelopment strategies have been shaped by provisions in federal legislation. Federal regulations have provided incentives for specific types of redevelopment (for example, highways, housing, mass transit), from one time period to the next. Another source of programmatic similarity among the big cities' redevelopment schemes, however, is the role played by redevelopment in the political economy of the city. Most large cities of the United States experienced similar problems of slowed growth after World War II. As groups of business and government leaders have cast about for strategies to support central city growth, they have frequently arrived at the same "solutions" to their problems. Philadelphia was one of the first cities to undertake large-scale redevelopment, so it is not surprising that other cities often used Philadelphia's projects as models for their own redevelopment.

Why Redevelop?

The City of Philadelphia, and especially its Central Business District (CBD), have traditionally been the focal point of economic activity in the Delaware Valley. Yet, as we noted in the preceding chapter, suburbanization has also been present in the region throughout its history. This "persistent dualism" (as historian William Cutler called it[5]) between growth at the center and on the periphery did not present great problems to the city until recent decades, as the impact of global and national economic transformations became apparent.

On the surface the city's problems appeared as a lack of growth and a physically obsolete infrastructure. Recall that until 1950 the populations of both the City of Philadelphia and the seven suburban counties surrounding it were growing. After 1950, however, the city's population began to decline while that of the nearby suburban areas continued to grow. Increasingly through the 1950s and 1960s, business and industry as well as residents moved to the suburbs, building modern facilities in New Jersey or Montgomery County and draining the city's tax base in the process. Between 1954 and 1977, for example, the number of retail establishments in Philadelphia's CBD decreased by 32 percent and the CBD's share of retail sales in the region went from 15 percent to 6 percent.[6]

Infrastructure problems were rampant. By the late 1940s Philadelphia was generally considered to be a "worn-out city," with 60 percent of its industrial buildings obsolete and 30,000 properties vacant.[7] The built environment had suffered from lack of investment since the 1920s because of the Depression and wartime strictures. In addition, the city's physical plant was largely made up of what Warner called "the inheritance of the industrial metropolis": old manufacturing lofts, narrow streets clogged with auto and trolley traffic, railroad tracks at grade level, and tiny houses crammed onto every available piece of land. The very features that had signified progress in earlier times had now become impediments to investment in Philadelphia.

These surface problems of shrinkage and obsolescence were another manifestation of the changing nature of the city's economy. As we point out in Chapter 2, the nationwide decline in manufacturing, a result of global shifts in investment, hit Philadelphia with particular ferocity after World War II. Redevelopment officials recognized the importance of this shift early in the postwar period. They decided to try to stimulate economic growth and to reinforce the city of Philadelphia as the economic center of the Delaware Valley region. In effect, this meant successfully competing with the nearby suburbs for business, industry, and residents. It meant successfully drawing private investment into the City and into the CBD. It meant strengthening the forces toward centralization to compensate for those tending toward decentralization. These goals have driven the types of projects undertaken.[8]

The most important goal of redevelopment was to prevent the central city from being eclipsed by its suburbs, and managing transportation routes was one tactic in their struggle. Automobile travel was facilitated by the construction of a network of highways into and through the city, the widening of city streets, and the construction of parking garages at highway exits.

Commuter access was enhanced when the two commuter rail lines were connected, high-speed transit lines to the suburbs were added, and existing subway and elevated lines were extended. As much as possible, planners tried to route through the CBD by making it the functional center of the regional transportation network.

Another tactic was to provide or strengthen amenities in the central city that would focus attention on it as the hub of the region. New sports facilities, museums, convention facilities, and shopping centers were planned, and historic areas were slated for improvements. Universities and hospitals were targeted for retention and expansion, not just for the jobs they provided but for the public visibility they brought to the city.

The second goal of redevelopment has been to overcome physical obsolescence—that is, to replace the remains of the manufacturing city with new facilities for the corporate economy emerging in the city. Downtown factories and warehouses, old railroad tracks and stations, narrow streets and alleys were replaced by skyscrapers surrounded by broad plazas, modern office buildings, attractive hotels and restaurants, and new retail outlets. In addition to aiding the downtown service sector, redevelopment would provide the new technological and infrastructural bases needed for modern industry and trade. The port was improved, the airport expanded, routes were provided through the city for oversized rail and truck loads, and new first-class industrial space was constructed.

Finally, redevelopment aimed to change the distribution of the population in the metropolitan area to correspond with the changing function of the city. Redevelopment officials tried to increase Philadelphia's white middle-class population and thereby lessen the proportion of the poor, unemployed, and minority groups living in the city. Slums and skid rows were demolished. Deteriorating colonial housing was refurbished. High-rise apartment buildings were constructed. Residential density was reduced and open space provided in neighborhoods. Making the transition to a corporate service economy implied remaking the city to attract and retain the professional white-collar classes as residents and to downplay the presence of the poor and working classes.

Trends in Redevelopment

Throughout the postwar period, from the establishment of the Redevelopment Authority in 1946 to the reorganization of the Office of Housing and

Community Development in 1987, three types of activities have claimed the bulk of public and private money spent on redevelopment: housing, transportation, and economic development. The proportions of each type, the locations chosen for them, and the populations served by new projects have differed from time to time, however.

In its earliest phase, the 1940s and early 1950s, redevelopment emphasized the removal of slum housing. The city cleared large tracts of land in the most "blighted" areas of the city (particularly Lower North Philadelphia) and sought developers to build new housing there. Planners envisioned a mix of public, private, and cooperative housing to replace the demolished units. They planned a companion "new town," Eastwick, to be built in the southwestern part of the city to absorb the displaced population. By 1957 city officials decided that the residential program was a failure because demolition proved more costly than anticipated and because developers were not interested in buying the cleared land.[9]

The cost and frustration they encountered in rebuilding the city's deteriorated neighborhoods led redevelopment officials in the late 1950s to scale back the residential program and turn its emphasis from clearing tracts of land to rehabilitating existing housing units. In addition, they decided to downplay North Philadelphia as a redevelopment site and to concentrate more funds on Center City, where private investors had already begun some significant rebuilding.[10] In 1960 Mayor Richardson Dilworth (1956–1962) unveiled the Plan for Center City, which projected an integrated downtown of new highways, mass transit facilities, parking garages, shopping centers, and rehabilitated housing. The showpiece of this new downtown strategy was the renewal of Society Hill as a chic residential district for white middle-class professionals. Changes in the federal legislation facilitated this shift to downtown development; after 1954 more diversified urban renewal projects were permitted and massive federal highway funds became available.[11]

In the 1960s continued emphasis on Center City prompted protests from residents of renewal areas. The most prominent grievance was displacement, but other important issues were the lack of low-income housing construction and the demolition of historic buildings. These conflicts over redevelopment reached a crescendo in the 1970s. Neighborhood organizations became more vocal and more politically sophisticated in their attempts to influence the redevelopment process. They especially criticized the city for not spending more in the poorest neighborhoods, for breaking up neighborhoods with highway construction, and for spending federal funds on

Market Street East, Schuylkill Park, and other downtown projects. Yet the consistent protests had little success in diverting resources away from the CBD and out to the neighborhoods.

The 1980s have seen a renewed emphasis on economic development projects and Center City redevelopment. Mayor William Green (1980–1984) targeted the port and waterfront as high priorities for redevelopment, in line with his desire to make Philadelphia a center for international commerce and financial investment. Mayor Wilson Goode (1984–1992) has followed through with the strategies of his predecessors, pursuing the waterfront project at Penn's Landing and adding a massive convention center to the Market Street East complex. Moreover, Goode's city planning commission released in spring 1988 a new plan for Center City that projected unabated growth for Philadelphia's downtown: 80,000 new jobs, $4 billion in new investments, and 22 million square feet of new office development by the year 2000.[12] Philadelphia, the commission predicted, will have an advantage over its competitors like Baltimore and Boston, because it has large tracts of undeveloped land close to the center. The progrowth plan recommended that much of the new office development be directed into the high-rise corridor stretching west from City Hall and culminating in a new 30-million-square-foot complex on the Schuylkill River, just north of the 30th Street Railroad Station. Goode's administration, however, has also supported housing rehabilitation for low-income families and has recently targeted North Philadelphia for special coordination programs. During Goode's tenure, community activists attempted (unsuccessfully) to block the convention center project and (successfully) to gain the city's help in taking over privately owned abandoned housing.

The priorities in redevelopment, and certainly its speed, have varied somewhat from one decade to another, as federal funding has waxed and waned, and local administrations have changed. Community groups have been more or less angry, more or less politicized, and more or less organizationally capable of affecting policy decisions. Yet the basic dynamic of redevelopment is unmistakable: the emphasis has been overwhelmingly on downtown development rather than on neighborhood revitalization, no matter who the players happened to be. How do we explain the city's unfailing preference for investing in the center?

Two Case Studies

More detailed descriptions of the redevelopment projects undertaken in two areas of the city—one a low-income neighborhood and the other a downtown site—can provide us with some answers to that question. The two areas, Lower North Philadelphia and Market Street East, have been undergoing redevelopment continually since 1950. Their locations are depicted in Figure 4.1.

Lower North Philadelphia, which lies directly north of Center City, is made up of a collection of small neighborhoods. Some were originally independent towns that were incorporated into the city, other sections were immigrant neighborhoods surrounding industrial sites, still others were built as streetcar suburbs, and one section was originally a mansion district. The heart of Lower North Philadelphia became home to the city's largest concentration of blacks during the 1920s. Throughout the postwar period it has had the lowest levels in the city on all the standard economic and social indicators.

Because of the age and dilapidated condition of its housing and the pattern of mixed land use in the area, Lower North Philadelphia had the dubious distinction of being chosen as the first site for slum clearance under the 1949 federal redevelopment legislation. Between 1950 and 1962 more than 10,000 housing units were demolished, representing 85 percent of all housing demolitions in the city during that period.[13]

Land was cleared at a rapid pace. The city chose its sites for clearance on the basis of the physical deterioration in the block rather than on the basis of where developers were interested in acquiring land.[14] Thus, the Redevelopment Authority often found itself unable to sell off cleared land. Most banks and developers refused to invest in Lower North Philadelphia because they thought it too financially risky. In one case the city had to arrange to have a private developer take credit for a rental housing project that was really built by the Redevelopment Authority.[15]

The city itself took over a good deal of the cleared land, constructing public housing, schools, playgrounds, and other public facilities. This strategy, however, thwarted the intentions of the redevelopment program in several ways. First, public facilities did not add to the city's tax rolls. Second, federal legislation discouraged the use of redeveloped land for public housing, since public housing was thought to deter the purchase of land on the private market. Third, since the city simply did not have uses for all of the vast tracts of land that it had cleared, many of them remained vacant.

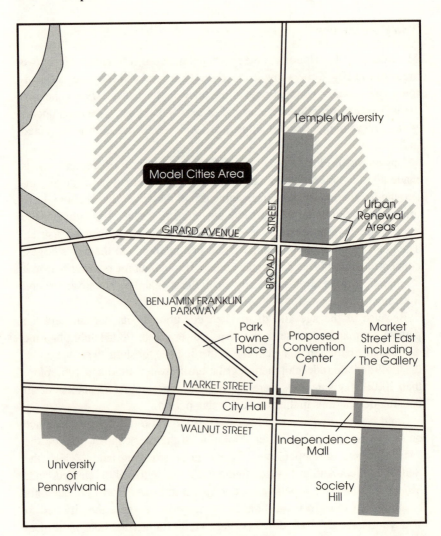

Figure 4.1 Center City and Lower North Philadelphia

Meanwhile, the social and economic problems underlying Lower North Philadelphia's housing conditions continued to exist. In 1956, when the Redevelopment Authority reviewed its progress, its members were surprised to discover that despite their efforts, slum conditions had not only persisted in Lower North Philadelphia but they had spread to new areas. They interpreted this to mean that although large-scale clearance was still a viable policy, it would be a slower and costlier process than they had anticipated.[16] Although the city spent nearly one-third of its urban renewal funds in Lower North Philadelphia between 1949 and 1970, it never achieved the large-scale redevelopment officials hoped for.[17]

When their plans for physical renewal failed to bear much fruit in North Philadelphia, planners shifted to a new target. Beginning in the late 1960s the emphasis on North Philadelphia changed from one of attacking physical deterioration to attacking social problems. First with the Community Renewal Program and then with the Model Cities Program, federal funds became available to bolster physical programs with social and economic policies aimed at fighting poverty. Philadelphia officials designated a portion of Lower North Philadelphia as the city's Model City area and between 1969 and 1975 targeted it for special health, education, transportation, and jobs programs as well as increased effort on housing construction and rehabilitation. To accomplish the latter, the Redevelopment Authority began a new phase of property acquisition in North Philadelphia and began to give loans and grant for homeowners to bring their properties up to code.[18] The lasting results of Model Cities in North Philadelphia, as elsewhere in the United States, were very limited. One reason may be that the Model City strategy of improving Lower North Philadelphia's conditions was undercut by the chair of the City Planning Commission, Bernard Meltzer. Meltzer initiated a policy of land clearance and landbanking in the early 1970s, on the grounds that many "nonviable" neighborhoods would at some future time be able to attract private investment if the land were vacant and available at a low price.[19]

Another reason for the limited successes (which we see more clearly with hindsight) is that these problems were not amenable to the types of solutions being offered by the federal and state programs of urban renewal, Model Cities, and later revenue sharing or enterprise zones. The redistribution of jobs, credit, and sound housing across the metropolitan area created a cruel and virtually iron-clad developmental template for inner-city neighborhoods. As the example of Lower North Philadelphia shows, these programs did not, and could not, have the leveraging effect on the private sector that was dreamt of in their political justification.

Much of the housing that was constructed in North Philadelphia under the housing programs of the urban renewal and Model Cities era was public housing, especially large-scale high-rise or combined high-rise/low-rise projects. Contrasted with earlier eras, when public housing was considered a temporary way station on the path to economic integration, the philosophy of the 1960s was that public housing was a place to contain groups characterized by long-term poverty and social problems. Despite the massive construction of the postwar era in these housing units, the waiting list

Table 4.1 Investment in
North Philadelphia, 1980–1985
(in millions of dollars)

Type	Public	Private
Housing	165.0	20.5
Commercial	6.7	10.1
Industrial	51.0	11.5
Institutional	0.0	123.0
Public facilities	13.1	0.0

Source: Philadelphia City Planning Commission *North Philadelphia Plan: A Guide to Revitalization* (1987).

for public housing has exceeded 10,000 households for most of the years from 1965 to the present day.

One response to the shortage of public housing units was to use federal aid programs to house persons in existing housing. Using renewal dollars and various FHA and Section 8 subsidies, the local government became an increasingly major actor in Philadelphia's real estate market, purchasing single units or small multifamily structures to house public-housing families. This had the effect of exacerbating the racially charged atmosphere in which the city's residents already tended to interpret their housing decisions, given that the vast majority of public-housing residents were black. Thus, a large portion of the "scattered site" public-housing units ended up being placed in already ghettoized North Philadelphia.

In the 1980s North Philadelphia received renewed attention and investment from both the public and private sectors. Table 4.1 shows the amount and types of investments made in the area in the first half of the decade. Some of the housing investment from private sources is due to gentrification now occurring around the edges of the district. (Interestingly, the area undergoing gentrification has recently been officially recategorized as part of Center City.) North Philadelphia also became an issue in the 1987 mayoral campaign, when Mayor Goode pledged to spend half of the city's $60 million Community Development Block Grant in that part of the city. Despite these highly publicized efforts, however, the area as a whole has continued to decline in socioeconomic terms, and the consensus is that redevelopment never "caught on" in North Philadelphia.

Let us turn now to an example of the city's more favorable redevelopment record downtown. In contrast with the Lower North Philadelphia redevelopment projects, those on Market Street East have been considered an enormous success. Market Street is the major east-west axis of the city, and the Market East projects have covered an eight-block area stretching east from City Hall toward the Delaware River. These few blocks, which housed three of the city's four department stores, had become a problem by the 1950s. Several storefronts were vacant, and many of the businesses that remained were small shops selling low-priced goods to a low-income, largely black, clientele. Since Market Street was a key route between City Hall and the newly refurbished historic district including Independence Hall, the city was interested in making it more attractive for shoppers and passing tourists. Furthermore, Market Street East was a symbolic gateway to the downtown since it contained one of the major access routes to Center City, the Reading Railroad Terminal.

In the 1960 Plan for Center City, planner Edmund Bacon presented a multi-use complex of transportation (railroad, subway, bus, and auto), shopping, and office space covering several blocks of Market Street East. This megastructure was designed to be a four-block-long concourse, open to the sunlight, linking subway and commuter rail service, below street grade level. Rising above this, at appropriate intervals, were four very substantial office towers. On the other side of the office towers would be a bus terminal and parking garage, completely isolating the downtown retail area from direct access of the rest of the city.

The first formal action on the project was the federal approval in 1969 of a tunnel to link the Reading Station east of City Hall with the Pennsylvania Railroad's Suburban Station on the west side. This "commuter tunnel" was designed to bring more people into Center City and to give improved access to Market East from the western suburbs. It was intended to reinforce the downtown district as the region's transportation hub. Because of engineering problems, funding problems, and resistance from nearby businesses and residents, the construction of the tunnel was delayed many times. Started in 1978, it was finally completed in 1984 at a cost of some $300–400 million.

In 1974 plans for the next portion of the project were announced—the first major retail space in Center City since 1931. This was an enclosed, multilevel mall of 125 shops and restaurants covering the block between 9th and 10th streets, anchored by a new Gimbel's department store on the west and connected by a skywalk to the existing Strawbridge & Clothier store on the east. The project was a joint venture by the City of Philadelphia and James Rouse, each putting up half of the construction costs. The complex would be owned by the Redevelopment Authority but leased to Rouse for ninety-nine years. The Gallery, as it was named, opened in 1977 and proved to be such a success that it was followed by a companion project, the Gallery II, which opened in 1983 in the block between 10th and 11th streets.

The Gallery project was the linchpin of the reconstruction of East Market Street. The Reading commuter railroad station was moved to the rear of the Gallery II, and the original Reading Station, a historic and architecturally significant building, was converted for office use. Although the city had originally had difficulty finding developers for the office building planned for Market East, the success of the Gallery induced investors to build three office towers (in piecemeal fashion) in the Market Street Corridor.

One of the most controversial aspects of Market East's development was the proposal to build the city's new convention center in the area. In 1983 the Reading Company submitted a proposal to build a 1-million-square-foot (five city blocks) convention complex centered on its former train shed adjacent to the Gallery. Many small business owners threatened with displacement and community activists opposed to further spending on downtown development joined forces against the proposed center. The city's business leaders and public officials, however, wanted a new, large convention center, and they wanted it to be centrally located. They argued that the city had a big investment to protect in Market East and that the convention center was expected to bolster downtown businesses.[20] Although several other sites were put forward as being less expensive, more accessible, and more in scale with such a large edifice, the city ultimately accepted the Reading proposal.

Although disputes among politicians have halted the construction process from time to time or changed its direction, the Market Street East project has never failed to draw sufficient private investment dollars, from the 1940s when Independence Mall was built to the year 2000 when the convention center will be in operation. In contrast to the Lower North Philadelphia case, the city has seldom lacked investors to put money into the area or developers to come up with plans for the real estate. Market East projects have repeatedly been threatened by political pressure to reallocate the public funds involved but almost never by economic withdrawal of the private resources necessary to carry them out. The outcome in nearly every case has been the completion of the Market East projects, albeit at a slower pace than anticipated.[21]

The important distinction, then, between redevelopment efforts in these two parts of the city lies not so much in different governmental policies as in the behavior of the private sector. Publicly sponsored redevelopment "worked" downtown, where investors were eager to put private money into public projects. By contrast, the city's willingness to put public resources into Lower North Philadelphia could not draw private investors into those neighborhoods they saw as "nonviable."

The Political Economy of Redevelopment

From the turn of the century until World War II, economics and politics were distinctly separate spheres in Philadelphia. A Republican machine ran political affairs with little interference from business leaders, as long as politics did not interfere with their profits. In exchange for turning a blind eye to political corruption, the businesses were left unregulated by the politicians. This tacit bargain began to break down in the 1940s, fueled by scandals and the deterioration of public services.

Beginning with the end of World War II, business and political leadership groups in the city became increasingly intertwined. In 1948 a group of business leaders began a new organization called the Greater Philadelphia Movement (GPM), aiming to "get Philadelphia moving again" by ending the economic stagnation prevalent in the city. Those who spearheaded the effort were not part of the established business community. In fact, they were rivals of the Chamber of Commerce, which represented the large manufacturers, transportation firms, and other businesses that had dominated the city during its industrial era. Although all corporate heads, the members of GPM represented the newly emerging industries of the service sector: banks, law firms, insurance companies, and the like. Their partners in the redevelopment initiative were the Young Turks, a political reform group interested in city planning. Seeing physical planning, political reform, and economic vitality as interrelated issues, these two groups formed the core of Philadelphia's progrowth coalition as well as the movement for urban redevelopment.[22]

Business and government leaders cooperated through an array of public-private partnerships in Philadelphia. These were of two kinds: quasi-public agencies and coordination groups. The quasi-public agencies were established to perform certain tasks, for example, Old Philadelphia Redevelopment Corporation to oversee the construction of the Society Hill project, and Philadelphia Industrial Development Corporation to arrange financing for expansion of manufacturing businesses. The coordination groups, such as the GPM and its successors, brought business leaders and public officials together (with an occasional labor member) to set the municipal agenda and coordinate activity on it. Both types of groups have proliferated since that time and have become the normal way of doing business in the city.

To understand Philadelphia's business involvement in downtown redevelopment, we can examine the national context. In the postwar period, public-private planning groups emerged in a number of cities with similar economic histories. Pittsburgh, San Francisco, New York, New Haven, Boston, and other older cities all had some form of a "leadership planning committee" set up by business leaders to influence the city planning process. Redevelopment and highway planning were normally the first issues that these groups tackled.[23] Why has redevelopment been of such universal interest to business groups? Three answers to this question that have been advanced in the literature on urban political economy are, we believe, relevant to explaining the Philadelphia experience.

One explanation for business involvement in redevelopment comes from the "capital logic" school of thought. This argument stresses the changes that take place in the nature of the accumulation (profit-making) process and the varying "requirements" for accumulation in different stages of development. Within this framework, redevelopment is seen as a way of getting rid of the physical and social relations of an older stage of capitalism and initiating the new ones necessary for the emerging stage. In postwar Philadelphia this meant removing the infrastructure and social classes remaining from the industrial city to make way for the entrance of "postindustrial" or service-sector businesses and workers.[24]

Philadelphia's redevelopment programs spurred the transformation from the industrial to the postindustrial city. By 1985 the Philadelphia City Planning Commission could legitimately claim: "Downtown Philadelphia is poised for significant growth and development in its office core, having completed a difficult transition from its former role as manufacturing and wholesale center to its role as a service center" and that this transformation was accomplished because the "1963 plan . . . convincingly promoted a vision of Center City as a modern and attractive urban center that would arise from a concerted effort on the part of government to improve transit, highway systems, and public open spaces."[25] In addition to these changes, we can add the removal of warehouses and manufacturing lofts, railroad tracks and terminals, the wholesale food market, small retail facilities, rooming houses, other facilities characteristic of industrial Philadelphia.

The second theoretical perspective that helps explain the involvement of business in redevelopment is the theory of land values. According to this framework, investments in property lose their market value over a period of time. This occurs because the built environment always represents "the dead hand of the past," since having done one thing with a piece of property precludes doing something else with it. The "something" that one has

done is based on current economic conditions, which will change in the future. Since building tends to occur in cycles linked to the general state of the economy, numerous structures and in fact whole sections of cities lose their market value together. Redevelopment allows for revalorization of land by clearing away the old structures, which have become impediments to new investment. Thus, the "normal" process of economic growth requires periodic destruction of previous investment sunk into the built environment.[26]

As this theory would predict, investors in the city's real estate market have been interested in raising property values in the downtown area. Since this is difficult to achieve on an individual basis, they have looked to government-sponsored redevelopment as a way of increasing values over large portions of the city at once. Commenting on the Society Hill project, for example, Albert M. Greenfield, a prominent real estate investor and chair of the city planning commission, argued, "The reason that nothing is moving and nobody has bought down there is because nobody has been given a guarantee that his investment will be protected and the climate of the whole area improved." Greenfield went on to insist that "the entire 1000 acres southeast of Independence Hall, an area that formed one quarter of center-city Philadelphia, should be certified for urban renewal."[27] Thus, redevelopment was perceived as a mechanism for revalorization of downtown property.

The third theory that informs our understanding of redevelopment is that of the relationship between the government and the private sector. Although private investors uphold the sanctity of private investment decisions, there comes a time when private decisions create (or are incapable of overcoming) some obstacles of growth. There may not be agreement within the capitalist group on the necessity or appropriateness of concerted actions to address the obstacles. Government therefore steps in and coerces certain decisions to prevent chaos or to reverse economic stagnation. For example, in Philadelphia private investment decisions had created situations such as obsolete infrastructure that necessitated redevelopment of the built environment. Private decisions were insufficient to effect a coordinated redevelopment program. Thus, the government (at both the national and local levels) assumed control of the coordinating process, with the acquiescence of the investor class.[28]

The role of the public sector (the federal Department of Housing and Urban Development, the local city planning commission, the Redevelopment Authority, the Industrial Development Corporation, and the like) has been multifaceted. Public agencies have coordinated projects, providing planning options and bringing together disparate private interest groups. They have used their legal powers (chiefly through eminent domain) to overcome resistance of property owners and reduce the potential costs of acquiring property. Public agencies have also played the role of legitimators, removing the responsibility for urban redevelopment from private investors and justifying programs on the grounds of the common good. Finally, the public sector has provided some funds for redevelopment, primarily in the form of start-up or preparations aspects of the projects rather than major construction funds, which have been mostly privately generated.

Notwithstanding the important supporting role that government agencies have played from time to time, Philadelphia's redevelopment has ultimately been privately controlled. With a few exceptions, projects have been initiated either by private developers or by public agencies with assurance of private developers' cooperation. Private investors have provided the major funding for redevelopment projects, even when the initial plan was generated by a public agency. Most importantly, private investors have defined the limits of acceptable projects by investing or not investing in them. Thus, they have used a tacit veto power over the redevelopment process, which has eventually grown to be an agenda-setting power. Over the years the implicit control of the private sector within the public-private partnerships has become more explicit. For example, in the shift from the federal Urban Renewal program to the Urban Development Action Grant program, public agencies lost control over the definition, site selection, and planning of projects and became primarily conduits for private developers to assemble financing for their projects.

Despite the fact that redevelopment has been privately controlled, however, it may not have been possible for the private sector to have accomplished redevelopment (especially on such a grand scale) by itself. Roseman has shown that private investment was on the increase in Philadelphia's CBD after World War II, even before the publicly sponsored redevelopment projects were begun.[29] But because Center City was still considered a high-risk area for investment, it received proportionately less investment than did nearby suburban areas. Mayor Clark's housing coordinator William Rafsky recalled in 1983:

I would disagree with the statement . . . that the lending institutions were gung-ho for urban renewal during the time when we were first getting started. . . . The best illustration I can give you is Park Towne Place [a luxury high-rise project]. . . . The developers needed financing for $12 million. They went to all of the banks and couldn't get Philadelphia banks to put up the money. . . . The developers at our urging go to New York, and out of New York the best they can get is, "We'll put up 50% if you can get Philadelphia banks to put up 50%." . . . The mayor decided he would bring all the banks together . . . and we almost bludgeoned them to make the $6 million matching loans.[30]

Why was it so difficult to obtain investors? One explanation for Philadelphia's problem was local investors' extreme reluctance to risk venture capital. Even the projects constructed during the urban renewal heyday of the 1960s were mostly financed by out-of-town capital.[31] In 1979 John Gallery, then the city's director of housing and community development, complained that many potential projects in city neighborhoods outside of the CBD were begging for developers as investors continued to prefer suburban sites.[32] By the late 1970s, however, a few investors had become more enthusiastic about the potential profits to be made in city neighborhoods. A developer working with the highly successful firm headed by Willard Rouse expressed the company's "bullish" approach toward urban real estate in the 1980s: "If we believe that this piece of dirt has value it will have it. Liberty Place [a skyscraper built by Rouse] created value on Market Street—North Philadelphia has value also." [33]

Overall, the region's business leadership has assessed redevelopment as a necessary but risky proposition. They have expressed little commitment to redevelopment per se, only redevelopment as it becomes profitable. That is why the city has found it difficult to obtain the cooperation of the private sector in many instances and virtually impossible to obtain it for projects outside of Center City.

City officials did not appreciate the imbalance of power between themselves and the private investors when they undertook redevelopment originally. They were as surprised at the wild success of the Center City projects as they were at the failure of North Philadelphia slum projects.[34] Planners had calculated that if city land was as cheap as suburban land and available in large amounts, developers would find it as attractive as suburban land and begin building in the city again. They did not foresee that banks and developers would refuse to go into certain areas on the basis of past investment patterns and calculation of current profitability. In short, no incentives were powerful enough to induce investors into some parts of the city, and the city officials were powerless to change their minds. They ended up settling on a de facto "strategy" of giving investors incentives to invest in projects that were already potentially profitable, since those were the only ones investors wanted to invest in anyway. As one analyst summed up the problem: The agencies "that control urban renewal in fact reinforce the 'decisions' of the marketplace . . . [and have contributed] not only to the dynamism of the downtown districts but also to the decay of the remainder of the city." [35]

The Outcomes: Who Pays? Who Benefits?

Before deciding whether the redevelopment of the city has been "successful," we should ask, "successful for whom?" The city administration, in carrying out an economic analysis of its projects, concludes that redevelopment is a success. Since 1970 the city has been making money on redevelopment, in the sense that increases in tax assessments on redeveloped properties have outstripped losses.[36] City officials also point out that Center City's "role as a regional service center is now firmly in place," [37] and that Center City has remained "a place of job opportunity" for city residents.

A more useful type of cost-benefit comparison, however, is that which examines the gains and losses to the different social groups affected by the process, rather than to the city as a whole. When examined in the light of a social-group analysis, redevelopment can be seen to have helped to reinforce the existing dichotomy between the haves and the have-nots in Philadelphia.

Let us take the issue of employment. One of the goals of redevelopment was to strengthen the city as the economic core of the region. How has this translated into employment for the residents of the city? As we saw in Chapter 2, the job distribution within the metropolitan area still favors the suburbs over the city. As a whole, the city is still losing jobs (although at a slower rate than previously), but since 1976 the number of jobs in Center City has been growing. Redevelopment has, as planned, helped to stop the "hemorrhage" of jobs to the suburbs, but job growth has been occurring in Center City rather than in other areas of the city.

If this were simply an issue of where jobs are located, it would not be very significant. After all, Philadelphia does have a transit system that provides good access to Center City from every part of town. The real significance of the growth of Center City and the accompanying decline of jobs in other areas is in the types of jobs that have been growing compared with the types that have been declining. The largest proportion of the Center City jobs are in the financial sector and in general services. These are different kinds of jobs from those that are being lost in the other parts of the city, which are predominantly manufacturing and retail jobs.[38]

If present trends continue, the employment distribution in the city will become more polarized into the high- and low-wage sectors of the post-industrial service economy, with fewer opportunities for those workers displaced by deindustrialization to regain their previous employment and income standings. The point is not that these trends have been caused by redevelopment, but rather that redevelopment has not—and we argue cannot—help redistribute job opportunities downward. Rather, redevelopment has reinforced these economic trends, playing "midwife to the emerging corporate economy that now characterizes the major cities." [39]

Turning to housing, we find that redevelopment has also reinforced the polarization of housing opportunities described in the preceding chapter. Middle- and upper-middle-class whites now have more opportunities to live near the CBD, and the increase in high-wage, white-collar jobs in Center City has sent more white, affluent workers into the area's housing market. Two-thirds of Center City housing units are now occupied by single people living alone, and the median income in the area has risen to nearly double the median for the city as a whole. Center City has become a hot area for real estate investors; more than 4,000 housing units (mostly rental) were added to the existing stock between 1970 and 1980 alone, and there the construction was sustained throughout most of the 1980s. Property values soared, with 45 percent of owner-occupied housing in Center City in 1980 worth more than $100,000, compared with only 5 percent of the housing in the metropolitan area. [40] In real estate terms, even the definition of "Center City" has changed; the old boundaries of Vine and South streets have been replaced by the "Center City Corridor" of Girard to Washington avenues, more than doubling the size of the area considered "desirable" by white professionals. [41]

On the other hand, black, Hispanic, Oriental, and white working-class neighborhoods close to the center of the city have been eroded, either through demolition as in Society Hill and along South Street or through gentrification as in Spring Garden, Northern Liberties, and Second Street. Chinatown has been hemmed in by redevelopment projects on all four sides, having lost land to Independence Mall, the Gallery, the Vine Street expressway, and the Convention Center. The nonwhite population of Center City dropped from 23 percent in 1950 to 10 percent in 1980 and is continuing downward. [42]

Outside of Center City, too, poor and nonwhite people have had to bear the brunt of the demolitions and displacement from redevelopment projects. For example, between 1950 and 1980 North Philadelphia lost 35,000 housing units (net), and its average property value dropped from 60 percent to 40 percent of the city's average.[43] These demolitions were never matched by positive construction of units to replace the ones destroyed, despite the variety of federal programs aimed at the inner city.

As early as 1959 Philadelphia's Fels Institute Community Leadership Seminar had discussed the issue of class bias in the urban renewal program. The questions posed were "Are those hurt most the least able to afford it?" and "Are middle-class standards of 'blight' relevant to the people living in the houses to be demolished?" In raising these questions, Philadelphians were acknowledging that governmental policy itself (as opposed to poverty, the nature of the housing market, and so forth) may contribute to unequal outcomes for city residents.

One manifestation of class bias has been the differing plans for different populations. From the very beginning of the redevelopment program, it was intended that the poor black population of North Philadelphia be "dispersed" to Eastwick's new town and to the suburbs, while a concentrated effort was made to "get the white leadership back" into Center City.[44] A second but closely related issue is the differential negative impact of the programs on different groups. If redevelopment is to be considered a necessary step toward progress, then who has absorbed the costs of that progress? The most important cost, displacement from homes and businesses, has been borne overwhelmingly by the poor, the nonwhite, and owners of small businesses.[45]

This pattern has not gone unnoticed by the victims of progress. Hardships stemming from redevelopment have over the years spawned many organizations to resist the process. In the 1950s residents and small business owners attempted to block demolitions in the area of Independence Mall; in the 1960s, around Drexel University, Temple University, 15th and Market, Pine Street, and South Street; in the 1970s, near the University of Pennsylvania, Chinatown, Market Street East, and Spruce Street, just to name a few of the more famous confrontations. The height of neighborhood-based opposition to city-sponsored redevelopment occurred in the late 1970s, with groups boycotting the Gallery at Market East, squatting in abandoned houses in North Philadelphia, and organizing coalitions to redirect the city's community development program.

Neighborhood organizations had a long history in Philadelphia, but until the 1960s they were mostly homeowners' associations and federations of block clubs. As such, their agendas concentrated on property values and city services in their areas. In the 1960s, however, neighborhood-based groups became increasingly politicized, partly as a result of the local implementation of federal programs.[46] Urban Renewal, for example, had created local project area committees, some of which took their role of "maximum feasible participation" seriously. When the federal funding base for urban programs shifted in 1974 to the Community Development Block Grant (CDBG), new groups emerged to influence local decisions about how the funds would be spent.

Two grassroots groups with different organizing and political philosophies dominated the local policy debate: Philadelphia Council of Neighborhood Organizations (PCNO) and the North Philadelphia Block Development Corporation (NPBDC). PCNO was founded in 1975 as a coalition of existing neighborhood-based organizations. As an umbrella organization representing 250 groups, it eschewed racial or geographical emphases for an overall "pro-neighborhood" approach. Its lobbying campaigns emphasized increasing the proportion of CDBG money allocated to housing and neighborhood programs as opposed to downtown development programs. The NPBDC, begun in 1976, was organized to lobby for increased community development funding to the predominantly black area of North Philadelphia west of Broad Street. As a mass-based rather than organization-based group, it had no permanent membership but gained much media attention by holding frequent rallies and dramatic protests, calling attention to the presumed racially biased pattern of public spending.

The two neighborhood-based groups had different approaches to politics. PCNO, headed by a Catholic priest without political aspirations, had no electoral program of its own but acted as a citizen lobby to strengthen and coordinate neighborhood groups' activities. Its participation in the political process was indirect: interviewing candidates and endorsing those who most closely conformed to the neighborhoods' policy agenda.[47] NPBDC, on the other hand, became an electoral vehicle for its founder, Milton Street, who was elected to the state legislature, and his brother, John, who was elected to City Council. Although Milton proved too much of a maverick for public office, John has continued to be reelected and has been an important leader of the pro-neighborhood forces on Council throughout the 1980s.

Community groups, however, have been in the position of fighting rearguard actions rather than shaping policy direction. One "victory," the adoption of a relocation program for displaced residents, took place after the bulk of displacement had already occurred.[48] Another, defeating the Crosstown Expressway along South Street, proved to be a Pyrrhic victory since virtually all of the original businesses in that area left during the protracted negotiations, and most of the residents were displaced by subsequent gentrification. Overall, though neighborhood organizations have succeeded in limiting some of the worst aspects of redevelopment, they have been unable to maintain a broad political movement to shape the overall direction of the program.

There is an interesting political irony in the fact that redevelopment helped to strengthen the city's growing network of community organizations in the 1960s and 1970s—organizations whose target was most frequently city government. A further irony, however, is that many of these community leaders "joined the system" in the 1980s by taking jobs either in the city administration or in a number of related quasi-public agencies. As the 1990s open, the remaining community organizations are increasingly turning from political protest groups into self-help housing-development corporations, vying for city and foundation funds for their own programs, and today's activists complain that the level of community organizing is at a low ebb.

Conclusions

Redevelopment has changed the city of Philadelphia physically in a way that has facilitated the economic and social transformations taking place in the region and nation. It has provided new spaces for the growing corporate service industries of the CBD. It has counteracted the flow of jobs and residents to the suburbs, strengthening the city as the economic center of the metropolitan area. It has helped to "recapture" Center City as a prime residential location for the white professional population.

Although redevelopment has involved both the public and private sectors, it has been driven by the private sector more than the public. The impetus for undertaking redevelopment was and still is to generate private economic growth, with the corollary that, "of course," private growth will be good for the public sector as well. The public-private partnerships have been an acknowledgment of the fact that neither the public nor the private sector could have effected redevelopment alone—the private sector lacked adequate coordination mechanisms and the public sector lacked adequate funding.

This point is underscored by the fact that the redevelopment projects in areas like North Philadelphia have failed while those in Center City have succeeded. Redevelopment programs are designed to leverage private investment money and have been held hostage by private investors' assessments of the profit-making capabilities of the projects. Although the city has spent enormous amounts of seed money to lure investors into less desirable areas of the city, its efforts have been futile, since the investors think their money can be spent more profitably elsewhere.

Although it has generated economic growth in the city, redevelopment has not redistributed the benefits of that growth downward. Rather, it has tended to reinforce the positions of wealth and poverty in the city as a whole. In traditional economic theory, wealth generated at the top of the income pyramid should trickle down to those at lower levels. Although it is true that real estate developers are making money on the redeveloped Philadelphia, few good jobs have trickled down to poorer city residents. Instead, the jobs generated by redevelopment in Center City (like new jobs generated nationally in the 1970s and 1980s) have contributed to increased polarization in incomes of city residents.

Furthermore, the city's low-income and minority populations have borne the brunt of the hardships presented by the redevelopment process. Evictions, demolitions, displacement, loss of employment, and other forms of dislocation have hurt the low-income and minority populations disproportionately. They have often organized and fought back, but their efforts have not been sufficient to produce major changes in the thrust of the programs.

The most striking finding is the widening contrast between the neighborhoods of the city as a whole and the newly revitalized Center City. As elsewhere, the growth of the office economy in Philadelphia has resulted in the erection of a gleaming new facade over the ruins of the commercial and industrial past. These symbols have become identified with prosperity and have encouraged observers to equate downtown development with regional economic progress. Meanwhile, however, the old industrial neighborhoods have continued to decline, the ghettos have continued to suffer abandonment and neglect, and neighborhoods that have become gentrified have displaced long-term residents.

5

Race, Class, and Philadelphia Politics

Our position herein has been that any plausible account of Philadelphia's changing neighborhoods, its downtown redevelopment, and even its race relations in the period since World War II must begin with the region's economic transformation from a manufacturing hub to a service center. That transformation, as we have seen, brought decay to many of Philadelphia's older factories and communities, at the same time intensifying downtown commerce and spawning new industrial and residential nodes in the suburbs.

In politics, just as in other features of Philadelphia life, the economic transformation changed many well-established patterns. In the preceding chapter we noted the intertwining of business and political leadership during the 1950s in the Greater Philadelphia Movement. Several decades later the heads of the region's largest corporations are no longer so visible in local politics. As Philadelphia has lost corporate headquarters, its branch offices and branch plants are managed by transient CEOs who see the city as a temporary career stop rather than a permanent home. Most often living in the suburbs, people in this group have less incentive than those of the preceding generation of business leaders to participate in Philadelphia's civic and political affairs. With the shrinking manufacturing base, industrial unions have become marginal players in city politics. These previously powerful forces in city politics have lost ground to a new generation of political leadership that is largely neighborhood based. In this increasingly divided city, neighborhood-based politicians find it more and more difficult to reach accommodation with one another. To the extent that the new service economy is reinforcing class and racial inequalities in the region, the political demands voiced by different constituencies have become incompatible.

As a result, the structure of politics in the region has fragmented during the postwar period. The steady dissolution of the Democratic coalition over forty years made it more and more difficult for *any* organized group within the city to redirect public priorities. The combination of this political fragmentation with the fiscal austerity of the 1970s and 1980s virtually condemned the municipal government to the status quo.

The Dissolution of the Ruling Postwar Coalition

As described in Chapter 4, Philadelphia entered the postwar era with a surge of reformist energy directed against the century-old Republican machine. Needing a mass base, the business people, professionals, and members of the civic elite who led the reform movement found their allies in the city's downtrodden Democratic organization. A coalition of patricians with regular "rowhouse" Democrats was built on the prospect of finally throwing the corrupt opposition out of City Hall. But almost as soon as they had achieved a charter change and captured the office of mayor for their standard bearer, Joseph Clark, the parties to this tenuous alliance began to quarrel among themselves.

Many observers have noted that our society never developed class-based parties in the same way that the Europeans did. Rather, American political parties have tended to be structured as broad coalitions that cross class lines. The coalition fashioned by Philadelphia reformers in the 1950s—linking progressive middle and upper-middle-class whites with trade unionists, the city's black community, and ward politicians of the regular Democratic party—resembled the national coalition forged by New Deal Democrats. And like the national Democratic party, Philadelphia's Democratic organization has been prone to factionalism. In fact, the political history of postwar Philadelphia can be read chiefly as the story of struggles within the Democratic party.

Let us recall briefly that at the national level the Democratic party since World War II has been dominated by three main factions: labor, blacks, and a reform faction sometimes called "New Politics" Democrats. The balance of power among these factions shifted considerably during the 1960s. Union members, who had contributed 38 percent of Adlai Stevenson's vote in the 1952 presidential election, accounted for only 32 percent of George McGovern's vote in 1972. At the same time the black Democratic vote grew, from only 7 percent of the 1952 Democratic presidential vote to 22 percent of the 1972 vote for McGovern. Meanwhile, the New Politics Democrats emerged as a middle-class, college-educated, and liberal constituency, motivated more by issues than by the politics of patronage and compromise.[1]

The inherent tensions within this national alliance were obvious in 1968 from the large number of white working-class voters who defected from the Democrats to support the populist George Wallace, running as a third-party candidate. Wallace Democrats were found disproportionately in urban working-class districts where whites lived next to expanding black populations. A researcher who visited those precincts one year after the 1968 election stressed the racial dimension of the Wallace vote:

> Each Wallace precinct was like another outpost marking the borders to which Negro residential movement had pushed. On some streets the families who had voted for Wallace in 1968 were already gone, the area having turned entirely Black by 1969. Other streets simmered with the strains of neighborhood transition. At still other points, the Whites had drawn an unyielding line that permitted no Blacks to pass.[2]

Similar racial and class strains marked postwar politics in Philadelphia. Almost immediately after defeating the Republican machine in 1951, the Democrats became embroiled in conflicts pitting the upper-class reform mayor, who was determined to stamp out patronage, against the ward politicians, who saw patronage as the normal spoils of victory. This tension between the reformers and the regular Democrats has remained a powerful dynamic in the party ever since, complicated further in the 1970s by the emergence of a third major element within the party: black politicians who remained independent of the other two factions.

When the second of the reform mayors, Richardson Dilworth, resigned in order to run for governor, he was succeeded by James Tate, the City Council president whose roots were in the old-style patronage politics of the regular Democratic party. Tate had to fight to become the party's candidate in the next regular election; the party chair preferred to run a reformer instead and sought to deny Tate the nomination. Tate won, but then four years later the party refused to nominate him for reelection. Tate ran against the party organization in the primary and defeated the party's more reform-minded candidate.

By the late 1960s the party's fragmentation appeared serious enough to influence Mayor Tate's thinking about grooming his successor. In his memoirs Tate explained his choice of the swaggering police commissioner, Frank Rizzo, to succeed him:

One thing that was becoming obvious was that the old Democratic coalition of the City Committee, organized labor, the working class whites, liberals, and blacks and other minorities, was breaking down. The working class whites, for example, who were not able, or did not choose to leave the city, were developing increasingly Republican tendencies. . . . I felt that Rizzo could bring the white working class vote back into the Democratic Party.[3]

Rizzo repeated Tate's experience of running against his own party organization in his reelection bid of 1975. The Democratic organization refused to endorse Rizzo for reelection to mayor, yet Rizzo achieved an impressive victory for himself and for the eight City Council candidates who represented his rump organization.

With Rizzo's successor, Mayor William Green (1980–1984), the liberal reform element of the party was satisfied, but not the "rowhouse" Democrats. Green was a Kennedy-style liberal Democrat who became mayor after a long congressional career. Green's Washington experience had not prepared him for the rough-and-tumble of big city politics. Almost as soon as he took over city hall, Mayor Green made enemies of public employee unions by stubbornly refusing to negotiate wage increases despite marches by the police, threats of walkouts by fire fighters, and a fifty-day strike by public school teachers. He disdained the brand of ward politics that dominated the City Council and allowed the Democrats' patronage machine to atrophy. To party regulars, Mayor Green seemed aloof—a man who avoided going into the city's neighborhoods to press the flesh. That assignment he left to his managing director, Wilson Goode, who used his visibility in the Green administration to launch his successful campaign for mayor in 1983.

At last the Democrats appeared to have a candidate who could reconstruct the splintered party. Wilson Goode claimed the support not only of downtown businesses but also of neighborhood groups whose municipal services had improved during his term as managing director. White reformers saw Wilson Goode as a hard-working administrator with a record of honest, efficient management of the city's operating departments. Black Democrats lined up solidly behind this candidate who had worked effectively for inner-city neighborhoods as managing director, and who symbolized greater opportunities for blacks. Goode's campaign even made accommodation with the party regulars in pro-Rizzo, working-class white wards along the river and in South Philadelphia. In return for the ward leaders' support, Goode offered his endorsement to some of their hand-picked candidates for lower-level offices and patronage jobs in his administration. Goode's coalition-building efforts paid off. He won the 1983 election in a campaign that never took on an overtly racial tone.[4]

Yet a mayoralty that began with great promise was crippled almost beyond recovery in May 1985 by the city's disastrous confrontation with a small extremist commune known as MOVE. In a largely black neighborhood of West Philadelphia that had been threatened by violence from the commune's residents, the police erected barricades around the MOVE house and ultimately dropped explosives on it, setting off a fire that killed all eleven MOVE members inside the house and destroyed two city blocks.

In addition to destroying human lives and more than sixty homes, the incident also destroyed Wilson Goode's hopes of being the politician who would put the city's fractured political majority back together. No longer did Goode enjoy the unqualified support of black Democrats, some of whom saw the city's decision to drop a bomb on a residential area as a racist act. Business leaders were appalled at the lapse in managerial control that led to the incident; a blue-ribbon investigating panel accused the mayor of abandoning his command responsibilities in the emergency. And many white liberals were shocked at the use of such brutal force to quell a neighborhood disturbance. Although Wilson Goode was able to reestablish his control over municipal operations, he did not regain the personal loyalty that would have allowed him to act as the peacemaker among quarreling party factions.

Surveying the returns from the past thirty years of electoral history in the city, one might be tempted to ask whether the factionalism within the party has really created problems for Philadelphia Democrats. After all, Democratic voters have consistently outnumbered Republicans 4 to 1 in the city, and the party has held onto almost all public offices in the city government. Since 1951 the Republicans have never even come close to regaining the dominant position they held before World War II. The City Council has included only two or three Republicans out of a total membership of seventeen throughout most of the postwar period. And for most of that time the Republicans held their seats, not because their vote totals justified it, but because the city charter requires that the minority party hold at least two seats. This overwhelming electoral advantage enjoyed by Democrats, however, belies the party's weakness as an organization.

How is this weakness reflected? As we have already seen, the party lacks the fundamental ability of strong party organizations—that of controlling nominations. Not since the early 1960s had the party been able to assure the nomination to the candidate of its own choosing. Both Mayor Tate and Mayor Rizzo ran successfully in Democratic primaries against their own party leadership. And by 1983, when Frank Rizzo and Wilson Goode faced each other in the Democratic primary for mayor, the party organization actually refused to take sides at all, remaining both formally and operationally neutral in one of the most important political contests of the postwar period.

Perhaps the most convincing evidence of the Democratic party's dissolution lies in the almost invisible races for judgeships. Political insiders consider these races to be the easiest nominations for the party to control, because they involve candidates who have no public recognition, running for an office that few voters care about. By the mid-1980s the party leadership could not even control these nominations. In 1985 and 1987 unendorsed judicial candidates won nominations by obtaining support from maverick ward leaders and from outside organizations like the American Bar Association.

Nor does the party have a monopoly on instructing Democratic voters. In every election the party organization provides a "sample ballot" that is distributed both door-to-door and at polling places to remind the voters which candidates have the party's endorsement. But individual Democratic candidates often print their own sample ballots, urging their supporters to vote for their preferred slate, which may or may not correspond to the city committee's slate. In preparing for the spring primaries of 1988, the city committee faced so much splintering among the ward leaders that its leadership took the unprecedented step of giving each individual ward leader the money to print his or her own personal ballot choices. The result was that 175 different versions of the "official" city committee ballot circulated on primary day.

The reform element in the party has displayed a distaste for patronage, and throughout much of the postwar period the party has exercised only weak control over patronage appointments to municipal jobs and to state jobs (during periods when the state government was held by Democrats). Individual Democrats often go directly to administrators in state or city government to request appointments for ward committee members, constituents, or others, without consulting the party leadership in the city.

In recent elections the Democratic party has not even been able to provide sufficient "street money" to its 3,500 committee people. Traditionally, the party set aside at least $50 to reimburse each committee person for election day expenses and efforts. Since the mid-1970s, however, Democratic committee people in wards throughout the city have frequently received their street money from individual candidates running in their districts, rather than from the Democratic city committee. Individual ward leaders have become capable of raising their own money and fielding their own organization without the party's help. In the November 1984 election, for example, one ward leader commented: "It finally came home to roost. Not only was there a lack of street money from the City Committee— but nobody cared. There wasn't a committeeman on the street who didn't have money." [5] In short, Philadelphia elections during the past thirty years have increasingly become a free-for-all in which the fact that a candidate wears the "Democratic" label means little about his or her attachment to the party organization. Philadelphia Democrats these days might well echo Will Rogers's observation in the 1920s: "I belong to no organized political party. I am a Democrat."

Why the Fragmentation?

One commonly heard explanation for the disintegration of the Democratic organization is the extraordinary loss of party leadership in the past fifteen years through criminal prosecutions. It is true that Philadelphians have witnessed an unusual number of removals of local Democratic politicians from office for criminal activity, including the City Council member in 1976 who accepted bribes to influence the granting of concessions at Philadelphia Airport, the state senator who was convicted in 1978 of using his office for racketeering, the three Council members caught in the Abscam net in 1980, and the Council member convicted in 1987 for soliciting a bribe to influence legislation assisting a waterfront development project. Although each one of these incidents jolted the party temporarily, the reasons for its decline are far more deeply rooted.

The party's weakness can be traced to its internal divisions into three main factions: reformers, rowhouse "regulars" (a group that once included many union members), and black Democrats. The schism between the upper-middle-class reform element of the party and its working-class party regulars mirrors a widening gap in the region's occupational and income structure. The shift toward a two-tier service economy that we have described is reflected in the divergence of interest between those who hold professional, technical, and managerial jobs in the corporate offices that are flourishing in the region, and those employed by the declining manufacturing sector and the low-paid service sector.

As the economic fortunes of these factions diverge, so do their political

Table 5.1 Revenues received per capita by
local governments in selected cities, FY 1986

	Local taxes	State aid	Federal aid	Local taxes as percentage of total
Philadelphia	$ 749	$188	$100	72%
Chicago	417	132	88	65
New York	1,180	809	181	54
Detroit	474	377	132	48
Baltimore	478	464	164	43
Boston	425	616	116	37

Source: Pennsylvania Economy League, *Revenue and Expenditure Comparisons: Philadelphia vs. Selected Major Cities* (Philadelphia, 1989).

preferences. They want different things from local government. Political leaders representing rowhouse Philadelphians struggle to maintain the city's basic services to neighborhoods—especially public education and public safety—while keeping taxes from escalating. Voices speaking for the city's downtown interests emphasize the value of using the city's resources for economic development. Taxpayers, they say, must be willing to invest in convention centers, waterfront development, and other large-scale projects in order to ensure future growth. Meanwhile, liberal reformers argue that local government must provide some services for the city's most disadvantaged citizens—its poor, its homeless, its drug and alcohol abusers, AIDS victims, abused children, and others.

Cutbacks in federal aid to the city since the mid-1970s have forced city officials to rely more heavily on local resources. Table 5.1 shows that compared with other major American cities like Boston, Chicago, and Detroit, Philadelphia derives a higher proportion of its local government revenues from its own tax base, while receiving a smaller proportion from federal and state subsidies. This unusually heavy reliance on local resources increases the public perception of political struggles over local expenditures as zero-sum games in which every choice in favor of economic development subsidies to corporations and to downtown projects is a choice against basic services to neighborhoods. In this climate the alliance among liberal reformers, downtown business leaders, and rowhouse Philadelphians has proved difficult to sustain.

What about the political role of labor unions, a key element in the Democrats' national coalition? With manufacturing leaving the city, unionized workers have provided less and less support for Democratic officeholders.

The earlier importance of industrial unions in local politics lay, not so much in their ability to dominate the city's policy priorities, but rather in their function as the main vehicle connecting workers to political institutions.

Michael Peter Smith has pointed out that the growth of nonunion jobs in low-paid, part-time, temporary work, as well as the growth of the informal sector in America's cities, has implications for working people's interactions with political institutions. (We are using the term "informal sector" to include the untaxed and unregulated production and exchange of services and goods by those who are self-employed, by unprotected wage laborers who engage in piecework done at home, and by other sub-contractors who work "off the books.") Rather than being connected to political life through trade unionism, the new low-wage workers and participants in the informal sector are more likely to be connected to the political system through their residential communities.[6] New immigrants are especially likely to be tied to their residential communities by bonds of language, religion, and custom, and to lack the experience, common to earlier immigrants, of participation in large, industrial work places. The eclipse of industrial unions removes one important integrating vehicle from city politics.

At present the most politically potent of the labor unions are the public employee unions, whose membership numbers about 20,000 and whose interests clearly lie in continuing support for public services. Yet the political power of the municipal employees is not an unmitigated blessing for the Democratic party. Mayors Tate and Rizzo demonstrated in the 1960s and 1970s that when the local budget is expanding, officeholders can secure the loyalty of municipal employees by negotiating favorable contracts. In the tighter fiscal conditions of the late 1970s and 1980s, however, it became more difficult to buy labor support with generous settlements, and therefore more difficult to keep municipal unions within the Democratic fold. Both the downtown business community and the city's taxpayers expressed increasing resentment toward union demands.

Adding to the growing income disparities among the different segments of the Democratic coalition is an emerging pattern of racial polarization within the Democratic electorate. Ever since the Democratic reformers took possession of City Hall, blacks have represented a substantial constituency within the Democratic electorate, but only recently have they begun to vote as a bloc and to support an independent black leadership. In the first few decades following World War II black turn-outs were low, despite the fact that northern urban blacks had once demonstrated participation rates nearly equivalent to whites. From 1950 to 1960 the difference in registration rates between Philadelphia whites and blacks widened, with the black percentage declining from 44 percent to 41 percent, while the white rate increased from 52 percent to 55 percent. This was the third consecutive decade that blacks' registration rate had declined.[7] Blacks were not only registered in smaller proportions than whites; they consistently turned out to vote in lower proportions as well.

Yet if we look at registration and turn-out figures in the early 1980s, we see a dramatic change in the level of black participation. In the election year of 1983, for example, 98 percent of the city's eligible black voters were registered. In that year's election black voter turn-out exceeded the city-wide average for the first time in Philadelphia's history. Moreover, the black community was more financially involved in Democratic politics than ever before. Local newspapers estimated that of the approximately $5 million that mayoral candidate Wilson Goode spent on his campaign, $2 million had been contributed by blacks (twenty times the amount of black contributions to any previous mayoral candidate). Preceding Wilson Goode's second election in 1987, registration figures showed about even numbers of blacks and whites on Democratic voter rolls.

What accounts for the startling rates of black political participation in recent elections? To explain the ascendancy of black mayors and legislators in American cities, it is commonplace to observe that black empowerment has resulted from the shifting numerical ratio of blacks to whites. And it is true that the massive exodus of whites from Philadelphia since 1945 has created an increasingly black electorate. Yet, if changing demographics were the only explanation, then we would expect to see a gradual emergence of bloc voting and leadership formation from the time that suburbanization got under way. Instead, until well into the 1970s the traditional pattern prevailed, in which black participation was channeled through a white-dominated party. Black candidates did not generally make election appeals based on race, nor did the black electorate vote on the basis of race. Instead, the city's black voters staunchly supported the Democratic party from the 1940s to the mid-1970s, registering and voting overwhelmingly as Democrats, whether the party's candidates were black or white. Writing about conditions in the mid-1960s, one scholar commented: "Blacks did not participate in politics through a Black political machine in Philadelphia. . . . Black politicians, successful and aspiring alike, publicly acknowledge that the white-dominated city political organizations determine which Blacks are nominated and elected."[8] One reason was that the party organization successfully squelched attempts to build black political organizations, using such defensive tactics as redrawing the boundaries of legislative districts to dilute the concentrations of black voters and coopting vocal black leaders into the structure of the party and the municipality. An example of successful cooption is Mayor Tate's handling of the War on Poverty programs of the 1960s, which furnished federal funds to create community-based programs in some of the city's poorest neighborhoods. The mayor devised a governing structure that offered to black community leaders an opportunity to control some patronage within the organization but not to build an independent political base. Unlike Chicago, New York, and Detroit, the War on Poverty in Philadelphia "never encouraged independent political activities that could significantly alter power relationships." [9]

This is not to deny that black activists in the 1960s often protested against the city's political and economic institutions, their chief target being the urban renewal program, as Chapter 4 mentions. At the height of protest activity, from summer 1963 to summer 1965, black organizations conducted seventy-eight demonstrations, boycotts, and picketing campaigns against businesses and government offices. [10] The most dramatic symbol of black protest in Philadelphia was the August 1964 race riot, described in Chapter 3, which took place in North Philadelphia. By the time it ended, there were two dead, more than three hundred wounded, and $3 million in damage to property.

Yet the racial confrontations of the 1960s did not lead to electoral separatism among blacks. Black voters continued to support white candidates within the framework of the Democratic party. For example, in the Democratic mayoral primary of 1971, a black candidate ran against two white contenders, one of whom was Frank Rizzo. Surprisingly, it was not the black candidate who received the majority of black votes; that distinction went to Rizzo's white opponent. (Nevertheless, the three-way split of the votes allowed Rizzo to win the primary with only 48 percent.) In that race and several subsequent elections, many black voters supported white candidates over blacks.

The turning point for black participation in Democratic politics appears to have been the referendum of 1978 on whether to change the city charter to allow individuals to serve more than two consecutive terms as mayor. The mayor in question was Frank Rizzo, who wanted to remain in office past 1979 but who needed a change in the charter to permit him to run for an unprecedented third term. Black Philadelphians enthusiastically joined the forces opposing Rizzo's charter change. Rizzo's opponents led a massive voter-registration drive in the inner city, enrolling more than 62,000 additional black voters. Blacks turned out at about the same rate as whites for the referendum and voted solidly against the charter change. In the same black wards where about one-third of the vote had gone to Rizzo in 1975, fully 96 percent of the voters rejected his bid for a charter change in 1978.[11]

The charter change referendum signaled a new recognition among political observers of a black voting bloc, self-consciously supporting black political candidates. For the first time in 1979 a group of black Democratic ward leaders met to hear presentations from the major candidates and to endorse its own slate, independently from the city committee. Many commentators on Philadelphia politics have interpreted the emergence of a black voting bloc as one more sign of the growing racial separatism in the city, a trend that is reflected in the increasing residential segregation of blacks that we document in Chapter 3. These commentators reason that the increasing isolation of blacks into separate neighborhoods breeds a separate set of political interests—interests that can truly be understood and promoted only by black political leaders. When black incumbent Wilson Goode ran for renomination against a white Democratic challenger in the primary of May 1987, headlines in the local media stressed the racial polarization among Democratic voters: "Goode's Win Came in a Vote Along Racial Lines."[12] "Tally Indicates Race was Primary Fulcrum,"[13] and "A Campaign in Black and White."[14] Some political forecasters even spoke of a time when blacks would completely dominate the Democratic party in Philadelphia and white Democrats would migrate to the Republicans, producing a racially based party system.

Our analysis challenges the assumed link between residential segregation and the emergence of the black voting bloc. To examine this link, we collected data on the racial composition of the vote for black candidates in three successive mayoral primaries: 1979, 1983, and 1987. In each of these three years the Democratic primary was a contest between a black candidate and a white candidate. (In 1979 black attorney Charles Bowser lost to the white candidate, Bill Green. In both 1983 and 1987 black candidate Wilson Goode beat his white opponents, Frank Rizzo and Edward Rendell, for the Democratic nomination.) Not surprisingly, we found that in all three primaries the number of black voters in each ward was highly correlated with the size of the vote for the black candidate (see Table 5.2). The slight dip in the correlation coefficient in 1983 probably reflects the dramatic increases in black registrations just before that campaign. Total Democratic registrations rose by as much as 25 percent in some of the most heavily black wards of the city, as Goode's supporters signed up first-time voters, some of whom did not turn up on election day at the polls. Nevertheless, these coefficients suggest the remarkable base of support that the black electorate provided for these black candidates.

Having said that, however, we must also observe that in the most heavily

Table 5.2   Correlations of votes for black candidates with number of blacks registered to vote in Philadelphia

	Pearson correlation coefficient	Significance
1979 Democratic primary (Bowser vs. Green)	.987	.000
1983 Democratic primary (Goode vs. Rizzo)	.962	.000
1987 Democratic primary (Goode vs. Rendell)	.987	.000

Table 5.3   Proportion of registered Democrats voting for the black candidate in the city's most heavily black wards

Ward	Voting for Bowser, 1979	Voting for Goode, 1983	Voting for Goode, 1987
3rd	58%	64%	60%
4th	56	63	59
6th	50	61	53
11th	48	57	52
16th	47	62	53
28th	49	59	53
29th	47	61	49
32nd	44	61	50
44th	53	60	56
47th	34	55	40
60th	50	63	58

black wards of the city the pattern across the three elections was *not* one of increasing support for the black candidates. Instead, we see in Table 5.3 a surprising decline from 1983 to 1987 in the percentage of black Democrats supporting the black primary candidate. In these eleven wards, where more than 90 percent of registered Democrats were black, the voters turned out for the black candidate at the rate of 48 percent in 1979. With an increase of about 25 percent in Democratic registrations before the 1983 mayoral primary, mainly achieved by Wilson Goode's campaign, the black candidate in 1983 picked up a larger proportion of the registered Democrats—60 percent. Then, in his bid for renomination in 1987 following the MOVE tragedy, Wilson Goode suffered both from declining registrations in these wards and from lower levels of support from those who remained on the voting rolls. As the black candidate in 1987, Goode was supported by only

Table 5.4 Correlations of the index of segregation, 1980, and the extent of black nonsupport for the black candidate

	Pearson correlation coefficient	Significance
1979 Democratic primary (Bowser vs. Green)	.449	.000
1983 Democratic primary (Goode vs. Rizzo)	.634	.000
1987 Democratic primary (Goode vs. Rendell)	.652	.000

53 percent of the registered Democrats in the wards that were supposed to have been his strongholds.

If we move beyond the most heavily black wards of the city to consider all sixty-six wards, we see in Table 5.4 a pattern that contradicts much of the popular commentary on racial polarization in segregated neighborhoods. For in fact, black segregation in the wards of the city was *positively* correlated with the degree of black *nonsupport* for the black candidate in the three mayoral primaries. To put it another way, black voters were less likely to turn out for the black candidate in heavily black wards than they were in wards where they constituted a numerical minority. One reason may be that the most segregated wards tended to be low-income areas, and low-income voters universally have lower turn-out rates than more affluent voters. That hypothesis is at least partially confirmed by Table 5.5, which shows the extent of black nonsupport for Wilson Goode's candidacy in the 1987 primary. It confirms that Goode suffered fewer defections in the middle-class black sections of the city (Overbrook, Wynnefield, Mount Airy, and Oak Lane) than in the poorer neighborhoods of North and West Philadelphia. It may also be that black voters who find themselves living in white-dominated neighborhoods are more motivated to demonstrate racial solidarity by supporting black candidates. If that is true, then the increasing racial segregation in Philadelphia will not contribute to black political solidarity and may even make it more difficult for black politicians to mobilize supporters in black neighborhoods. This pattern of nonparticipation of many low-income blacks should caution those who assume that the key to encouraging more participation by minority and low-income citizens is to reform the country's voter registration system.[15] Even when they are registered, low-income minority voters do not necessarily turn out to support the candidates who symbolize their interests.

Table 5.5   Proportion of registered black voters not supporting
the black candidate in the 1987 Democratic mayoral primary

In predominantly black wards of West Philadelphia		In wards changing from white to black		
3rd	36%	19th	56	(West Kensington)
4th	37	40th	35	(Eastwick)
6th	43	43rd	38	(Hunting Park)
44th	39	46th	42	(Cobbs Creek)
60th	37	48th	49	(Southwest Philadelphia)
In predominantly black wards of North Philadelphia (west of Broad Street)		In wards changing from black to white		
11th	45	2nd	45	(Queen Village)
16th	45	15th	45	(Fairmount)
28th	45	27th	40	(Penn/Drexel)
29th	46			
32nd	47	In wards with middle-class blacks		
47th	57	10th	33	(Oak Lane)
		22nd	29	(Mount Airy)
		34th	27	(Overbrook)
		52nd	30	(Wynnefield)
In predominantly black wards of North Philadelphia (east of Broad Street)				
14th	50			
20th	45			
37th	48			
43rd	38			
49th	42			

Blacks are not the only minority group with a significant stake in Philadelphia politics, though they are by far the largest. A growing segment of the citizenry is Hispanic, of whom Puerto Ricans constitute the largest single group. Hispanic residents are highly segregated, over half of them living in only 15 of the city's 364 census tracts. Nonetheless, because they represent less than 10 percent of the total population, they do not yet dominate any electoral districts for either the City Council or the state legislature. The one Hispanic member of the City Council, Angel Ortiz, was elected at-large rather than to represent a district, and he therefore cannot concentrate his efforts on issues of interest to the Hispanic community.[16]

The Business Community and Philadelphia Politics

Surveying the fragmentation of the majority party in Philadelphia during the postwar period, one might guess that the city's business community has simply moved in to dominate an otherwise chaotic situation. Much of the literature on postwar urban politics highlights the direct influence that business coalitions have had on politics and redevelopment programs.[17] For example, Chapter 4 describes the pivotal role played by business people in the reformers' City Hall administration in the 1950s. Given the high level of business activism in those early days of Democratic control and the growing weakness in the party coalition, it would be easy to assume that business has consistently dominated municipal politics since the 1950s. But such an assumption would be wrong. In fact, business activism in local politics has been sporadic during the postwar period, with long periods of inactivity punctuated by spurts of direct involvement.[18]

From the "power elite" theory of C. Wright Mills, to the pluralist paradigm developed by Robert Dahl, to Harvey Molotch's depiction of the city as a "growth machine," observers of business dominance in urban politics have tended to focus on the extent to which business people, as individuals and in groups, participate in politics in order to shape government to their own purposes. But as the Philadelphia case shows, it is not only through the political actions of business men and women that business interests shape governmental decisions.

If the protection of business interests by urban regimes were purely the result of business lobbying, then we would expect policy makers to respond always to those segments of the business community that are most vocal and most involved in local politics. "Business" is not a monolithic bloc with a single set of interests. Within the urban economy there will always be significant differences in the interests of small and large firms, or the interests of firms operating in different sectors. We show in Chapter 4, for example, that in the 1950s the politics of redevelopment pitted business people representing the new service sector of the city's economy (real estate, bankers, lawyers, insurance companies) against business people associated with the declining manufacturing sector. In that case the former set of interests, represented by the GPM, clearly triumphed over the latter set of interests, organized in the Chamber of Commerce.

Among the least active participants in urban politics are executives of absentee-owned plants, whose interests are not tied to the locale in the same way that banks, real estate developers, and metropolitan newspapers are. Research suggests that branch-plant managers are typically not motivated to participate [19] and may even be instructed not to participate by their superiors.[20] Yet their absence from the political scene does not mean that policy makers have neglected their interests. On the contrary, city officials have increasingly catered to the needs of mobile manufacturing firms, offering tax concessions, infrastructure improvements, customized training programs, development subsidies, and other benefits. Why? Because those firms with the smallest stake in the city find it easiest to abandon Philadelphia, taking jobs and tax revenues with them. To keep them in the city, public officials must serve their interests, even though those interests are not expressed through the political process.[21] In short, there is no one-to-one correlation between business activities and business influence, as a review of Philadelphia's postwar politics will show.

Chapter 4 describes the Greater Philadelphia Movement (GPM) as an alliance created in 1949 to represent the views of civic-minded bankers, lawyers, and business people. As a tax-exempt organization, GPM was technically prohibited from direct political activity. But its political influence was detectable in all of the major undertakings of the reform movement. Many of its members, though registered as Republicans, backed the Democratic reform mayors, Joseph Clark (1952–1956) and Richardson Dilworth (1957–1962). GPM pushed for the formation of a citizens' commission to redraft the city charter and saw to it that the commission's membership included thirteen downtown business people and lawyers, many of them members of GPM, compared with only two elected officials.

The *Philadelphia Bulletin* admiringly labeled the GPM "the cream of civic group giants," the "powerhouse of Philadelphia's citizen elite," and "the combat and control center of the city's movers and shakers." [22] After the election of the first reform mayor in 1951, a number of GPM's members took positions in the new government, most notably as managing director and commerce director, two key cabinet appointments. One insider's history of the Philadelphia reform movement documents the constant communication and collaboration between GPM's board and mayors Clark and Dilworth.[23]

Operating largely through direct personal contacts, this link between organized business and the reform administrators was never institutionalized, and GPM's access to City Hall virtually disappeared during the term of Mayor Tate, the old-style patronage politician who succeeded the reformers in the early 1960s. Business influence waned because of the business community's active opposition to Mayor Tate's bid for reelection in 1967. In that year most of the city's business leaders and the GPM as an organization supported Tate's Republican opponent. Narrowly winning reelection, Mayor Tate then broke off relations with GPM.

The GPM's relationship with Tate's successor, Frank Rizzo (1972–1980), was more mixed. While Rizzo was still police commissioner, the GPM had strongly supported the police department's handling of a potentially explosive "revolutionary people's constitutional convention" sponsored by the Black Panther party at the North Philadelphia campus of Temple University. To the surprise of many Philadelphians, the three-day event was held without violent incidents, leading the GPM to send Commissioner Rizzo this congratulatory telegram: "Representatives of the GPM have personally observed abuse and provocation to which your men are often, on such occasions, subjected. We congratulate you and them for maintaining peace during the meetings at Temple University." [24] But as soon as Rizzo became a candidate for mayor, his relationship to GPM began to deteriorate. When the business coalition distributed a questionnaire to all the mayoral candidates, Rizzo refused to respond, asserting that he would not allow the city's business elite to interfere in the electoral process: "I will go directly to the people. In the end, it is the people who will accept or reject my programs." [25]

Once elected, Mayor Rizzo retained at least the lukewarm support of many Philadelphia business people because he held the line on taxes throughout his first four-year term. As soon as he was reelected, however, his administration disclosed an $86-million deficit that forced him to ask for a 30-percent increase in both the property tax and the real estate tax. An outraged Chamber of Commerce charged the mayor with concealing the operating deficit in order to get reelected and urged him to limit the tax increases and to prune patronage employees. Mayor Rizzo responded by blaming the city's economic problems on the "ineffectuality" of unnamed business executives, a response that alienated a large part of the business community.

It is not surprising, then, that the business community mobilized in 1978 to prevent Mayor Rizzo from changing the city charter in order to run for a third term. The "Charter Defense Committee" united the GPM (now called the Greater Philadelphia Partnership) with prominent black leaders. Funds supplied by the business community paid for highly successful voter-registration drives in the city's black neighborhoods and for radio advertisements opposing the charter change. After venturing into local politics for this short-term victory, the business community lapsed into silence again, appearing to play no more prominent a role during the term of Rizzo's successor, William Green (1980–1984), than it had during Rizzo's eight years in office.

In the early 1980s a group of the city's business leaders began a well-publicized campaign to regain influence over the city's development. They acknowledged having lost the standing and the confidence that the business community had once enjoyed; their efforts had become fragmented and unfocused. A long-range planning committee of the Chamber of Commerce charged that businesses had "failed to provide the larger community with the leadership it needs" to achieve economic development.[26]

The way to reestablish corporate influence, business leaders agreed, was to reorganize the modern-day incarnation of the GPM, to rename it the Greater Philadelphia First Corporation (GPFC), and to recruit its board of directors from among the chief executive officers of the region's largest corporations. Not content to work only by influencing local government, the new corporation would acquire its own working capital. Each of the twenty-seven corporations holding a seat on the board would contribute a minimum of $50,000 in annual dues in order to create a pool of funds that the new coalition could use to promote various economic development projects in the region. To direct the work of this ambitious coalition of banks, insurance companies, public utilities, and other business firms, the GPFC hired an executive director from a federal development agency who had served his first political apprenticeship under reform Mayor Joseph Clark.

In forming the GPFC, members of Philadelphia's business elite openly declared that they were seeking to enhance their political and economic influence: "Of course we are interested in having a more powerful leadership position. . . . We are willing to take risks, and put our reputations on the line to achieve progress and move Philadelphia ahead. This may be misunderstood as a power play for its own sake." [27] One of their first opportunities came in the mayoral election of 1983, when the business community enthusiastically supported the candidacy of W. Wilson Goode. Out of two dozen members of GPFC's board of directors, most of them Republican business people, only one made a personal contribution to the campaign of the Republican businessman who opposed Goode, while eleven directors were listed as personal contributors to the Goode campaign. Business leaders described Goode's appeal on the basis of his "apolitical and professional" approach to his previous post as managing director. They were impressed with his campaign strategy as well, particularly when, well before the election itself, Goode invited dozens of business people to help him with a search-and-screening process to identify qualified candidates for the top city jobs. The corporate volunteers were organized into search committees that reviewed and graded thousands of résumés, guiding the mayor-elect in his choice of cabinet officers, department heads, and other key figures in his new administration. This was the most direct participation in shaping a municipal administration that the business community had exercised since the days of the reformers.

The irony of Wilson Goode's term as mayor is that business's bold initiative in establishing the GPFC and its role in supporting and shaping the new administration produced only minimal advances for the business community's agenda. By 1987, the end of Mayor Goode's first term, board members of GPFC expressed a sense of disappointment in the coalition's accomplishments and called for its reorganization. Some business leaders who had avidly backed Goode's candidacy in 1983 shifted to supporting his opponent in the Democratic primary because they felt that their investment had yielded too little return.

By the same token, we can observe that during the periods when Philadelphia's business community was least active in promoting its interests, such as during the Tate and Rizzo administrations, city government pursued many probusiness programs. For example, an analysis of the city's capital spending practices under different mayors shows that in constant dollars, mayors Tate and Rizzo spent just as much on downtown capital projects as did the reform mayors of the 1950s who were far more directly linked to downtown business interests.[28] It appears, in other words, that the connection between activism and probusiness policies is not so direct as it has sometimes been portrayed. It is not necessarily true that when business people participate actively, their priorities will prevail. As we observed earlier, even a well-organized and well-funded business coalition that enjoyed direct access to City Hall in the early 1980s had only limited success in promoting its priorities. Unlike the "movers and shakers" of the 1950s, their counterparts in the 1980s were operating at a time when the fragmentation of the majority party had reduced the mayor's influence over City Council. Business leaders could no longer assume that if they gained mayoral support for their plans, the legislative body would fall into line. In fact, the split between the mayor and City Council was part of the impetus for forming the GPFC. The rhetoric of business leaders who spearheaded its creation in 1982 emphasized the lack of coordination in deploying the city's resources to advance its development; this was their way of describing the increasing fragmentation of political leadership.

Nor is it the case that business leaders must always participate actively in politics in order to have policy makers cater to their needs and preferences. It appears that even when the business community is not able to influence government in direct ways—by lobbying and campaign contributions and through direct personal contact with policy makers in private clubs and organizations—municipal policies may still be favorable to business interests. This suggests that there are *structural* factors linking business and government at the local level, quite apart from personal influence.

One of the important structures for ensuring that business interests remain protected, even when business people have lacked direct access to

City Hall, is the quasi-public authorities. Increasingly in Philadelphia, as in other cities throughout the United States, large-scale development projects have been planned and implemented by nonprofit development corporations that are independent of city government. Chapter 4 highlights the importance to the redevelopment program of these public-private partnerships, created specifically to ensure "significant input from the private sector into the policymaking process." [29] Most often, financial sponsorship of the projects under their control is shared between the public and private sectors, and sometimes involves federal or state funds as well.

Alternately labeled "corporations" or "authorities," these structures have proliferated since the reform era. One reason is that such independent authorities often find it easier to obtain financing for development projects than does the city government itself. Independent corporations can borrow for large projects without having the debt count against the municipality's total indebtedness.

Typically, these nonprofit development corporations are run by boards of directors that combine elected officials with business leaders. The expectation is that by placing major capital investment programs under the control of such boards, the city guarantees they will be operated independently of the political process. Having no direct political accountability, their managers are free to use only financial and technical criteria to make operating decisions. Ordinarily, civil service protections do not extend to employees of such independent corporations, giving managers more flexibility than political officials enjoy in hiring, promoting, and firing staff. And the clarity of their mission, when compared with the complex functions performed by general purpose government, makes it easier to evaluate their performance.

An equally important explanation for the popularity of development corporations, however, is their ability to insulate the development agencies from electoral pressure. One such corporation that nicely illustrates this insularity—even anonymity—is the Philadelphia Industrial Development Corporation (PIDC), formed in 1958 jointly by the city government and the Chamber of Commerce. Its mission is to stimulate industrial development by offering low-interest loans, locating industrial sites for new start-ups, and cutting red tape for businesses trying to deal with banks and local government agencies. PIDC raises most of its own operating budget through fees and land sales, supplemented by an annual subsidy of slightly less than a million dollars from the city government. Writing about PIDC recently, a Philadelphia political columnist told his readers that this agency "has a hand in just about every major development in Philadelphia, from Penn's Landing to the massive health care complex now being developed on the old Philadelphia General Hospital site in West Philadelphia . . . . All of which suggests a single nagging question about PIDC, to wit: How come you never heard of it?"[30]

The answer is, of course, that many development officials prefer to operate in relative anonymity, staying out of major political conflicts. We have portrayed Philadelphia's majority political party as increasingly fragmented and plagued by conflicts among its most important constituencies. While downtown business interests favor investing the city's scarce resources in large-scale redevelopment, populists in City Council have questioned the development agenda, stalling major projects like the convention center and a trash-to-steam plant. One way to minimize the impact of these debates on the redevelopment program is to put that program outside the reach of normal political processes. Politicians justify the creation of nonprofit corporations on much the same grounds that the reformers of the early twentieth century used to defend the establishment of many independent boards and commissions—by assuming that they will operate apolitically, basing their judgments on expertise. The consequences of this strategy are much the same as they were in the earlier period: to remove policy making from the public forum of the City Council and thereby reduce the policy makers' accountability to the electorate.[31]

A second consequence of the proliferation of these nonprofit corporations, and one that is less favorable to business interests, is the difficulty faced by any mayoral administration that attempts to coordinate their efforts. Because each one is set up with a specific assignment, a separate staff, and its own financing mechanisms, these "alphabet soup" agencies tend to operate on their own, rarely seeking to coordinate their efforts with those of other agencies, and sometimes actively resisting attempts by the mayor, the city planning commission, or the City Council to bring them into line. In the long run, this coordination problem is detrimental to the interests of the business community because it hampers the city's ability to control the spillover effects of individual projects on one another. The downtown business community in Philadelphia, as elsewhere, has supported city planning as a way of rationalizing market forces. Yet the proliferation of independent nonprofit corporations makes it more difficult to achieve such rationalization.

Populism and Minority Politics

Philadelphia's business elites in the 1980s have been troubled not only by the political fragmentation but also by what they perceived to be the increasingly populist, antibusiness stance taken by the City Council. Recent councils have exercised their authority in a number of ways that appear inimical to the interests of business. In doing so, the members of the Council have reflected the suspicions and apprehensions that their constituents in the neighborhoods feel about downtown development. Chapter 4 makes the point that, during the past twenty-five years, neighborhood groups have been mobilized time and again to protest developments that threatened their interests. Projects involving highways, high-rent housing, hospitals, universities, and office buildings have all, at one time or another, met with community opposition. As the power of Council members representing specific districts has increased, relative to the central leadership of the Democratic party, it has become more common for City Council members, individually or in small groups, to hold up major development projects in order to examine the question of who would benefit from their construction. Gone is the universal appeal of growth for its own sake. In the open, fragmented politics of the 1990s the question is, rather, growth for whose sake?

One recent example of the Council's opposition to a business-sponsored project is its refusal to approve plans for a large new incinerator to burn trash and recover energy in the form of steam heat. Facing a rapidly worsening crisis in solid-waste disposal, both Mayor Green in the early 1980s and his successor Mayor Goode sought to persuade the Council to endorse a new trash-to-steam plant, to be located at the Naval Yard in South Philadelphia. The Chamber of Commerce and other business groups made it clear that the trash crisis had driven up the cost of doing business in the city, and they outspokenly endorsed the trash-to-steam plant as a high priority for city action.

Residents of South Philadelphia, however, vigorously opposed having the plant sited in their neighborhood. They feared its potential for emitting dangerous cancer-causing chemicals into the air, and they protested as well against the damaging effects of traffic congestion and foul odors associated with its operation. Their district council member, allied with several at-large members of the City Council, succeeded in holding up the project for more than five years, despite intense lobbying by both the mayor and representatives of the business community. Ultimately, Mayor Goode withdrew the proposal rather than prolong his confrontation with the City Council.

The council's veto power has been applied not only to projects that threatened to disrupt residential neighborhoods but also to major downtown projects, the most notable of which is the massive $465-million convention center proposed for Market Street East. First conceived in May 1982, the project had the unqualified support of the mayor, the GPFC, and the Chamber of Commerce from the outset. Yet its value was questioned by city councilors who were not convinced it would bring anything but a massive new tax burden for their constituents in the neighborhoods. Few of its benefits, they predicted, would "trickle down" to rowhouse Philadelphia.

The majority of the Council took the position that, at the very least, the project should be structured to guarantee that a fixed share of construction jobs and contracts would go to minorities, women, and city residents, and they threatened to stall the project if their viewpoint did not prevail. One influential Council member warned: "I don't think the project can move forward without council support. And the position at this point is that a majority of the council favors not approving anything until they abide by affirmative action." [32] Although the affirmative-action question was rather quickly resolved to the Council's satisfaction, it was not until two years later that the Council finally voted to endorse the project.

Business groups cite other instances as well of the City Council's failure to sympathize with the concerns and needs of business. For example, Council members passed in the early 1980s a landmark plant-closing bill, becoming the nation's first municipality to require firms that want to close down to give workers two months' notice. As in most cities and states where such legislation has been considered, organized business groups warned that it would scare new businesses away from the city and unduly hamper those already there. The Council was undeterred by the warnings.

The Council's minority members have been especially vocal in representing the interests of neighborhoods—in particular, by demanding that the city's investments be spread throughout the city, rather than going exclusively to downtown projects. For example, reviewing the annual capital budget that was presented to the Council by Mayor Green in 1983, three of the Council's most powerful black members—its president, Joseph Coleman, and his fellow members John Street and Lucien Blackwell—joined forces to criticize the budget's downtown bias. Pointing to the heavy emphasis on downtown projects such as the proposed new convention center and waterfront development, John Street complained, "I don't call that a program that reflects any interest in the residents of the city. . . . We pay and we pay and we pay, and all we see is fancy buildings going up in the center of town." [33]

Minority City Council members have also been active supporters of various affirmative-action measures to improve economic opportunities for minorities in city-sponsored projects. In 1982 the Council enacted a set-aside ordinance (unanimously overriding Mayor Green's veto) requiring that 25 percent of the city's contract work go to prime contractors who use subcontracting firms owned and operated by minorities and women.[34] To oversee the code's implementation, the Council created the Minority Business Enterprise Council (MBEC) and watched its progress closely. Monitoring the MBEC's record, several Council members have complained that it has been too lax in its certification procedures. Granted, the agency showed a marked increase in business participation by minorities and women between 1984 and 1988—from about $43 million to $62 million. But local journalists reported that nearly half of the construction contracts awarded during MBEC's first two years went to companies that used minorities and women as fronts in order to obtain contracts.

Minority officeholders have focused special attention on the job opportunities that will be created by the proposed convention center, the largest single municipal development project in the city's history. We have already seen that the City Council threatened to hold up the project until it included hiring guidelines for minorities and women. State legislators as well, representing the city's minority neighborhoods, lobbied for minority hiring provisions when the convention center legislation passed through the statehouse in the spring of 1986. To the embarrassment of the city's mayor and business leaders who were pressing for state support for the project, nine out of twenty-two members of the Philadelphia delegation actually voted against the state's appropriation to support the Philadelphia convention center because the bill contained no assurances of jobs for minorities and women.

Philadelphia is not the only city in which minorities have focused their growing political power on jobs and contracts. This focus seems to be a pattern across the United States. One study of ten California cities concluded that the most dramatic changes associated with the increasing political integration of blacks and Hispanics were in the areas of city hiring and contracting.[35] Other researchers have shown the positive effect that the presence of black officeholders is likely to have on black employment within city government.[36] Nor should this finding surprise us, given the record of other groups that have risen to prominence in urban politics and used their position to gain access to municipal contracts and employment. Whether minority officeholders can continue to promote minority hiring in the 1990s remains to be seen, given the Supreme Court's recent rulings on affirmative action, particularly the 1989 decision to strike down minority set-asides in Richmond, Virginia. In April 1990, only months after the Richmond ruling, a federal judge declared Philadelphia's set-aside ordinance to be unconstitutional because of its similarity to the Richmond ordinance. And although both the mayor and City Council announced their determination to revive the set-aside provision by modifying its language, it was not clear that they would prevail in the courts.

So far, we have focused our attention primarily on minority members of the City Council. What about Philadelphia's first black mayor? How closely did he identify himself with the problems and needs of the black community? Wilson Goode's campaign rhetoric was resolutely nonracial. His 1983 campaign put forward a classic reform platform, pledging a more business-like approach to managing municipal government and a strong emphasis on economic development projects like the port and the convention center. Goode promised to deliver services more efficiently and create jobs by attracting and retaining business. He reminded his audience that there was no black or white way to deliver city programs.

Facing his reelection campaign in 1987, Goode was in an uncomfortable position. The MOVE incident had cost him much of his white liberal support, and his Republican opponent Frank Rizzo lured an estimated 40,000 white rowhouse Democrats to switch their registrations to the Republican party in order to vote for Rizzo. Thus, Goode's electoral base had narrowed considerably, and it was clear that he would have to rely more completely on black voters than in his campaign four years earlier. Recognizing this fact, Goode's campaign organizers worked intensively in the city's black neighborhoods, even while the mayor continued to downplay race as a factor in the campaign. There was, in short, a tension between the reality of Goode's electoral base (Goode won by drawing about 97 percent of the blacks who turned out) and the rhetorical style of his campaign.

Goode's agenda placed a heavy emphasis on economic development. The most visible of his administration's efforts were made on behalf of two massive downtown projects—the convention center and a waterfront development at Penn's Landing. Goode's drive for economic development has taken precedence over all other goals of his administration, even affirmative action. So determined was the mayor to secure the state legislature's final support for the convention center that, unlike the City Council, he was willing to agree to a legislative package that omitted any affirmative-action guidelines on the construction project—guidelines that the City Council regarded as necessary. Moreover, when the City Council in 1985 considered an ordinance to supplement the minority set-aside legislation by stipulating that not just construction contracts, but construction employment as well, would be governed by affirmative-action guidelines, the mayor opposed the bill. He vigorously opposed the measure that would have required any construction project of more than \$1 million that involved city funds to give at least 25 percent of total employment to minorities and 5 percent to women workers. Aligning himself with the business community, most of the construction unions, and the building contractors, Mayor Goode argued that such a law would impose unfair regulation on the construction industry and discourage investment. On this issue the mayor's view prevailed; the bill never made it out of committee to the floor of the Council.[37]

Another of the mayor's well-publicized economic development initiatives involved building fifty luxury skyboxes at the city-owned Veteran Stadium. Alarmed at the possibility that the Eagles football team might move out of Philadelphia, the mayor offered a package of incentives that included the new skyboxes and other improvements to the municipal stadium, a new practice field, increases in the team's percentage of revenue from stadium concessions, and a deferral of the team's annual stadium rent (\$800,000) for up to ten years.

At the same time that he invested political capital in these large-scale, widely publicized development ventures, the mayor was cutting city services and discouraging the construction of new community facilities on the grounds that the city's limited operating funds could not provide staffing for new recreation centers, libraries, and swimming pools. The difference in the levels of funding committed to downtown and neighborhood projects frequently brought the city's first black mayor into open conflict with black members of City Council.

Mayor Goode also found himself battling the city's major public employees' union, an organization with a largely black membership whose leaders had enthusiastically supported his election in 1983. In July 1986 the mayor withstood a twenty-day trash strike in order to demonstrate to those who were most concerned about the city's solvency that he was willing to resist the city workers' demands. Two weeks into the disruptive strike, which left mountains of garbage rotting in the summer sun, the president of the Chamber of Commerce praised Mayor Goode for his tough stand: "It's the fiscally responsible thing to do. . . . Sometimes you have to take strikes rather than give the store away." [38] Goode finally broke the strike by persuading the courts to issue a back-to-work order. Only a year later, in the midst of his reelection campaign, Goode commissioned a consultant's study on privatizing trash pick-up and then endorsed its conclusion that Philadelphia should contract out two-thirds of its residential trash collection and reduce the remaining crews from three or four workers to only two workers. The proposal threatened to eliminate the jobs of about 1,500 sanitation workers, prompting an outpouring of bitter protest from several of the city's labor leaders who had previously supported Goode.

How do we explain the mayor's willingness to emphasize downtown economic development and fiscal stability as highest priorities, even when it brought him into conflict with black Council members and union leaders? Why would he risk alienating the black community that had supported his candidacy so solidly? Research done in other cities suggests that Wilson Goode was not alone in his approach to his job. Other minority mayors have been caught between downtown business coalitions and their popular electoral base: "Increasingly, black mayors were placed in a quasi-colonial posture: they depended upon black votes to guarantee their success at the polls, but once elected, they often implemented public policies that contradicted their constituency's material interests." [39] Particularly when it comes to matters of city finance, taxes, and indebtedness, the attitudes and policies of black officeholders are seldom distinguishable from those of whites.[40]

Unlike legislators who represent only their district in City Council or in the state legislature, mayors must run for office in a larger and more heterogenous electorate. For them, being narrowly identified with the black community alone is a drawback. Wilson Goode echoed the campaign speeches of many other black mayoral candidates around the country when he stressed that he would be the "mayor of all the people of this city." There is a strong incentive for black mayors to demonstrate that they can be responsive to other important constituencies in the city.

Conclusion

In a spring 1987 interview with the *Philadelphia Inquirer* Mayor Wilson Goode publicly acknowledged that he did not control the city's Democratic party: "I do not profess to be a party boss." He downplayed the importance to a mayor of party leadership. Running the party, he declared, was a minor concern compared with running a city government.[41]

In making such a statement, the mayor was expressing his well-known preference for seeing urban government primarily as a matter of efficient administration, not street-level politics. He was also seriously understating the extent to which his party's fragmentation had hampered his ability to lead city government. Philadelphia is known for its strong-mayor form of government, one of the products of the 1951 charter reform. Compared with the mayor of Chicago, for example, Philadelphia's mayor has a much stronger grip on city government. Yet the city's chief administrator finds it difficult to move the machinery of government in rational, purposive ways. Increasingly, Philadelphia is moving toward a model of local politics that Douglas Yates has labeled "street-fighting pluralism"—an extreme pluralism of political, administrative, and community interests that is "fragmented to the point of chaos." [42] Without a reliable support coalition in the City Council, even a mayor with a clear and consistent set of policies cannot effectively pursue them. As we have seen, the balkanization of the city's development agenda in dozens of autonomous, quasi-public corporations makes it extremely difficult to coordinate the city's larger construction projects.

We have already made the point that Philadelphia's political fragmentation has made it increasingly difficult for business interests in the city to advance their agenda, even when they enjoy direct access to City Hall. City Council has frequently challenged the wisdom of trickle-down strategies that channel investments to downtown development in the expectation that their benefits will spill over into the neighborhoods. Does the reduction of corporate influence mean that the policy-making process is now more responsive to other groups in the city, particularly excluded groups seeking social change? Probably not.

The same fragmentation that frustrates business lobbyists frequently defeats the efforts of community and public interest activists as well. Neighborhood advocates, environmentalists, consumer activists, tenants' rights organizations, and other similar groups may find it easy to gain a sympathetic hearing from one or more political leaders in the city. But the hyperpluralism of urban politics makes it extremely difficult to forge effective coalitions to push for policy change. In the absence of a strong political center, "there is no mechanism to achieve or protect the goals sought by these new groups. The result is often a stalemate, which is a victory for the status quo." [43]

Not only does the political fragmentation defeat social change, it also hampers local officials' capacity to act as mediators or brokers among communities in conflict. Philadelphia has always been a city of neighborhoods whose interests diverged, sometimes dramatically. Ethnic rivalries as well as religious and class differences have divided the city's residents for at least a century and a half. The Republican political machine that dominated Philadelphia from 1850 to 1950 acted as a mediating institution, employing the wealth that it extracted from the burgeoning industrial economy to buy political stability. By making side payments to ease community discontent, by coopting rival political leaders, and by brokering conflict within the confines of the party, the machine was able to bridge the gaps among ethnic groups and classes. As recently as the 1960s, Mayor Tate could still use the patronage and money available through the federal War on Poverty to coopt emerging black community leaders. But the loss of federal funds in the late 1970s and 1980s and the accompanying cutbacks in the city workforce (from about 39,000 public employees in 1978 to only 24,500 in 1988) severely restricted the supply of patronage, contracts, and other resources traditionally used to buy political support.

The loss of political capital occurred at the very time when, as earlier chapters have shown, inequality among groups and communities was increasing in the city. The transformation of the region's economy after World War II has produced an uneven pattern of decay and redevelopment, widening the gaps between income groups and generating competition and conflict between races at the lower end of the income scale. There is a kind of circular relationship between the changing economic reality and Philadelphia's political disintegration. We have portrayed the growing inequalities among groups and neighborhoods as one factor that has weakened the majority political coalition. And once weakened, the city's political institutions can do little to mediate the conflicts that inevitably result from those inequalities.

6

The Prospects for City-Suburban Accommodation

The governmental boundaries that separate the city from its surrounding suburbs, constant since 1854, have stymied any real efforts at regionalism, which many people see as the key to social and economic progress. The recognition that the metropolitan area functions as a single economic unit has led many of the region's leading citizens to conclude that the multitude of local and county governments that do business in the region must be brought into greater harmony. Interjurisdictional competition must be replaced with cooperation.

To many readers, the word *regionalism* sounds an echo from the 1950s and 1960s, when a series of national reports on governmental reform promoted the idea of local government consolidation to overcome the proliferation of jurisdictions in the nation's large metropolitan areas.[1] Consolidations were attempted in several dozen large American cities, but when these efforts failed in most cases, interest in regionalism waned during the 1970s. In Philadelphia, that interest may be reviving.

In previous chapters we stress the widening disparities, both demographic and economic, among the different parts of the region. But those disparities do not, in and of themselves, rule out the possibility of regional cooperation. There is, after all, a very significant precedent for such cooperation in the city's history. In 1854 Philadelphians, led by business leaders, endorsed the consolidation of the city of Philadelphia, comprising what is now the CBD, with the surrounding county of Philadelphia. The twenty-eight boroughs, townships, and districts that, along with the city, made up Philadelphia county were a disparate collection of communities with strong, separate identities. Some, like Kensington and Southwark, were industrial enclaves. Others, like Germantown, were still largely rural. And many of these previously separate jurisdictions were ethnically differentiated. However diverse in character, they functioned increasingly as an economic unit in mid-nineteenth century, and the consolidation of 1854 transformed this economic unit into a political unity.

These days no one is touting governmental consolidation as a realistic alternative for the Delaware Valley. The first and most obvious problem with that idea is that the regional economic unit now spans two states—Pennsylvania and New Jersey. Short of governmental consolidation, however, are many forms of regional cooperation, and many groups in the Delaware Valley, particularly business groups like the GPFC, have asserted that regional accommodations would help the region to compete more effectively in the national and international arenas. The city's facilities, especially its airports, research universities, and cultural and recreational amenities, are significant assets in attracting firms to all parts of the region. At the same time, suburban expansion provides economic opportunities for city residents because it enlarges the market for the city's goods and services. Logically, it makes sense for the city and its suburbs to pursue economic development cooperatively, a point made graphically in a recent cartoon on the editorial page of the *Philadelphia Inquirer* (see Figure 6.1).

For many of the firms doing business in the region, the political boundary lines that separate counties and townships have little operational meaning. Many of the region's retailers, for example, sell to the regional market rather than to a strictly local market. Similarly, banks, insurance companies, realtors, and many other providers of business and personal services appeal to customers throughout the region. And employers of all kinds draw on a workforce and a network of suppliers that spans the entire region. Such firms would benefit from greater coordination among the separate jurisdictions that tax them, provide their economic infrastructure, and impose regulations on their business operations.

For example, suburban developers are among the strongest advocates for more regional planning. Many developers would rather deal with a strong, professional regional planning apparatus than with a variety of small, non-professional township boards. Under Pennsylvania law the responsibility for zoning and land-use planning is lodged at the local level. County governments have weaker control over zoning and planning than in many other states, and regional coordination is nonexistent. One of the region's largest and most successful developers complained of Philadelphia's suburbs: "I would guess that 90 percent of the undeveloped land is subject to amateur hour when it comes to planning," and then he went on to say of regional planning that "the average builder with any degree of sophistication would support it wildly, if it meant you were dealing with professionals." [2]

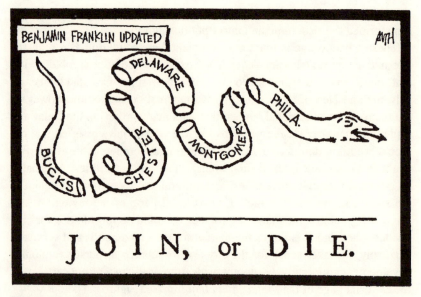

Figure 6.1   Cartoon urging regional cooperation
Source: Philadelphia Inquirer, May 13, 1988.

The business community's enthusiasm for regionalism has not been matched by an equally positive response from the region's politicians. Business people, who see the entire Delaware Valley as their arena, are much more vocal supporters of the idea than are politicians whose fortunes are tied to narrow geographic constituencies. The difference in these two perspectives was dramatically illustrated in 1981 when the president of Fidelity Mutual Life Insurance Company announced that he would move his company office out of the city to a suburban office complex, taking 500 jobs with him. The move was dictated, he explained, by a calculation that his largely clerical and computer-based operation would save more than $20 million in ten years by moving to northern Delaware County. At the same time, however, his company saw good reasons to invest in luxury condominium and hotel development in central Philadelphia and therefore proposed to invest more than $50 million in a combination of projects within the city, even as the company moved its corporate operation out of town.

Fidelity Mutual's announcement, made without any prior consultation with the city's development officials, so incensed Philadelphia mayor Bill Green that he retaliated immediately by denying the company permission to spend $10 million turning its old art deco headquarters building into condominiums. In doing so, he was defending the city's narrow political interests against a business's interest in placing its investments strategically within the region. A local development expert explained the maneuver this way: "How can a mayor take a statesmanlike view regionally when everything he has to do militates against it? . . . We really are an integrated economic unit trying to act like we're not."[3]

A similar announcement by a second major insurance company in 1987 prompted a bidding contest that pitted ten different possible sites in the region against one another. The Cigna Corporation announced its search for less expensive office space for 4,400 employees in the summer of that year and allowed six weeks for bidding by interested developers from the city and three suburban counties. By the deadline, the company had received proposals for six sites within the city, two in Montgomery County, and one each in Chester and Delaware counties. This time, faced with the prospect of losing $7 million in annual revenues from wage taxes as well as many other spillover benefits of Cigna's presence downtown, the city government went all out to defeat its competition. Among the city's weapons was its ability to secure a $10 million Urban Development Action Grant (UDAG) from the federal government to subsidize new office construction, and its offer to take over the office space then occupied by the insurance company and pay off the last five years of Cigna's lease. The city government could make this gesture, valued at about $39 million, because it could use the space to relocate city workers who were then scattered in office buildings around the city. The city's package of incentives was irresistible; Cigna executives chose to stay in Philadelphia. Their decision prompted the Chamber of Commerce of one suburban office center, King of Prussia, to complain that the city's use of $10 million in federal subsidies to compete against its own suburbs was unfair and short-sighted.

Periodically the city's mayor holds a summit conference with leaders of suburban counties and townships. These meetings invariably generate more rhetoric than action, given the overwhelming incentives for political leaders to protect their own turf. The closest the region comes to having a forum for cooperative planning and action is a relatively weak body, the Delaware Valley Regional Planning Commission. Created in 1965 by an interstate compact between Pennsylvania and New Jersey, it includes the eight counties of the SMSA plus one additional county in New Jersey (Mercer). Its primary function has been to fulfill the role of clearinghouse for proposed federal funding. Its role in this regard has declined in recent years, as federal grants for sewer and water projects and other types of local infrastructure have declined. Its other work has consisted mainly of transportation planning for the region. Unfortunately, the representatives from the various counties and the state governments who sit on the regional commission have no authority to commit the resources or policies of their respective units, and as a result, this body has never wielded significant power. Moreover, the separate counties' support for regional planning has historically depended upon what they were getting out of it. So, for example, when a dispute broke out in the late 1970s about how much of the commission's federal planning grant should be used for its own purposes and how much should be passed through to county planning departments, the city and several suburban counties simply withheld their annual support payments to the commission until they received satisfactory allocations.

Barriers to Political Cooperation

The integrating mechanism in the metropolis, we have suggested, is more the market than government. Why do the mayors, county commissioners, township supervisors, and others at the heads of governmental units have such difficulty finding common ground? Why have they resisted pressures from the business community for more regional cooperation? Without question, the most important cleavage line in the region is that between the city of Philadelphia and its surrounding neighbors. Enormous differences in politics and resources divide the periphery and the center.

No distinction between Philadelphians and their suburban neighbors is more clear-cut than that of political affiliation: whereas city dwellers are overwhelmingly registered as Democrats, the Republicans dominate the surrounding counties by margins of two to one and even three to one. Only rapidly growing Bucks County has a situation that approaches a competitive two-party system, largely because the communities in lower Bucks County, closest to the city border, have many more registered Democrats than the more remote townships. All of the suburban counties, in fact, have seen a recent surge in Democratic registrations in the areas nearest Philadelphia, yet the majority of new suburbanites continue to register Republican. That means that even though the Democrats have made some inroads at the township level, Republicans consistently sweep any election involving a countywide office. As one discouraged Democratic leader in Chester County lamented, "The Republicans can put up someone who is barely mediocre. . . . In order to wage a credible campaign, [the Democrats] have to put up someone who is practically a saint."[4] His Democratic candidate for Congress had just spent an unprecedented sum of money waging a vigorous campaign yet lost to a Republican incumbent who campaigned only fitfully, declined to debate his opponent, and was nearly inaccessible to the media.

The issues of greatest concern to suburban voters appear to be taxes and services, growth management, and environmental preservation. Occasionally, a Democrat is able to appeal successfully to voters on the basis of these concerns. The most visible example is Democrat Peter Kostmayer, who has won several terms in the U.S. Congress by pledging to protect the environment and quality of life for his normally Republican constituents in Bucks County. That same Republican electorate in Bucks County temporarily installed a Democratic majority on their county Board of Commissioners in the early 1980s, again on an environmental platform: the Democrats promised to challenge the construction of a pumping station on the Delaware River that would divert water for a nuclear power plant. Environmentally conscious voters rejected the project in a 1983 nonbinding referendum and hoped that the Democratic county commissioners they elected that same year would stop the pump. But once the issue had been resolved (a judge ruled that the project must go forward despite political opposition), the county's electorate returned to the fold, reinstalling a Republican-controlled Board of Commissioners.

Admittedly, the Republicans' overwhelming advantage in voter registrations does not tell the whole story of suburban politics. For in fact, there are significant differences among Republicans from county to county. Ironically, the most solidly Republican county in the region—Delaware County—is run by leaders who often sound more like the Democratic City Committee than like their counterparts in the other suburban counties. At the western edge of the city, Delaware County contains many rowhouse communities that spilled over the city boundaries before World War II and were settled at a time when the Republican organization still controlled Philadelphia politics. Many blue-collar residents of those areas retain their party loyalties to this day. Their social conservatism contrasts with the liberalism of white-collar Republicans who predominate in other, more affluent suburban counties. Commenting on his blue-collar constituents' tendency to vote a straight ticket, a Delaware County Republican leader contrasted his voters to those of nearby Montgomery County, the most affluent county in the state: "There's a lot of conscience liberals when you have money. You don't vote a straight ballot because that would be going along with the masses. We don't have that type of thinking in Delaware County." [5]

Unlike the lawyers and other professionals who control party organizations in other suburban counties, Delaware County politicians are more likely to be small business owners. One current Republican leader, for example, runs a private security firm, has been compared to the young Frank Rizzo, and identifies Chicago's late boss Richard Daley as his political model. The Delaware County party operates more direct patronage than other county parties, awarding courthouse jobs to many party officials. (In other suburban counties, by contrast, the spoils of victory are more likely to be contracts for legal work or other services.) And campaigning in Delaware County is more likely to involve door-to-door solicitation than the direct-mail and big-ticket fundraisers that are common in other parts of the region. Within the county itself, differences in political outlook and style have begun to emerge as the more affluent communities in the northern part of the county have increased in population and in power, challenging the dominance of lower Delaware County. A decade of layoffs and plant closings in the factory towns of Chester and Marcus Hook has widened the split between the two ends of the county.

Whatever political sympathy for Philadelphia's problems might arise in lower Delaware County and several of the other older suburbs, unfortunately, is overshadowed by the single biggest political issue in city-suburban relations: the wage tax. Throughout the postwar period the city has levied the wage tax on all workers who held jobs in the city, regardless of where they lived. Suburban politicians have always bridled at what they regarded as taxation without representation. Their constituents who commuted into Philadelphia to work have had no voice in electing the City Council that set the tax rates, but they were expected to pay the tax anyway. As the suburbs grew and gained clout in the state legislature, they used this forum to protest against the unfair levy. In 1977 they gained a legislative cap on the tax rates for nonresidents working in Philadelphia. Thus, in 1983 when the city needed additional revenue, it could raise the tax rate only on its own citizens. Under the current two-tier system, city residents pay a tax of 4.96 percent on wages earned in the city, while suburbanites who hold jobs in Philadelphia pay 4.31 percent.

Not satisfied with the cap, state legislators representing the Philadelphia suburbs have continued to press for reductions in the rate levied on their constituents. Their tactics have included trading their votes on other forms of legislation favorable to the city in exchange for a tax cut. In spring 1986 several dozen state legislators from communities on the city's border tried to block a state appropriation to support the construction of Philadelphia's proposed convention center. Despite the Republican governor's contention that the project would be a boon for all of southeastern Pennsylvania, these suburban Republicans voted against it, openly declaring that their opposition was a tactic designed to force concessions on the wage tax. Although they were unable to defeat the appropriation, their success in delaying its passage added to the general climate of suspicion that marked political relations between the inner and outer rings of the region.

For Philadelphia officials to relinquish the revenue they obtain by taxing suburban workers would be to exacerbate the already substantial differences in the tax burdens carried by their constituents, compared with suburban taxpayers. As in virtually all major American cities, the erosion of manufacturing and of the city's residential neighborhoods has affected the tax base that supports urban services. The stagnation in the tax base has meant that Philadelphia taxpayers must bear an increasingly heavy load (see Figure 6.2).

Estimates of the tax burden carried by middle-class households in city and suburbs show Philadelphia's tax burden to be about 40 percent higher than the regional average (see Figure 6.3). The city also levies a tax burden on businesses that is far higher than the region as a whole—45 percent higher for manufacturing, 95 percent higher for wholesale trade, and 50 to 60 percent higher for most of the services.[6]

The lower *average* tax burden for suburbanites does not mean that all suburban townships are equally fortunate. In fact, some of the older suburbs near the borders of the city are facing a serious tax squeeze because of a rapid rise in the school-age population starting in the mid-1980s. These are the pre-Depression suburbs, found mainly in Delaware and Montgomery counties, located along the rail lines that first threaded their way through the countryside beyond Philadelphia's borders around the turn of the century. As the region's first bedroom suburbs, they are filled with older houses and little industry or commerce of their own. For a decade prior to the mid-1980s their populations were made up more and more of "empty nesters" whose children had grown up and moved away.

With the region's economic and housing boom, these inner suburbs began attracting more young families with school-age children. As a result, township officials, many of whom were boarding up excess classrooms and selling off schools a decade ago, are now facing a rising demand for schools. Without developable land or commerce and industry, their tax bases are either stagnating or, in some cases, declining. In one Delaware County school district, for example, the total value of taxable property dropped 19 percent from 1981 to 1987, while taxes went up 25 percent in order to serve the influx of school-age children.[7]

Other suburban townships with open land for development are gaining so much revenue from developers' fees, building permits, and taxes on real estate sales that they have little need to raise property taxes. Pennsbury, a

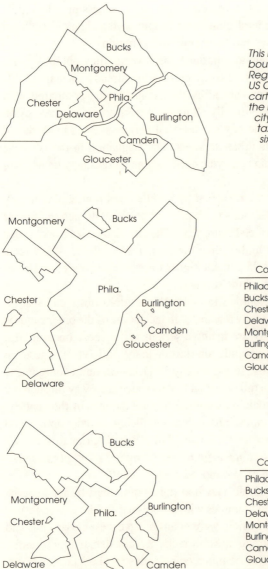

This map shows the geographic boundaries of the Philadelphia Region as defined by the US Census Bureau. The cartograms below show how the real estate tax base in the city declined while the total tax base in the region grew six–fold.

1956

County	Valuation	Per-cent
Philadelphia	$5,997,811,000	53%
Bucks	783,130,000	7%
Chester	528,375,000	5%
Delaware	1,673,693,000	15%
Montgomery	1,765,129,000	15%
Burlington	107,078,000	1%
Camden	359,316,000	3%
Gloucester	100,400,000	1%
Total	$11,294,932,000	

1986

County	Valuation	Per-cent
Philadelphia	$20,179,635,000	28%
Bucks	10,529,012,000	14%
Chester	1,533,518,000	2%
Delaware	8,743,710,000	12%
Montgomery	15,432,479,000	21%
Burlington	6,965,098,000	10%
Camden	6,053,131,000	8%
Gloucester	3,838,566,000	5%
Total	$73,275,149,000	

Figure 6.2   Shift in taxable property base in the Philadelphia region, 1956–1986

Sources: Pennsylvania Statistical Abstract, New Jersey Municipal Data Book.

Note: The values shown are for the estimated market value of real estate.

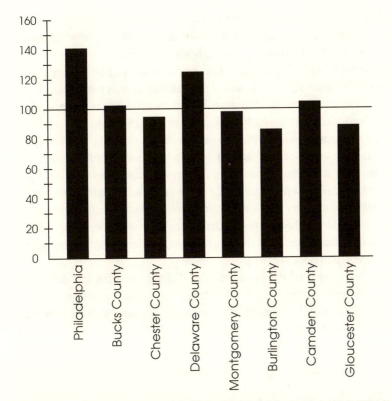

Figure 6.3 Tax burden for middle-income households across the Philadelphia
SMSA (100 = average tax burden for SMSA)
Source: Thomas Luce and Anita Summers, *Local Fiscal Issues in the Philadelphia Area* (Philadel-
phia: University of Pennsylvania Press, 1987), p. 80.

small community in Chester County, offers a good example. Since 1960
this sparsely populated farming community has changed into a booming
residential area. In 1987 the revenues from the real estate sales tax and
building permits covered almost half of the township's total expenditures,
and the township's anticipated surplus actually exceeded its entire budget.[8]

One comprehensive study of metropolitan Philadelphia in 1965 suggested that although differences among jurisdictions' tax resources were an
important barrier to cooperation, an even more significant impediment was
the difference in the social rank of their populations (defined by the researchers as educational and occupational differences).[9] The authors discov-
ered distinct patterns of taxing and spending in different types of suburbs:
industrial and commercial suburbs favored spending on physical infrastructure and on services to business, such as police, fire, and streets; densely

populated residential suburbs spent money on trash collection, parks and recreation, and planning; lower-density suburbs spent very low amounts on all services except planning; and high-status suburbs were particularly notable for spending on libraries, in addition to an array of other services.[10] The authors' opinion surveys indicated that the residents of high-status suburbs were more concerned with amenities than residents in lower-status suburbs, who seemed more interested in keeping taxes down.

Interestingly, the one notable issue on which the residents of both high-status and low-status suburbs agreed was the importance of keeping out undesirables. If anything, the residents in lower-status communities were even more adamant than higher-status communities that this should be a significant responsibility of local government. In both kinds of jurisdictions the respondents thought that undesirables' moving in was more likely to arouse community reaction than virtually any other problem, including zoning, taxes, and poor services.[11]

When they examined the initiatives that different suburbs had taken by 1965 to work cooperatively with other jurisdictions, these researchers observed that "given a choice as to the selection of partners to an agreement, cooperation occurs among municipalities with similar social rank and tax resources, in that order." [12]

Opportunities for Regional Cooperation

Despite the dramatic differences in political viewpoints and available resources in the city and suburbs, there is one important constellation of issues that promises to bring city and suburban leaders together, on the basis of hard-headed self-interest, not altruism or public-spiritedness. That set of issues involves the region's physical infrastructure—the "life support system" of the metropolitan area composed of its roads, bridges, mass-transit system, ports and airports, water mains, sewers and other waste disposal systems. Economists sometimes refer to these structures as "economic overhead capital" because they undergird the regional economy. Infrastructure policies are among the ways that governments influence markets. The role they play in directly supporting the productivity of the private sector means that these systems command the attention and support of business groups.

Philadelphia's business community in the 1980s became increasingly troubled by the deteriorating condition of the region's infrastructure. As in many other American cities, the agencies responsible for transportation, utilities, and other major systems had been deferring maintenance for decades in order to save money. By the mid-1980s the consequences of that pattern were so visible and alarming to business leaders that the GPFC commissioned a study of the region's infrastructure, with estimates of how much money would be needed to correct existing problems.

This study, completed in 1985, concluded that large parts of the infrastructure system were literally falling apart, and that the region would need to invest a total of $10.5 billion to halt the deterioration.[13] To allow the downward slide to continue would virtually ensure the region's defeat in its economic competition with New York, Baltimore, Boston, and other East Coast cities.

Transportation

Particularly acute are the problems created by the transportation infrastructure. Early postwar planners had envisioned a 105-mile network of expressways criss-crossing the region "to move people and goods quickly, cheaply and conveniently."[14] The city's 1960 Comprehensive Plan proposed a total of twelve concentric and radial expressways (see Figure 6.4), of which only two have been completed. One by one, these projects were abandoned because of citizen opposition and lack of funds. In retrospect, it seems a blessing to many that these ambitious plans were never completed; they would have driven six-lane highways through many stable communities and further sapped the vitality of center city by making suburban locations even more accessible. Yet there is little doubt that their absence (particularly the absence of cross-town expressways) slows travel in the region. Moreover, it increases the burden on the existing expressways. The GPFC's 1986 study concluded that 28 percent of the region's highways are so run down that they "may be barely tolerable for high-speed traffic."

Mass transit is another system whose current condition is worrisome to business leaders. Although it is operated by a regional authority, the region's mass-transit system hardly reflects a commitment to city-suburban cooperation. In fact, since its inception in 1964 the Southeastern Pennsylvania Transportation Authority (SEPTA) has mainly been an arena for conflict between the city and suburbs. The authority, which controls bus, trolley, subway, and commuter rail services in the city and four suburban counties within Pennsylvania, is governed by a board representing each of the five counties and the governor of the state. The central point of contention has been financing the system. Having no dedicated tax base, as many other regional transit systems around the country do, SEPTA depends en-

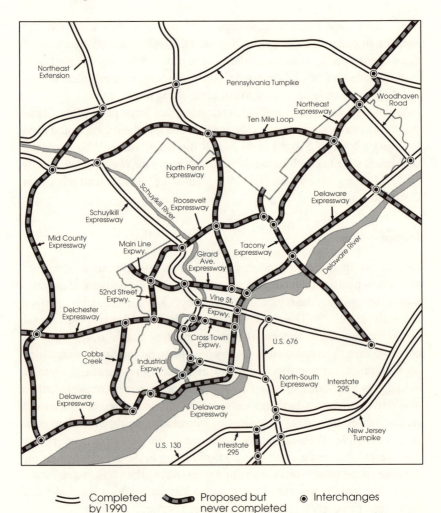

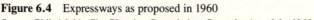

| ⎯⎯ | Completed by 1990 | ⬤ | Proposed but never completed | ◎ Interchanges |

Figure 6.4 Expressways as proposed in 1960

Source: Philadelphia City Planning Commission, *Re-evaluation of the 1960 Comprehensive Plan for Philadelphia* (Philadelphia, 1979).

tirely on annual contributions from the city, county, and state governments. The city complains that the suburbs do not shoulder their rightful share of the cost. Though they account for one-fourth of the system's ridership, the four suburban counties furnish only about 15 percent of its local aid.

Critics argue, too, that suburban riders enjoy more than their share of the subsidies distributed by the authority. This happens because SEPTA is divided into a city division, which operates all the subways, trolleys, and buses in the city, and a rail division, a collection of suburban passenger trains that came under SEPTA's wing when the Penn Central and Reading railroads went bankrupt. The SEPTA board oversees both divisions, allocating its revenue in such a way that suburban rail riders pay a lower proportion of the cost of running their trains than city riders pay toward the cost of their buses and subways. The authority acknowledges this apparent favoritism toward its more affluent customers but contends that the costs are higher on the rail lines. If asked to bear this higher cost themselves, suburban riders would be far more likely than city riders to desert the transit system. After all, more affluent suburban commuters could simply drive to work.

To many observers, the imbalance in the treatment accorded to city and suburban divisions is an inevitable result of unequal representation on the SEPTA board. The suburbs control eight of the eleven seats on the board. Periodically critics call on the city to pull out of the regional authority altogether and run its own buses, trolleys, and subways independently. Less extreme proposals have envisioned the expansion of SEPTA's board so that votes would be more evenly distributed between city and suburbs.

The absence of a regional perspective is evident in the transit authority's failure to deal effectively with the growing phenomenon of "reverse commuting." While smaller percentages of suburbanites are commuting inward, larger numbers of city dwellers are traveling outward. More reverse commuters are leaving the urban core to travel to jobs in suburban establishments. Since the mid-1980s the region's economic boom has added more than a quarter of a million new jobs, a large number of which are low-wage jobs in retail, service, and "back office" jobs like telephone sales or data processing in suburban locations. Suburban shopping malls are festooned with "Help Wanted" signs, and ads for office workers fill the newspapers. Increasingly, Philadelphians are filling these entry-level jobs. For example, at Prudential Insurance, which doubled the size of its workforce in Montgomery County to nearly 7,000 between 1983 and 1987, there were more than 1,250 Philadelphia residents on the payroll by 1987.[15]

Yet workers living in Philadelphia are unlikely to move to a suburban community in order to take such low-paying jobs, and even those who want to, find it impossible to afford suburban housing. City dwellers must therefore commute long distances for these low-paying entry-level positions in shopping malls, retail stores, fast-food outlets, and corporate centers in Cherry Hill, Fort Washington, the Main Line, and the Route 202 "high tech" corridor. The most important suburban magnets are in Montgomery County, which by 1980 had become a net *importer* of workers, a role previously played only by the city of Philadelphia in this region. The problem is one of mismatch: the city has the low-cost housing stock in the region, while the suburbs increasingly have the entry-level jobs.

Suburban developers and economic development officials complain about the difficulty of luring new companies to suburban office parks once they discover how hard it is to get entry-level employees to work at these locations. Some economists now predict labor shortages in some suburban counties, possibly serious enough to hamper the suburbs' economic expansion.

These concerns have spawned a number of experiments to match inner-city workers with suburban jobs. For example, one innovative program, Project Transition, linked together the Philadelphia Department of Public Welfare, two large companies that operate suburban fast-food restaurants, and a local university. The welfare department identified job candidates, and the university placed them with participating restaurants. Graduate students worked as "job coaches" helping the new workers to become acclimated to their jobs.

The single greatest obstacle to such employment schemes is the lack of adequate transportation for the workers. The region's transportation network was designed by postwar planners to focus entirely on accommodating commuter traffic from the suburbs into the central business district. It offers few options to reverse commuters whose jobs are typically located several miles away from the nearest suburban train station.

True to the historical tradition of privatism, a number of the region's entrepreneurs have operated outside the bounds of government to try to work out solutions to regional transit problems on a private basis. One good example is a privately operated shuttle service created by some suburban firms to assist reverse commuters recruited from the inner city. Some businesses in Valley Forge, for example, recruit prospective employees at inner-city locations and then lease vans to transport them each day. At another suburban office park, the Great Valley Corporate Center, the developer arranged to share the cost for five SEPTA buses to carry employees back and forth from the nearest train station on the commuter rail line into the city. Still another developer of several suburban business parks organized its major tenants to subsidize service from Philadelphia to the expanding Route 202 corridor through Bucks, Montgomery, and Chester counties. After only four months the bus line was breaking even. In yet another project two King of Prussia malls along with a major pharmaceutical company and a real estate firm have contributed $70,000 to improve SEPTA bus service in the King of Prussia area.

As intriguing as these private efforts are, they will not be enough to solve the region's problem of mismatch between job opportunities and labor pools. That task is one for the region's public transportation system, and we predict that the business community will exert increasing pressure on city and county political leaders to achieve greater cooperation in transportation planning.

Port Facilities

Another element of the region's infrastructure that is badly in need of refurbishing is its port, which has ranked high among U.S. seaports since the colonial era. Since World War II, however, the port has suffered in competition with other cities in the mid-Atlantic region, particularly Baltimore, Washington, and Norfolk. One of its main difficulties has been the absence of a strong regional authority, similar to New York's Port Authority. Such a body nominally exists, in the form of the Delaware River Port Authority (DRPA), but it serves a much narrower function than New York's multipurpose authority.

Created in 1951 and governed by sixteen commissioners who come in equal numbers from New Jersey and Pennsylvania, the DRPA's main interest has been in building and maintaining four toll bridges and a commuter rail line that span the Delaware River, connecting Philadelphia to the suburban towns of New Jersey. In the early 1970s a coalition of intergovernmental reformers made a serious attempt to enlarge the scope of cooperation by proposing a three-state authority (Pennsylvania, New Jersey, and Delaware) to unify the operation of the ports of Philadelphia, Camden, and Wilmington. Its responsibilities were to include not only the ports in the region but also airports, bridges, and mass transit. The attempt failed, not only because of its ambitious scope but also because even then SEPTA's aging system was seen as a financial liability that might drag the entire authority into debt.

Even the more limited mission carried on by the DRPA since 1951—operating toll bridges and one commuter rail line between Philadelphia and New Jersey—could not be characterized as an entirely successful example of regional cooperation. Critics charge that two of the authority's four bridges were costly mistakes, constructed in the early 1970s as the result of political horse trading between the mayor of Philadelphia and a suburban state legislator. Mayor James Tate wanted the Betsy Ross Bridge on the northern stretch of the river, to connect northeast Philadelphia with New Jersey. State Senator Clarence Bell wanted the Commodore Barry bridge to the south of Philadelphia, to span the river between the city of Chester and New Jersey. The two formed an alliance to get state funds; Tate wooed the Democrats in the state capitol, while Bell lined up the Republicans. As a result of their success, the two bridges were built and have been draining the authority financially since they opened in the early 1970s. Neither has attracted the number of cars projected, largely because the expressways that would have connected the spans to the area's highway system were never built. (Those roads were part of the ill-fated highway network mentioned above.)

The failure of the two bridges to generate the expected toll revenues has meant that their operation, as well as the deficits generated by the authority's high-speed commuter rail line to New Jersey, have been constantly subsidized by the receipts of the two more heavily traveled bridges, the Ben Franklin and Walt Whitman. And it has meant that the regional port authority generates virtually no surplus that might be invested in upgrading the port.

By 1980 the prospects for regional cooperation to improve the port were bleak enough that Philadelphia's Committee of Seventy recommended that the city give up its regional efforts. The nonpartisan watchdog group suggested that Philadelphia, along with Bucks and Delaware counties, form their own port organization rather than relying on the ineffectual regional authority. No significant initiatives were taken, and the port's downward slide continued throughout the early 1980s. From 1979 to 1988 total cargo shipments for the port declined by fully one-third.[16] Meanwhile, the terminal operators in Philadelphia's and Camden's ports spent more energy competing with each other for cargo then competing with the ports in New York, Baltimore, and Virginia. The approximately twenty shipping lines regularly serving the region moved back and forth across the river from Pennsylvania to New Jersey, shopping for the lowest priced docks, but the region's total cargo base did not expand.

In the late 1980s the attitude of business leaders shifted once more; again they began talking about the value of a single three-state "super agency" to take over port development. The prospect of a regional solution to the problem captured the interest of some of the area's strongest political leaders. Then-Congressman James Florio of New Jersey (who is now New Jersey's governor) and Thomas Foglietta of Pennsylvania held hearings on port unification in Philadelphia in March 1988, followed by a summit meeting among the governors of Pennsylvania, New Jersey, and Delaware to discuss the concept. By July 1989 Pennsylvania's legislature had passed a bill creating the Philadelphia Regional Port Authority, a new state agency to coordinate the operation of docks in Philadelphia, Bucks, and Delaware counties as a first step on the road to an eventual interstate compact. Though this should have been an easy step, requiring no lengthy or difficult negotiations, the state and city immediately became embroiled in a year-long dispute over how much the new agency would pay to acquire the city-owned docks and warehouses along the river. Finally in July 1990 the city turned over all of its piers and terminals to what it hoped would be a precursor to unified planning and marketing efforts for trade on both the New Jersey and Pennsylvania sides of the river.

Solid Waste

Yet another infrastructure issue that appears likely to foster more regional cooperation is the solid waste crisis that is worsening throughout the region. Every day the City of Philadelphia and the four Pennsylvania suburban counties create about five pounds of trash per person,[17] the bulk of which ends up in a dozen major landfills that ring the metropolitan area.

As the capacity of these suburban landfills is rapidly exhausted, suburban counties are restricting the city's ability to dump trash within their limits in order to preserve the existing capacity for their own townships. With many regional landfills closed, city trucks have been forced to cart more than a half-million tons of raw trash each year to disposal sites more than fifty miles away. Some of the city's garbage is now hauled as far as Maryland and Ohio. A highly controversial plan to ship Philadelphia trash to a Houston landfill was abandoned in early 1988, when the mayor and city council of Houston threatened to sue the hauler. At the same time, a ship cruised the Caribbean for eighteen months, looking in vain for a country that would allow it to dump tons of Philadelphia incinerator ash.

Suburban counties as well are feeling the effects of the competition for landfill space. Although many of them are still able to dispose of trash closer to home, the pressure on landfill space has driven up the cost rapidly. One reason for the limited disposal space is the fact that state law in Pennsylvania gives the responsibility for municipal waste planning to local governments rather than to county or regional bodies. Few localities are willing to accept the presence of landfills within their boundaries, and they can successfully use regulations to block any such proposals. The result is an acute shortage of landfills.

Foreseeing no easy resolution to this shortage of landfills, many of the region's communities have turned to plans for trash-to-steam incinerators such as the ill-fated one proposed for South Philadelphia. As we point out in Chapter 5, the city's proposal to build a massive new trash-to-steam plant in South Philadelphia touched off a political struggle that raged for more than five years, finally ending in the defeat of the proposal. Meanwhile, suburban planning officials have proceeded with their own plans for trash-to-steam incinerators. Besides taking care of their own trash problems, suburban officials expect to enrich their coffers by processing trash from outside customers.

So widespread was the enthusiasm for this alternative in the suburban counties that by 1987 at least sixteen such plants were being considered within a fifty-mile radius of Philadelphia. The prospect of even half that many plants going into operation in the region has alarmed critics of the incinerator technology, who are calling for voluntary regional agreements on when and where such plants will be built. Of the many problems besetting the region that could benefit by a cooperative effort, this one appears to be one of the most likely to prompt concerted action.

How Realistic Are the Prospects for Regionalism?

Our optimism about the prospects for regional accommodations on such issues as solid waste, transportation, and the port is founded on several observations. First, as we noted earlier, these infrastructure systems are directly supportive of private-sector activities, and their improvement therefore gets strong support from the region's business leaders. Admittedly, the fact of business support alone would not guarantee progress; as we have seen, the business community has not always succeeded in promoting its agenda in recent years. However, building and maintaining infrastructure is exactly the kind of governmental function that has most often been successfully handled by regional bodies in other metropolitan areas. More regional authorities exist to operate water and sewer lines, airports, bridges, tunnels, and public transit systems than to oversee services like police, public welfare, and public schools. The reasons seem to be that the region's physical systems require large capital expenditures that can be shared, that they benefit from economies of scale, and that their activities are generally less value-laden than human services. Hence, these are the areas in which the region's political leaders are most likely to overcome the barriers to regional cooperation.

We noted earlier that once before in Philadelphia's history a collection of separate communities came together to forge a single consolidated political unit. Why, then, does regional cooperation appear so difficult to achieve in the last decade of the twentieth century? One hundred years of economic development in the Delaware Valley have changed the relationship between the urban core and the periphery. In 1854 each of the twenty-eight boroughs and townships surrounding Philadelphia had its primary external economic relationship to the urban center. Before the automobile, the metropolis was characterized by mass participation in centrally located facilities and institutions.[18] Residents, companies, and institutions of all kinds were tied to the center by a rail network used by all classes. In that earlier time the gradual integration of various sections of the region occurred, not as they linked with each other, but as each community became linked to the center. It was the dominance of the center that forged economic unity in the region. In the late twentieth century the urban core does not play the same pivotal role.

Today's suburbanites display a declining sense of affiliation with the city. More and more of them lead lives entirely outside the city's boundaries. Substantial numbers of newcomers to the region's suburbs in the 1970s and 1980s were not moving there from Philadelphia, but from some other suburb. Thus, they had no long-standing tie with the center.

The decreased daily interactions between Philadelphia and its surrounding counties reflect changes in commuting patterns. In 1960, 25 percent of suburban residents commuted to a job in the city. By 1980 only 18 percent of suburbanites commuted to a city job. By 1980 the census showed that there were more workers commuting between suburban counties than there were commuting from the suburbs into Philadelphia. In six of the seven suburban counties most residents who had jobs worked in the same county in which they lived. This insularity was most pronounced in the New Jersey suburban counties, where 77 percent of employed residents had jobs in New Jersey.

The growing detachment of suburbanites from the urban core suggests to us that political strategies to promote regionalism will work only if they appeal to suburbanites' self-interest, rather than to any sense of obligation or loyalty to the city center. Such strategies are not impossible to conceive. The specialized character and economic roles played by different parts of the region may lead to complementarity as well as to conflict. We have suggested that infrastructure issues are ones on which the interests of the city and suburbs intersect, despite their increasingly disparate populations. The challenge to political leadership is to see beyond the sharp differences in income levels, lifestyles, and ethnic or racial composition that divide city and suburbs (and sometimes divide suburb from suburb) and to recognize the opportunities for mutually beneficial cooperation.

Without question, the most important prerequisite to regionalism is to forge a workable political coalition inside the city, without which Philadelphia leaders have no hope of negotiating effectively with their suburban counterparts. The handicap that Philadelphia carries as a result of its political disarray is reflected in several of the regional issues we have touched upon in this chapter. For example, we have observed how the city's interests in the regional transit authority are often overridden by suburban politicians, who insist on subsidizing suburban rail commuters at the expense of city bus and subway riders. This quarrel remains unresolved within SEPTA, partly because the political forces within the city's majority coalition cannot agree. Neighborhood organizations, City Council members, and others who represent city transit riders are the most vigorous critics of SEPTA's performance. Representatives of the downtown business community, however, take the position that the heavy subsidies to the suburban railway are absolutely necessary to the survival of the core office and retail district. Without reasonably priced rail service, the central business district could not compete successfully against suburban office complexes. Without unanimity among city political forces, there is little prospect of pressuring SEPTA to change its policies.

In another instance, the city's difficulty securing state funds for its proposed convention center resulted from conflict, not only between city and suburban legislators, but *within* the city's legislative delegation. Despite strong pressure from Mayor Wilson Goode and the business community, a half-dozen Democrats representing Philadelphia districts voted against the project, citing as their reason the failure to stipulate affirmative-action quotas for the jobs and contracts to be generated by the construction. As with the regional transit authority, the city failed to present a united front and thereby weakened its bargaining power with suburban politicians. On the whole, Philadelphia receives a lower level of state funding for its programs than many other big cities across the nation (consult Table 5.1 in the previous chapter). The gradual disintegration of the ruling Democratic coalition in recent decades, which we sketch in Chapter 5, has weakened Philadelphia's position in the state legislature and in regional bodies like the transportation authority. As Sam Bass Warner observed about an earlier period in the city's history, no amount of vigor displayed by the region's business leadership can substitute for a strong, unified, and public-minded political establishment.

7

Alternative Scenarios for Philadelphia's Future

Throughout this volume we have interpreted Philadelphia's social and political relations primarily as a reflection of the region's economic currents, which are in turn the products of national and global economic trends. We have argued that patterns of neighborhood change, racial conflict, and fragmentation within the predominant political party are all directly tied to the economy's distribution of wages and investment capital. In Philadelphia, as in other American cities included in this series, the distribution of resources and life chances generated by the regional economy is increasingly uneven. Is this trend toward racial and class inequality likely to continue?

To the extent that the regional economy continues its shift toward services, inequalities will persist. The reason lies in the distribution of jobs generated by the new service economy. We report in Chapter 2 that the occupational distributions of blacks and whites are increasingly similar. Still, blacks are at some disadvantage. Whereas whites distribute themselves across all major job categories, black workers have found employment primarily as operatives or as clerical or service workers. Blacks are underrepresented among professionals and managers. Hispanics, too, are disproportionately employed as operatives and service workers, and also as laborers. Unlike blacks, Hispanics are underrepresented among office and clerical workers. We document also the widening disparities in the incomes earned by those who hold the best jobs, primarily managerial and professional, and those who hold the less desirable jobs as clerical, sales, and service workers. Though employment is rising in the black and Hispanic communities at present, that does not mean that the income gap dividing them from whites is likely to narrow.

The growing inequalities among different segments of the region's population will continue to be reflected in its housing market. Those fortunate workers holding the well-paid professional and technical jobs will predominate in the suburbs, in some comfortable, tree-lined areas of the city like

Chestnut Hill, and in gentrifying neighborhoods close to downtown. In contrast, lower-wage workers will remain in vast stretches of rowhouses and in the older streetcar suburbs whose decline is discussed in Chapter 3.

Downtown Philadelphia will continue to be a strong center of office development, although the 1990s will not bring the same high level of office construction that the city experienced in the 1980s. The building boom of the 1980s dramatically changed Philadelphia's skyline, adding eight skyscrapers (including the landmark development of One Liberty Place, the first Philadelphia skyscraper to tower above City Hall) and expanding downtown office space by about a third. We expect, however, a significant slowdown in the pace of new construction in the next decade. At the close of the 1980s it was already clear that the Philadelphia market in commercial real estate was influenced by a national slowdown that many economists connected to demographic and labor market changes, specifically the end of the baby boom and a tapering off of the extraordinary rates at which women entered the work place in the 1970s and 1980s. Developers of several major office projects who had already secured planning permissions to build were stalled because they could not find tenants or financing. Occupancy rates in downtown offices had fallen below 90 percent, discouraging investors.[1]

The softening of the commercial market in office construction will probably make it more difficult for community activists to promote a policy of linked development similar to programs adopted by Boston and San Francisco and contemplated in Chicago by the late Mayor Harold Washington.[2] A coalition of thirty neighborhood organizations formed the "Money for Neighborhoods Coalition" in 1988 to press Philadelphia's mayor and City Council to follow the lead of other major cities in requiring all commercial developers of downtown real estate to contribute to neighborhood improvements outside the central business district. Specifically, the coalition proposed that in exchange for the permit to build downtown, developers should be obligated to pay into a trust fund an amount of money based on the square footage of their buildings. The trust fund could then be used to redevelop neighborhood housing and commercial strips and to support job training and day care for low-income workers.

In addition, the coalition proposed that the city donate to the trust fund the paybacks from developers who had received Urban Development Action Grants (UDAGs) from the federal government. During the life of that program the federal government lent more than $100 million to Philadelphia developers who must pay back these loans to the city rather than to the national treasury.

Although he declared himself willing to consider donating the city's

UDAG paybacks to such a trust fund, Mayor Goode rejected the idea of imposing an exaction on developers on the grounds that "it only works where you have the demand exceed the market supply, and I'm not sure we have that situation here. . . . We're trying to entice developers."[3] If the mayor and the City Council were unwilling to risk alienating developers in the office boom of the 1980s, they are even less likely to consider exactions in the slower real estate market of the 1990s.

Suburban governments, on the other hand, will increasingly impose developer exactions to fund the public improvements that must accompany new growth. As early as the 1960s suburban townships were asking developers to make "voluntary" contributions to ballfields or volunteer fire departments. But in the 1990s developers will increasingly be required to contribute to major community systems such as roads, water, and sewers. The irony is that conservative Republican municipal officials in the suburbs are taking a firm stance toward private investors: developers who stand to profit greatly from construction must pay for some of the negative externalities of their enterprise. At the same time, a Democratic, self-styled "progressive" administration in Philadelphia is unwilling to exact concessions from developers. The comparison illustrates the extent to which economic realities constrain political ideologies.

If the future of the service sector is unlikely to foster more economic equality among groups and communities in the region, what can we expect from future trends in manufacturing? There is disagreement among economists about how important manufacturing growth will be in the U.S. economy of the 1990s. Some see America's manufacturing base continuing to erode in response to overseas competition, pushing the nation to rely even more on its service sector. Others like Lester Thurow and his colleagues at the Massachusetts Institute of Technology predict a slowing in the growth of the service sector that will force the United States to restore its manufacturing sector.[4] If the Philadelphia region does participate in the kind of industrial restoration foreseen by Thurow, the new growth is likely to come in a very different form than the traditional manufacturing enterprises that provided the basis of nineteenth- and early twentieth-century growth.

What is this new form? In both Europe and North America, economists have detected a shift away from industrial systems based on the mass, assembly-line manufacture of standardized products (sometimes referred to as "Fordism") and toward a more flexible system of production. The shorter product cycles and higher demand for specialized goods in advanced capitalist economies have called forth new forms of production typically housed in smaller plants that have the ability to change product lines quickly and to manufacture smaller quantities of custom-designed goods—an ability that often depends on computerized technologies. Such plants rely more on skilled craft production than on assembly lines, and they tend to buy services and components from outside sources rather than producing them internally. Thus, this new flexible manufacturing generates networks of interdependent suppliers. Piore and Sabel have labeled the transition to this new industrial form the "second industrial divide."[5]

Because they are embedded in networks of subcontractors and suppliers, firms engaged in flexible manufacturing must be clustered geographically—a fact that holds promise for Philadelphia and other manufacturing centers with large numbers of skilled craft workers.[6] In Chapter 2 we note that the custom apparel industry has recently shown signs of reviving in Philadelphia. This is the classic example of an industry manufacturing upscale or highly specialized products that respond to the fragmentation of the consumer market into submarkets. It engages in short production runs with frequent shifts in product line. Composed of small to medium-size firms seldom having more than a hundred employees, the industry operates through subcontracting networks.

It is possible that other craft industries may take advantage of the city's labor force and its supply of vacant industrial structures to set up relatively small, non-assembly-line manufacturing plants, reviving a segment of the city's old industrial base. In a sense this trend would echo an earlier industrial period when Philadelphia's manufacturing base included a mixture of small and large establishments. As we observe in Chapter 2, that mixture was one of the factors in the city's industrial success in the nineteenth century. Moreover, it created a web of interconnections among contractors and subcontractors that helped to maintain the social and political order.

If they want to promote the latter-day version of that pattern, political and economic leaders must adapt city policies to that end. At a minimum, they must rethink the tax policies that currently favor real estate developers and some large service firms, to the disadvantage of small manufacturers. Since 1978 developers of commercial and industrial real estate have enjoyed a virtually automatic entitlement to a full forgiveness over five years of all property taxes on improvements made to property. This blanket abatement represents a massive and growing tax expenditure by the city. From 1984 to 1988 the number of properties involved grew from 1,131 to 3,371, and the city revenues lost each year increased from $8.9 million to $41.6 million.[7] Quite generous compared with abatement programs in other cities, the Philadelphia program is totally untargeted yet ends up giving the most benefit to center-city real estate because that is where developers prefer to build.

Others who enjoy favorable tax treatment are banks, insurance companies, brokerage houses, taxi and trucking companies, and utilities, whose liability for business taxes is far lower than manufacturing companies and other businesses. For example, a recent study by the city's Finance Department showed that manufacturing firms pay an effective tax rate of 2.35 percent of their gross receipts, whereas banks pay only .001 percent, insurance companies pay .007 percent, and brokerage firms pay .360 percent.[8] This favorable tax treatment for some large service-sector firms costs the treasury about $56 million annually. Any governmental effort to encourage new manufacturing must start by correcting inequities that place the tax burden on only a narrow segment of the business community.

However, public policy must go further than tinkering with the tax structure if government is to act as an economic catalyst. The problem calls for a strategic approach to economic development that differs from the region's "come one, come all" stance toward new developers and new firms. To create and sustain the interdependent networks that are crucial to flexible manufacturing, planners would begin with a careful analysis of market trends, technological developments, and product lines and would select a series of development targets. They would use subsidies selectively to attract and support the types of firms that fit into the subcontracting networks. Because labor must be flexible to meet the requirements of small employers, the city would build employment programs that constantly retrain workers and match them to jobs. And because the subcontracting networks cannot function without all of the pieces in place, the city would move quickly to replace any firms that shut down. Lest the reader think that this prospect sounds completely unattainable, we cite the example of the "Montachusetts" region in central Massachusetts—a declining industrial region whose shift toward flexible manufacturing is documented in a study by Peter Doeringer and his coauthors.[9]

Yet even if the region were to succeed in reviving small-scale manufacturing, we cannot assume that the emergence of this new kind of economic activity would reduce social and economic inequalities. Earlier Fordist forms of manufacturing spawned a system of labor relations that included standardized job categories, wage rates, and fringe benefits negotiated collectively between labor and management. At its peak this regime supported entire neighborhoods of working-class families and even propelled many of the region's households into the middle class. The newer forms of industrialization can support a small core of skilled, high-wage workers, but they also typically require unskilled labor. In order to achieve maximum flexibility, employers "tune their payroll numbers as sensitively as possible to the ups and downs of production," [10] hiring and laying off employees with great rapidity, using part-time and temporary workers whenever possible, and putting out a large proportion of their work to subcontractors who operate in the informal economy. The subcontractors seek out marginal groups in the labor force—immigrants, women, and teenagers—and offer them minimal pay in unregulated, unprotected working environments. So no matter how great a volume of such economic activity is generated in the region, these enterprises will provide upward mobility only for their owners and limited numbers of workers.

No matter which economic forecast is more accurate—a continuing shift toward service-sector firms, or a mixture of services and new manufacturing—our conclusion is the same: Philadelphia cannot grow its way out of social and political inequality. By itself, economic revival promises neither to close the income gaps between the well-paid and low-paid segments of the population nor to channel additional investments into the region's weakest housing markets. Economic growth may even widen the distinctions between the best-off and worst-off communities. Thus, trickle-down strategies are inadequate. It is futile to expect that the region can simply grow its way out of poverty, racism, and inadequate shelter and education. These problems must be addressed by direct, not indirect, remedies: health and nutrition programs for poor children, employment and training, housing and community-development programs for declining neighborhoods.

These days it is almost impossible to sustain these kinds of programs at the local level. Local officials in the United States have always been reluctant to adopt policies with visibly redistributive results for fear that businesses and middle-income residents would leave the city to escape paying for services for the have-nots.[11] In the 1990s we can expect to see that attitude strengthened in cities like Philadelphia, where the base of middle-income employment has shrunk dramatically and the divide between those who pay taxes and those who consume services has widened. The city's first budget for the new decade was a harbinger of things to come.

When Mayor Goode conducted a series of twenty-two town meetings in spring 1989 to garner support for a proposed tax increase, the angry residents who attended the neighborhood hearings overwhelmingly opposed the tax hike, while at the same time demanding more police and fire protection and improved sanitation services. A blue-ribbon tax advisory panel gave the mayor exactly the same message, rejecting the tax increase and calling for increases in basic housekeeping services. As a result of public pressure, the city's budget for fiscal year 1990 raised spending on police, fire, and sanitation while making massive cuts in social services, including a 50-percent cut in the city's AIDS program and a 40-percent cut in funding for homeless shelters. Single, able-bodied adults would no longer have access to shelters, and the city halted new admissions to its program for mentally ill street people. Reporting this dramatic shift in the priorities of city government under the headline "Goode Slashes Social Aid," the *Philadelphia Inquirer* announced, "the mean season has begun." [12]

Philadelphia's incapacity to sustain services for the poor is no different from the problem facing other large cities. Urban administrations across the nation face the constant threat that the owners of homes and businesses will move to escape paying for the poor. That is why virtually all serious analysis of America's social welfare policies comes to the same conclusion: support for the urban poor must come mainly from the states and the federal government. This is true even when local economies are expanding, as has happened in the Philadelphia region in the 1980s. Economic expansion alone will not eradicate the social inequalities that redistributive programs are aimed at reducing. At best, economic growth may generate additional tax revenues to help local governments cope with the damaging effects of inequality. It will assuredly not obviate the need for government action.

Appendixes

Appendix A
The Index of Dissimilarity

The index of dissimilarity measures the differences in the distributions of different population groups (for example, blacks, whites, or members of different nationalities) over census tracts. If the different populations were evenly distributed across all census tracts, there would be no difference in their distributions—the index would be 0. On the other hand, if both groups were located in census tracts that were racially homogenous—if there were no racially integrated areas—their geographic distribution would be completely different. The index of dissimilarity would be 1.0.

Appendix B
Economic Transition: Further Data

This appendix contains detailed analyses of job data developed in summary form in Chapter 2. The depth of the analyses involved would have drawn attention away from the central points of that chapter. At the same time, the materials are important to a full understanding of the economic shifts facing the Philadelphia area. Hence, we provide these materials here for further reference.

Detailed Job Change Data

The discussion in Chapter 2 of job changes in the Delaware Valley points to the crucial distinction between city and suburbs, and to the different distributions reported at different wage levels. In particular, Table 2.3 and Figure 2.4 are used to support our major conclusions. Although these reflect the general pattern of changes, it should also be noted that these changes did not apply equally across all industries.

Neither the table nor the figure reveals the contributions of each level of earnings to the total amount of change that occurred. In other words, as jobs increased in the suburbs and decreased in the city, what role did low-, moderate-, and high-paying jobs play in this change? Where did most growth occur? Decline? And did this differ from city to suburb?

To answer this question, one must compute change in the total number of jobs and ask what fraction of this total change occurred in each earnings category. This fraction or percentage indicates the contribution of each level of earnings to the total net change in jobs.

The manner in which these percentages are computed can be illustrated by the use of data from Table B.1. In the City of Philadelphia the difference between the number of jobs in the lowest earnings category in 1987 (93,021) and the number of city jobs in the lowest category in 1980 (80,868) is equal to 12,153. The total net change is equal to the difference between the total number of city jobs in 1987 (648,987) and 1980 (670,247), that is, 21,260. The lowest group's percentage of total net change is, then, $(12,153/21,260) \times 100 = 57.2$. In this instance, employment in the category grew by 9,580 during a period when total net employment diminished; because total net change is negative, the percentage is negative, even though employment expanded in the category. Conversely, if employment in the category had dropped, the percentage would be positive because both the change in the category and the total change would carry negative signs. The percentages thus carry "counterintuitive" signs, a problem solved here by multiplying these changes by -1 where total net change is negative. Thus, declines in jobs carry a negative sign, and growth a positive sign. Because the number of jobs lost or gained in any one category can be greater or less than the total net change, the absolute value (that is, ignoring positive or negative signs) or changes can sum to a total *greater* than the total net change (which is the sum of positive and negative changes); a category's percentage of total net change can be greater than 100 percent. However, over all categories, the positive and negative percentages will add to plus or minus 100 percent.

Table B.1 provides this information for the city and the suburbs. As you read the table, most of your attention should go to the third and fourth columns, which show the net gain or loss in jobs by earnings category, as well as the proportion of the total gain or loss which this represents. The last column shows that in Philadelphia low-wage jobs contributed 57.2-percent growth in the face of a net job loss overall. The share of moderate-wage jobs fell by 329.5 percent while the percentage of high-wage jobs contributed a 172.3-percent increase. In the suburbs, not only did overall employment grow, but the three earnings groups shared roughly equally in the growth.

City and suburbs have clearly experienced the economic transition of the region differently. Though there has been broad, even growth across

Table B.1   Employment change in the city and suburbs
of Philadelphia by level of earnings, 1980–1987

Earnings level	1980 employ-ment	1987 employ-ment	Change 1980–1987	Proportion of net change accounted for
City of Philadelphia				
Less than half of median	80,868	93,021	12,153	57.2%
Half to twice median	555,586	485,532	−70,054	−329.5
More than twice median	33,793	70,434	36,641	172.3
Total	670,247	648,987	−21,260	100.0
Suburban Philadelphia				
Less than half of median	180,832	240,556	59,724	30.0
Half to twice median	814,837	886,542	71,705	36.0
More than twice median	50,867	118,791	67,924	34.2
Total	1,046,536	1,245,889	199,353	100.0

Table B.2   Employment change in the Philadelphia
metropolitan area by level of earnings, 1980–1987

Earnings level	1980 employ-ment	1987 employ-ment	Change 1980–1987	Proportion of net change accounted for
Less than half of median	261,700	333,577	71,877	40.3%
Half to twice median	1,370,423	1,372,074	1,651	.9
More than twice median	84,660	89,225	104,565	58.7
Total	1,716,783	1,894,876	178,093	99.9

suburban earning categories, the city has experienced a hemorrhage of
moderate-earnings jobs. The overall pattern is more clearly seen in Table
B.2, in which the metropolitan area as a whole is examined. It is rather
clear from these data that both upper and lower earnings categories have
shared in the recent growth of jobs in the region, but that middle-income
jobs—a very broad category—have evidenced little change at all. Taken
together, these two tables paint a picture of a city losing its middle-income
jobs to the suburbs and becoming more polarized in its job opportunities.
Many disputes between city and suburbs may also be traced back to this
fundamental disparity in the way in which these areas have experienced
economic change.

These data appear to challenge assertions that the middle class is absolutely declining, in that they seem to show that decline may depend upon
the location of employment. The divergent paths taken by the city and

Table B.3 Industry shares of job change by wage level
for Philadelphia and its suburbs, 1980–1987

Industry	City of Philadelphia			Suburbs		
	Less than median	Half to twice median	More than twice median	Less than median	Half to twice median	More than twice median
Agriculture/Mining	0.2	0.3	−0.1	1.2	2.9	0.4
Construction	2.0	−3.2	2.5	2.4	27.7	6.1
Adv.-Technology Manufacturing	0.4	−15.5	11.3	−0.2	−40.8	31.0
Other Manufacturing	−5.2	−53.7	8.2	−0.8	−64.8	1.4
Transportation/ Communications/ Utilities	−5.0	−24.3	32.3	−0.3	−2.4	10.8
Wholesale	1.5	−9.0	7.2	2.5	11.5	11.6
Retail	82.3	−5.8	0.1	53.3	25.6	2.1
Finance, Insurance, Real Estate	−4.6	0.5	16.4	1.2	42.0	10.9
Adv.-Technology Svcs.	−2.4	−4.1	8.6	−1.0	18.0	11.8
Other Business Svcs.	64.0	8.1	5.9	27.7	31.7	3.2
Consumer Svcs.	3.4	7.8	3.3	10.2	22.9	5.3
Nonprofits	−36.6	−1.1	4.3	3.7	25.7	0.2
(N)	(9,581)	(71,176)	(40,331)	(39,397)	(45,254)	(43,974)

Source: Computed from data tapes from the New Jersey Department of Labor and Pennsylvania Department of Labor and Industry.

suburban industrial structures may have produced a situation in which the industries that generate middle-income jobs in the city differ from those in the suburbs. Designed to examine this question, Table B.3 describes industry shares of the changes in low-, moderate-, and high-income jobs for the city and its suburbs. It demonstrates that the sources of job change in the 1980s were both similar and different in the city and its suburbs. In both places the loss of manufacturing jobs dominated the loss of middle-income jobs. But in the city, eight out of the twelve industrial categories lost middle-income jobs, whereas in the suburbs only three did. Surprisingly, the city's advanced technology manufacturing fared little better than other manufacturing; it, too, lost ground as the provider of middle-income jobs. For sources on defining advanced technology industries, see Chapter 2, note 8.

Growth in high-income city and suburban jobs differed substantially in its industrial origins. In Philadelphia the top three sources of high-income jobs were transportation/communications/utilities, finance, insurance, and real estate, and advanced-technology manufacturing—with the first source being three times as large as the last. In the suburbs the picture is reversed: advanced-technology manufacturing produced fully 31 percent of the gain, whereas transportation/communications/utilities, wholesale, finance, insurance, and real estate, and advanced-technology services each contributed a much smaller proportion.

The data presented in Table B.3 also suggest that the transition from manufacturing to service sector is complicated by the suburbanization process. Thus, the region's transition to a service economy has meant a loss of middle-income manufacturing jobs for both city and suburbs, but the city has been threatened by declines in mid-level jobs in other sectors as well. Further, some of the disappearing middle-income manufacturing jobs appear to have been replaced by high-income manufacturing jobs. One possible explanation is the substitution of machines for middle- and low-income workers; another is the movement of production offshore, with executives and design personnel left behind. The latter strategy has been heavily employed in the apparel and computer industries—both of which have a strong presence in the region. Probably both trends are at work, but the available data do not allow exploration of the issue.

Appendix C
Income Differentials by Race

It is observed in Chapter 2 that the changing economy of the region had clear implications for the income inequality between whites and blacks. The analysis presented there of the factors linked to this inequality rests on a regression analysis of family income, which allows simultaneous discussion of racial, family, and job patterns as they interact with one another. That is, this process allows an assessment of the relative importance of each factor in explaining the current split between black and white income levels.

To assess the cumulative effects of these factors, we conducted a multiple-regression analysis of family income, using both the characteristics of the family—race, family composition, and number of wage earners —as well as individual characteristics of the head of the household—age, education, and industrial sector of employment. The results of this analysis, presented in Table C.1, provide an estimate of the relative importance of

Table C.1   Effects of race, family, personal
characteristics, and industry on family income, 1987

Variable	B	Beta
Black	−8026.07	−.107627
Other	−4681.71	−.026513
Hispanic	−611.21	−.003477
Family characteristics		
Single male	−2999.12	−.025644
Single female	−10320.23	−.145452
Number of earners	11986.90	.464558
Age of head	270.86	.153842
Education of head	2141.44	.249392
Employment of head		
Manufacturing	4159.95	.057269
Export services	6906.04	.117095
(Constant)	−21174.38	
Multiple R	.69	
R square	.48	

these factors in determining family income. The average income of white families was $36,964 in 1988. For black families, it was $19,229. Once we take into consideration family structure, number of wage earners, and the age and education of the head of the household, differences in the incomes of black and white families are reduced from $18,000 to $8,000, represented in the B for black families. This persistent inequality suggests a continuing separation of white and black income levels, even when leading socioeconomic factors are controlled. We regard this as strong, though not conclusive, evidence for the effects of racism and racial discrimination in employment.

The results of the regression analysis also suggest that the number of wage earners in the family and education levels of the wage earners stand out from the other significant factors, as evidenced in the relative strength of the beta weights. The age and female-headed family factors are next in order of importance.

What this analysis provides is a clearer picture of how multiple factors interact to produce racial inequality. The residues of past discriminatory patterns (represented in the $8,000 differential of black versus white income once other factors are controlled) combine with family patterns and education to produce the wide disparity in family incomes. Although this discussion is continued in Chapter 2 using simple cross-tabular data to illustrate these points in greater detail, its roots are in this equation.

Notes

Chapter 1

1. David Harvey, *The Limits to Capital* (Chicago: University of Chicago Press, 1982); John Logan and Harvey Molotch, *Urban Fortunes* (Berkeley: University of California Press, 1987).

2. Sam Bass Warner, *The Private City: Philadelphia in Three Periods of Its Growth*, 2d ed. (Philadelphia: University of Pennsylvania Press, 1987), p. 52.

3. Philadelphia City Planning Commission, *A City of Neighborhoods* (Philadelphia: City Planning Commission, 1976), pp. 12–13. The street grid and rowhouse became so ingrained in Philadelphia's physical development pattern that attempts to modify them have seldom been successful. Even after World War II, when the Far Northeast section of the city was being developed, the city planning commission had to battle developers who wanted to continue the grid pattern into that region, obliterating hills, streams, and other features of the landscape. Ultimately, the grid was broken for only a small section of the city.

4. Ibid., p. 19.

5. J. Thomas Scharf and Thompson Westcott, *History of Philadelphia* (Philadelphia: L. H. Everts, 1884), 3: 2239.

6. Bruce Laurie and Mark Schmitz, "Manufacturing and Productivity: The Making of an Industrial Base, 1850–1880," in Theodore Hershberg, ed., *Philadelphia: Work, Space, Family and Group Experience in the Nineteenth Century* (New York: Oxford University Press, 1981), p. 45.

7. Philip Scranton, *Proprietary Capitalism: The Textile Manufacture at Philadelphia, 1800–1885* (Philadelphia: Temple University Press, 1983).

8. Digby Baltzell, *Puritan Boston and Quaker Philadelphia* (New York: Free Press, 1979), esp. chap. 13.

9. Scranton, *Proprietary Capitalism*, chap. 8.

10. Laurie and Schmitz, "Manufacturing and Productivity," pp. 85–87.

11. Carolyn Golab, *Immigrant Destinations* (Philadelphia: Temple University Press, 1977).

12. For a description of Philadelphia's most important "bosses," see Harold Zink, *City Bosses in the United States: A Study of Twenty Municipal Bosses* (Durham, N.C.: Duke University Press, 1930), chaps. 9, 10, and 11.

13. W. W. Pierson, *Annals of American Academy of Political and Social Science* 29 (March 1907): 124.

14. Lincoln Steffens, *The Shame of Cities* (rpt., New York: P. Smith, 1984).

15. Baltzell, *Puritan Boston and Quaker Philadelphia*.

16. Delos Wilcox, *Great Cities in America* (New York: Macmillan, 1910), p. 253.

17. Zink, *City Bosses*, p. 201.

18. W. E. B. DuBois, *The Philadelphia Negro* (rpt., New York: Shocken Books, 1967), pp. 373–81.

19. Warner, *The Private City*.

20. Wilcox, *Great Cities in America*, p. 274.

21. Francis Biddle, *The Llanfear Pattern* (New York: Scribner's Sons, 1927), p. 233.

22. Kirk Petshek, *The Challenge of Urban Reform* (Philadelphia: Temple University Press, 1973), pp. 18–19.

23. Thomas Luce and Anita Summers, *Local Fiscal Issues in the Philadelphia Metropolitan Area* (Philadelphia: University of Pennsylvania Press, 1987), p. 34.

24. Warner, *The Private City*, p. 10.

25. Mark Alan Hughes, *Poverty in Cities* (Washington, D.C.: National League of Cities, 1989).

26. *Philadelphia Inquirer*, June 18, 1989, p. 12A.

Chapter 2

1. U.S. Senate Committee on Interstate and Foreign Commerce Special Subcommittee to Study the Textile Industry, *Problems of the Domestic Textile Industry* (Washington, D.C.: Government Printing Office, 1959); idem, *Problems of the Domestic Textile Industry* (Washington, D.C.: Government Printing Office, 1961); and idem, *Problems of the Domestic Textile Industry* (Washington, D.C.: Government Printing Office, 1963).

2. George Perazich and W. T. Stone, *Economic Effects of Textile Mill Closings in Selected Communities in Middle Atlantic States* (Washington, D.C.: U.S. Department of Commerce, 1963). Although generally considered apparel, hosiery and all knitted apparel are actually classified as textiles by the federal government.

3. William A. Reynolds, *Innovation in the United States Carpet Industry, 1947–1963* (Princeton: Van Nostrand, 1968); Steven S. Plice, *Manpower and Merger: The Impact of Merger on Personnel Policies in the Carpet and Furniture Industries*, Manpower and Human Resources Studies, No. 5 (Philadelphia: Wharton School, Industrial Research Unit, 1976).

4. David F. Noble, *Forces of Production* (New York: Oxford University Press, 1984); Philip Scranton and Walter Licht, *Work Sights: Industrial Philadelphia, 1890–1950* (Philadelphia: Temple University Press, 1986).

5. Edward B. Shils and Felix Goizueta-Mimo, "A Study of the Philadelphia Apparel Industry," mimeographed (Philadelphia: Southeastern Pennsylvania Economic Development Corporation, 1966), p. 28.

6. James Lardner, "Annals of Business, The Sweater Trade—I," *New Yorker*, January 11, 1988, pp. 39–73; also James Lardner, "Annals of Business, Global Clothing Industry—II," *New Yorker*, January 25, 1988, pp. 57–73.

7. Shils and Goizueta-Mimo, "A Study of the Philadelphia Apparel Industry."

8. Let us take an example from the apparel industry, historically one of Philadelphia's largest employers. Suppose a dress firm employs a $30,000-per-year pattern cutter to cut the fabric for a dress. Let us say the pattern cutter can cut enough fabric for 375 dresses each day and for 90,000 dresses each year. The production cost for each dress that is attributable to his earnings is then $30,000/90,000 = $.33. Now, suppose his employer chooses to replace him with a $300,000 computer-driven laser cutter and a $24,000 operator, which, together, can cut 50,000 dresses a day or 12 million per year. That portion of the cost per dress drops to $324,000/12,000,000 = $.03. But

only if all 12 million are sold. The company must sell more than 981,000 dresses just to break even! If the firm continues to sell its previous level of only 90,000 dresses, the cost per dress is $324,000/90,000 = $3.60. Thus, the firm must sell more dresses in order to pay for the machine and operator and make a profit. In order to do this, firms typically hire more sales and other nonproduction workers.

Several simplifications are involved in this example. Few firms employ but one pattern cutter, so the comparison really should be between a group of pattern cutters and a machine. In addition, one of the major differences between the use of pattern cutters and the machine is the setup time required to lay out the material and pattern in the first place. It is a significant fraction of total time for the pattern cutter and relatively trivial for the machine. However, despite these and other complexities, it remains the case that the greater fixed cost of operating the laser cutter requires substantially greater sales to produce a profit.

9. The list is based on research done by and for the U.S. Department of Commerce; it combines the lists of M. Boretsky, "The Threat to U.S. High Technology: Economic and National Security Implications," draft report, International Trade Administration, U.S. Department of Commerce, 1982; L. A. Davis, "Technology Intensity of U.S. Output and Trade," Office of Trade and Investment Analysis, U.S. Department of Commerce, 1983; and A. M. Lawson, "Technological Growth and High Technology in U.S. Industries," *Industrial Economics Review* (Washington, D.C.: U.S. Department of Commerce, 1982).

10. Although attention to the shift from manufacturing to service employment is fairly recent, the shift itself dates to at least 1920.

11. John F. Kain, "The Distribution and Movement of Jobs and Industry," in James Q. Wilson, ed., *The Metropolitan Enigma* (New York: Anchor, 1970), pp. 8–9; Roger W. Lotchin, ed., *The Martial Metropolis: U.S. Cities in War and Peace* (New York: Praeger, 1984).

12. Expenditures for military hardware jumped from $3.9 billion in 1950 to more than $17 billion in 1953; see Martin Schiesl, "Airplanes to Aerospace," in Lotchin, ed., *The Martial Metropolis*, p. 138.

13. David Elesh, personal interview with Henry Richner, Vice President, Philadelphia Chamber of Commerce, 1984.

14. Lester C. Thurow, "A Surge in Inequality," *Scientific American* 256, no. 5 (1987): 30–37.

15. We do not argue that the macroeconomic events are the sole cause of the decline of American manufacturing. Certainly, a case can be made for the contributions of mismanagement of firms, lack of realistic trade and industrial policies, and the industrial strategies of Japan, Hong Kong, Taiwan, Singapore, Korea, and other nations of the Pacific Rim. Our education of business leaders must also share some of the blame: no business school offers training in industrial processes and in understanding the organizational implications of technology. Tax and financial policies that reward short-term results are additional factors. However, we do argue that if domestic goods had not been at a price disadvantage, the decline of American manufacturing employment would have been considerably more gradual.

16. Kain, "The Distribution and Movement," pp. 8–10. Actually, Kain does not specify the kinds of industry, but there was far less need for continuous-flow production processes in most nondurable production. Although two of the nondurable goods

industries with the brightest future in the postwar era—chemicals and petroleum—had substantial employment totals in Philadelphia, both were among the most automated of all manufacturing industries and were therefore unlikely to generate many jobs.

17. Barry Bluestone and Bennett Harrison, *The Deindustrialization of America* (New York: Basic Books, 1982).

18. As Bluestone and Harrison are careful to note, some caution is required in interpreting these figures because they are based on analyses of the Current Population Surveys of the U.S. Census. In these, earnings data are somewhat inflated by the inclusion of overtime pay and income from multiple jobs.

19. Note clearly that the use of the median of average establishment earnings to define the earnings categories creates a definition of the middle earnings group that is very generous: in 1980 it incorporated 83 percent of the city and 80 percent of the suburban wage and salary workers. Thus, the growth of the low and high categories in both the city and suburbs represents groups that are genuinely extreme in terms of the earnings distribution. For example, those in establishments with average pay more than twice the median in 1980 constitute only *5 percent* of city and suburban workers. These facts are critical to understanding the implications of the changes in the job and earnings distributions examined below.

20. The figures were calculated from 1980 Public Use Sample data tapes supplied by the U.S. Census Bureau. The employment security data base covers private wage and salary employment in business establishments; the Public Use Sample describes persons. To make the two sets as comparable as possible, we limited the sample to persons with a current private wage and salary job who reported wage and salary income for 1979. Data on earnings in the employment security are for the first quarter of 1980. The median earnings in the census sample was $10,848; it was $13,729 (annualized) in the employment security data. Part of the difference between the medians is accountable from the fact that the census recoded all incomes above $75,000 to $75,000.

21. The actual numbers of jobs created, from low to high wage, were 59,724; 71,705; 67,924.

22. The data on which Table 2.4 is based do not provide direct information on full and part-time workers. To estimate the number of full-time workers, we obtained the average weekly hours worked for each of seventy-two industries from published and unpublished statistics from the U.S. Bureau of Labor Statistics and divided by 40. The resulting ratios gave the percentage workers in an industry exceeded or failed to work a 40-hour week. The actual number of workers in each industry was then multiplied by these ratios to produce an estimate of the number of "full-time equivalent workers." For example, in March of 1980 workers in the steel industry averaged 41.4 hours, so the ratio was $41.4/40 = 1.04$. If there were 500,000 steel employees, the number of 40-hour, full-time equivalent workers would be $500,000 \times 1.04 = 520,000$.

23. Support for the explanation also can be found in the 1980 Public Use Sample of the U.S. census, which shows that in 1980, 82 percent of city workers and 70 percent of suburban workers had work weeks under 40 hours.

24. *Wall Street Journal*, May 4, 1987, pp. 1, 20.

25. The focus on race, and in particular, on black-white differences, in this chapter is a simple recognition of a dominant theme in Philadelphia's development. The major referent of race has been the relationship between European-American communities of various national origins and the communities of African-American descent. Yet it is

also the case that this is not the only division in Philadelphia. As is apparent in the next chapter, for instance, a significant division exists between Hispanic and both European and African-American neighborhoods. Although systematic data are not yet available, recent work by Judith Goode will make discussions of stratification in Philadelphia much more complicated in the very near future. However, data limitations constrain this discussion to black-white differences.

26. These categories were isolated from a regression analysis performed on 1987 family incomes and reported in Appendix C. The results of this analysis demonstrate the relative weight of these factors in explaining black-white differentials in income.

27. The numbers can be interpreted as the percentage of one distribution that must be moved to make it identical to the distribution with which it is being compared. Please see Appendix A for an explanation of the index of dissimilarity.

28. We have combined occupational and industrial categories in order that similar classifications are used for each year.

29. W. L. Yancey and E. P. Ericksen, "The Antecedents of Community: The Economic and Institutional Structure of Urban Neighborhoods," *American Sociological Review* 44 (1979): 253–62; Stephanie Greenberg, "Industrial Location and Ethnic Residential Patterns in an Industrializing City: Philadelphia, 1880," in Theodore Hershberg, ed., *Philadelphia* (New York: Oxford University Press, 1981), pp. 204–232.

30. Again, all jobs are recorded as being where the respondent lives rather than where he or she works.

31. Although Table 2.7 suggests that there are no blacks in advanced-technology services, they are simply too few to register with one-decimal-point precision.

32. Some categories are anomalous, for example, the higher fraction of blacks than whites in suburban advanced-technology manufacturing. The relatively low numbers of workers involved (roughly 12,000 workers), plus the fact that much advanced-technology manufacturing is in fact an assembly-line or operative nature, would suggest that this finding may well be simply an artifact of the categories we have used to partition industrial types. Another surprise is the higher proportion of blacks than whites in craft work occupations in the suburbs. Perhaps the explanation is that the overall growth of suburban jobs of all types has afforded whites many alternatives to the traditional craft jobs, while blacks have remained more concentrated in such employment.

33. These findings were reinforced when earnings were compared across location and industrial structure. In poorer paying local service jobs, city and suburban earnings are the same, but in higher paying manufacturing and export service jobs, the suburbs pay substantially better. If incomes were recorded by location of job, the city median would be a higher percentage than the suburban. We also recognize significant industrial heterogeneity within these broad industrial sectors. Although the differences in earnings are broadly accurate, there are some significant variances within the broad sectors. For example, some of the industries we have grouped within the export sector pay more in the city than in the suburbs.

34. The decline in black employment rates may have begun earlier, but the data are not sufficiently comparable to include in the table.

35. John Kasarda, "Urban Change and Minority Opportunities," in Paul Peterson, ed., *The New Urban Reality* (New York: Brookings Institute, 1985), pp. 38–68.

36. The comparisons are limited to "prime" aged workers in order to limit the effect of age on the distributions. Workers above fifty-five entered the labor force with fewer

educational requirements, and workers under twenty-five will often have not completed their educations.

37. Part-time work is defined as work that occupied fewer than 35 hours per week. The Current Population Surveys ask for hours worked *at all jobs* last week. For this reason, the part-time definition undercounts part-time jobs, since some persons will have two or more jobs that together involve 35 or more hours.

38. Shils and Goizueta-Mimo, "A Study of the Philadelphia Apparel Industry," p. 16.

39. Anita Summers and Thomas F. Luce, *Economic Report on the Philadelphia Metropolitan Area 1985* (Philadelphia: University of Pennsylvania Press, 1985).

40. This figure comes from records of jobs reported to the unemployment compensation (ES202) programs of the states of New Jersey and Pennsylvania. Although the U.S. Census Bureau, in its *County Business Patterns*, measures the same population of business establishments, the ES202 is more comprehensive. The ES202 data are not available for the entire metropolitan area before 1980, and consequently the less adequate County Business Patterns data are used whenever longer-term comparisons are required.

Chapter 3

1. U.S. Bureau of the Census, *Annual Housing Survey* (Washington, D.C.: Government Printing Office, 1977).

2. Cushing Dolbeare, *Housing in Philadelphia* (Philadelphia: Public Interest Law Center of Philadelphia, 1988), p. 3.

3. Harvey Molotch, "Capital and Neighborhood in the U.S.," *Urban Affairs Quarterly* 14, no. 3 (1979): 289–312.

4. See Theodore Hershberg, ed., *Philadelphia: Work, Space, Family and Group Experience in the Nineteenth Century* (New York: Oxford University Press, 1981), for an extensive discussion of the history of Philadelphia's black community.

5. Kenneth Jackson, *Crabgrass Frontier: The Suburbanization of the U.S.* (New York: Oxford University Press, 1985).

6. C. P. Bradford, "Financing Homeownership: The Federal Role in Neighborhood Decline," *Urban Affairs Quarterly* 14 (1979); Barry Checkoway, "Large Builders, Federal Housing Programs, and Postwar Suburbanization," *International Journal of Urban and Regional Research* 4 (1980): 21–45.

7. Philadelphia City Planning Commission, *Comprehensive Plan: The Physical Development Plan for the City of Philadelphia* (Philadelphia, 1960), pp. 22–23.

8. U.S. Bureau of the Census, *State and Metropolitan Area Data Book* (Washington, D.C.: Government Printing Office, 1979).

9. David Bartelt, "Redlines and Breadlines: Depression Recovery and the Structure of Urban Space," mimeographed paper (Temple University, 1984).

10. David Bartelt and George Leon, "Differential Decline: The Neighborhood Context of Abandonment," *Housing and Society* 13, no. 2 (1986): 81–106.

11. Roman Cybriwsky, John Western, and David Ley, "The Political and Social Contribution of Revitalized Neighborhoods: Society Hill, Philadelphia and False Creek, Vancouver," in Neil Smith and Peter Williams, eds., *Gentrification of the City* (Boston: Allen & Unwin, 1986).

12. Thomas Clark, "The Interdependence among Gentrifying Neighborhoods: Denver since 1970," *Urban Geography* 3 (1985): 246–73; Richard Legates and Chester Hartman, "The Anatomy of Displacement in the United States," in Smith and Williams, eds., *Gentrification of the City*; S. Lipton, "Evidence of Central City Revival," *Journal of the American Institute of Planners* 43, no. 2 (1977): 136–47; Daphne Spain, "Indicators of Urban Revitalization: Racial and Socioeconomic Changes in Central-City Housing," in Shirley Laska and Daphne Spain, eds., *Back to the City: Issues in Neighborhood Renovation* (New York: Pergamon Press, 1980); Eileen Zeitz, "Reinvasion: A Neglected Form of Residential Segregation in Urban Areas," *Black Scholar* 9, no. 1 (1977): 41–45.

13. Chris Hamnet, "Gentrification and Residential Location Theory: A Review and Assessment," in D. T. Herbert and R. J. Johnson, eds., *Geography and the Urban Environment: Progress in Research and Applications*, vol. 6 (New York: John Wiley and Sons, 1984).

14. Richard Schaffer and Neil Smith, "The Gentrification of Harlem," *Annals of the Association of American Geographers* 76, no. 3 (1986): 347–65.

15. David Rose, "Rethinking Gentrification: Beyond the Uneven Development of Marxist Urban Theory," *Environment and Planning D: Society and Space* 1 (1984): pp. 47–74; Thomas Clark, "The Interdependence among Gentrifying Neighborhoods; Central Denver since 1970," *Urban Geography* 6, no. 3 (1985): 246–73; Schaffer and Smith, "The Gentrification of Harlem," p. 347.

16. Chester Hartman, "Comment on 'Neighborhood Revitalization and Displacement: A Review of the Evidence'," *Journal of the American Planning Association* 45 (1979): 488–91; Chester Hartman, Dennis Keating, Richard LeGates, with Steve Turner, *Displacement: How to Fight It* (Berkeley, Calif.: National Housing Law Project, 1982); Richard Legates and Chester Hartman, "The Anatomy of Displacement in the United States," in Smith and Williams, eds., *Gentrification of the City*.

17. Lynne Kotranski, "The Structure and Determinants of Urban Mortgage Lending Patterns: A Study of Philadelphia, 1968–1974" (Ph.D. diss., Temple University, 1981); Bartelt, "Redlines and Breadlines."

18. Ira Goldstein, "The Impact of Racial Composition on the Distribution of Conventional Mortgages in the Philadelphia SMSA: A Case Study" (Philadelphia: Temple University Institute for Public Policy Studies, Working Paper Series, 1987).

19. David Bartelt and George Leon, "Differential Decline: The Neighborhood Context of Abandonment," *Housing and Society* 13, no. 2 (1986): 81–106.

20. Phyllis Ryan, Ira Goldstein, and David Bartelt, *Homelessness in Pennsylvania: How Can This Be?* (Philadelphia: Coalition on Homelessness in Pennsylvania and the Institute for Public Policy Studies, 1989).

21. Cushing Dolbeare, *Housing in Philadelphia* (Philadelphia: Public Interest Law Center, 1988).

22. Our measure answers the question: If you were the average black person, what percentage of your local neighborhood's population would be black? It reflects the probability that someone who is black will encounter other blacks in his or her census tract. Similarly, for whites, it reflects the probability that they will encounter other whites in their census tracts.

23. See Appendix A for an explanation of the method of calculating the index of dissimilarity.

24. Lansdowne–Upper Darby Area Fair Housing Council, "Audit of John E. Wallace Real Estate—Century 21" (unpublished, 1978).

25. John Logan, "Fiscal and Developmental Crises in Black Suburbs," in Scott Cummings, ed., *Business Elites and Urban Development* (Albany: State University of New York Press, 1988), p. 338.

26. Sam Bass Warner, *The Private City: Philadelphia in Three Periods of Its Growth*, 2d ed. (Philadelphia: University of Pennsylvania Press, 1987), p. 53.

Chapter 4

1. On the creation of alleys and alley housing in the eighteenth century, see Sam Bass Warner, *The Private City: Philadelphia in Three Periods of Its Growth*, 2d ed. (Philadelphia: University of Pennsylvania Press, 1987) chap. 1.

2. Philadelphia City Planning Commission, *Center City and Its People* (Philadelphia: City Planning Commission, 1985).

3. Robert Beauregard, "Urban Form and the Redevelopment of Central Business Districts," *Journal of Architectural and Planning Research* 3, no. 3 (1986): 183–98.

4. Recall, for example, the expansion of the city's boundaries in the 1854 consolidation of the city and county, described in Chapter 1.

5. William Cutler, "The Persistent Dualism: Centralization and Decentralization in Philadelphia, 1854–1975," in W. Cutler and H. Gilette, eds., *The Divided Metropolis: The Social and Spatial Dimensions of Philadelphia, 1820–1840* (Westport, Conn.: Greenwood, 1980), pp. 249–84.

6. Beauregard, "Urban Form," p. 185.

7. Leo Adde, *Nine Cities: The Anatomy of Downtown Renewal* (Washington, D.C.: Urban Land Institute, 1969), p. 17.

8. The city's redevelopment goals have been articulated in several documents, e.g., Philadelphia City Planning Commission, *Comprehensive Plan: The Physical Development Plan for the City of Philadelphia* (Philadelphia, 1960), and "Job Creation and Retention," First Report of the Economic Recovery Task Force of the W. Wilson Goode for Mayor Campaign (Philadelphia, March 1983).

9. Nancy Kleniewski, personal interview with William Rafsky, August 2, 1983.

10. Penn Center, for example, was not a public redevelopment project but was privately funded and built, although with the active encouragement of Mayor Clark and the city planning commission.

11. On changes in federal priorities, see Mark Gelfand, *A Nation of Cities: The Federal Government and Urban America, 1935–1965* (New York: Oxford University Press, 1975).

12. Philadelphia City Planning Commission, "The Plan for Center City" (May 1988).

13. Community Renewal Program, *The Redevelopment Authority Program, 1945–1962*, City of Philadelphia, Community Renewal Program Technical Report No. 6 (Philadelphia, 1963), Appendix A.

14. Nancy Kleniewski, personal interview with Edmund N. Bacon, August 3, 1983.

15. Nancy Kleniewski, interview with William Rafsky.

16. William Rafsky, "A New Approach to Urban Renewal for Philadelphia," mimeographed report (Philadelphia: Office of the Development Coordinator, 1956).

17. The Yorktown–Progress Plaza development, consisting of a neighborhood of modern rowhouses adjacent to a suburban-style shopping plaza, is the prime example of what private market redevelopment was supposed to create in North Philadelphia. This successful private development, which has helped to retain some black middle-class households in North Philadelphia, has not been duplicated.

18. Francis M. Lordan, "Model Cities Project in North Philadelphia: $11 Million OKd for Ghetto Housing," *Philadelphia Bulletin*, August 22, 1969.

19. Peter Binzen, "Shall We Abandon 'Unlivable' Neighborhoods?" *Philadelphia Bulletin*, February 4, 1973.

20. Thomas Hine, "Convention Center on the Mall—Hmmm," *Philadelphia Inquirer*, August 5, 1984.

21. The Market East project, which had started as a planned megastructure in the vision of planner, Edmund Bacon, had gradually turned into strip development. This departure from original design was symptomatic of the breakdown of consensus within the political structure, the pressures and claims of the remainder of the city on development funding, the relative weakening of the reform elements within the elected government, and a breakdown of easy access to the elected government by business leaders, trends that are explored further in Chapter 5.

22. On pro-growth coalitions, see Harvey Molotch, "The City as a Growth Machine: Toward a Political Economy of Place," *American Journal of Sociology* 18 (1976): 309–332; and John Mollenkopf, "The Postwar Politics of Urban Development," in W. Tabb and L. Sawers, eds., *Marxism and the Metropolis* (New York: Oxford University Press, 1978), pp. 117–52.

On the Greater Philadelphia Movement, see Kirk Petshek, *The Challenge of Urban Reform* (Philadelphia: Temple University Press, 1973), and Nancy Kleniewski, "From Industrial to Corporate City: The Role of Urban Renewal," in W. K. Tabb and L. Sawers, eds., *Marxism and the Metropolis*, 2nd ed. (New York: Oxford University Press, 1984), pp. 205–222.

On the Young Turks, see Petshek, *Challenge of Urban Reform*.

23. See, for example, William Domhoff, *Who Really Rules?* (New Brunswick: Transaction Books, 1978); S. Fainstein, N. Fainstein, R. C. Hill, M. P. Smith, *Restructuring the City: The Political Economy of Urban Redevelopment* (London: Longman, 1983); Chester Hartman, *The Transformation of San Francisco*. (Totowa, N.J.: Rowman and Allanheld, 1984); Roy Lubove, *Pittsburgh* (New York: New Viewpoints, 1976); John Mollenkopf, *The Contested City* (Princeton, N.J.: Princeton University Press, 1983); and J. Allen Whitt, *Urban Elites and Mass Transportation: The Dialectics of Power* (Princeton, N.J.: Princeton University Press, 1983).

24. See David Gordon, "Capitalist Development and the History of American Cities," in Tabb and Sawers, eds., *Marxism and the Metropolis*; and Kleniewski, "From Industrial to Corporate City."

25. Philadelphia City Planning Commission, *The Urban Form of Center City* (Philadelphia: City Planning Commission, 1985), p. 83.

26. See, for example, David Harvey, "The Urban Process under Capitalism: A Framework for Analysis," *International Journal of Urban and Regional Research*, 2, no. 1 (1978): 101–131; and Neil Smith, "Toward a Theory of Gentrification," *Journal of the American Planning Association* 45 (1979): 538, 548.

27. Jeanne Lowe, *Cities in a Race with Time* (New York: Random House, 1968).

28. See, e.g., James O'Connor, *The Fiscal Crisis of the State* (New York: St. Martin's Press, 1973); and Mollenkopf, *Contested City*.

29. Cyril B. Roseman, "Public-Private Co-operation and Negotiation in Downtown Redevelopment: A Study of the Decision Process in Philadelphia" (Ph.D. diss., Princeton University, 1963).

30. Nancy Kleniewski, interview with William Rafsky.

31. Lou Antosh and Peter H. Binzen, "Business Leadership Fractured; Once-Powerful GPM Turns Flabby," *Philadelphia Bulletin*, October 17, 1972.

32. Walter F. Naedele, "Gallery in a Bind on Projects: Private Investors 'Flee' City," *Philadelphia Bulletin*, January 9, 1979.

33. Nancy Kleniewski, personal interview with Roy Diamond, July 24, 1987.

34. See Edmund N. Bacon, "What Was Attempted II: The Planning Story," in S. Newman, ed., *The Politics of Utopia* (Philadelphia: Temple University Department of Political Science, 1975).

35. O'Connor, *Fiscal Crisis of the State*, p. 136.

36. Redevelopment Authority of Philadelphia, *Annual Report* (Philadelphia: Redevelopment Authority, 1976), p. 42.

37. Philadelphia City Planning Commission, *The Urban Form of Center City*, pp. 84, 43.

38. Ibid.

39. John Mollenkopf, "Neighborhood Political Development and the Politics of Urban Growth: Boston and San Francisco 1858–78," *International Journal of Urban and Regional Research* 5 (1981): 15–39.

40. Philadelphia City Planning Commission, *Center City and Its People*.

41. Marc Kaufman, "Center City Sprawling Past Old Barriers," *Philadelphia Bulletin*, February 11, 1979.

42. Philadelphia City Planning Commission, *Population and Housing Characteristics for Philadelphia Census Tracts—1980 and 1970* (Philadelphia: City Planning Commission, 1983), and *Recent Historical Trends in Population, Housing, and Socio-Economic Characteristics of Philadelphia Planning Analysis Sections and Subsections 1930–1940–1950–1960*, Public Information Bulletin 11 (Philadelphia: City Planning Commission, 1966).

43. Ibid.

44. Mayor Dilworth, quoted in Lowe, *Cities in a Race*, p. 342.

45. Rafsky, "A New Approach;" Lowe, *Cities in a Race*, p. 340; *The Philadelphia Bulletin*, February 3, 1969; Community Renewal Program, *The Redevelopment Authority Program 1945–1962*.

46. The politicization of neighborhood organizations was probably also a function of the decline of the political machine, as discussed in Chapter 5.

47. Another indirect effect PCNO had on city politics was its close cooperation with a local liberal policy institute. The head of the institute was elected, with neighborhood support, to City Council and eventually was appointed as head of the city's housing and community development agency.

48. Conrad Weiler, *Philadelphia: Neighborhood, Authority, and the Urban Crisis* (New York: Praeger, 1968).

Chapter 5

1. Richard Rubin, *Party Dynamics: The Democratic Coalition and the Politics of Change* (New York: Oxford University Press, 1976). See esp. chap. 5, "The Changing Democratic Electorate and Elite Factionalism."

2. Samuel Lubell, *The Hidden Crisis in American Politics* (New York: Norton, 1970), p. 105.

3. James Tate, "In Praise of Politicians," *Philadelphia Bulletin*, January 23, 1974.

4. B. Ransom, "Black Independent Electoral Politics in Philadelphia and the Election of Mayor W. Wilson Goode," in M. B. Preston, L. J. Henderson, and P. Puryear, eds., *The New Black Politics*, 2d ed. (New York: Longman, 1987), pp. 256–89.

5. *Philadelphia Inquirer*, December 15, 1984.

6. Michael Peter Smith, *City, State and Market: The Political Economy of Urban Society* (New York: Basil Blackwell, 1988.)

7. J. H. Strange, "Blacks and Philadelphia Politics, 1963–1966," in M. Ershkowitz and J. Zikmund, eds., *Black Politics in Philadelphia* (New York: Basic Books, 1973), p. 122.

8. Ibid., p. 110.

9. J. David Greenstone and Paul Peterson, *Race and Authority in Urban Politics: Community Participation and the War on Poverty* (Chicago: University of Chicago Press, 1973), p. 28.

10. Strange, "Blacks and Philadelphia Politics," p. 114.

11. Sandra Featherman and William Rosenberg, *Jews, Blacks and Ethnics: The 1978 Vote White Charter Campaign in Philadelphia* (Philadelphia: Temple University Institute for Public Policy Studies, 1979).

12. *Philadelphia Inquirer*, May 20, 1987.

13. Ibid., May 21, 1987.

14. *Philadelphia Magazine*, May 1987.

15. A passionate case for reforming registration requirements is contained in Frances Fox Piven and Richard Cloward's recent book *Why Americans Don't Vote* (New York: Pantheon Books, 1988).

16. Eugene Ericksen et al., *The State of Puerto Rican Philadelphia* (Philadelphia: Temple University Institute for Public Policy Studies, 1985), p. 110.

17. For a summary of this literature, see John Logan and Harvey Molotch, *Urban Fortunes: The Political Economy of Place* (Berkeley: University of California Press, 1987), chap. 3.

18. For discussion of the tension between involvement and noninvolvement by business people in Philadelphia politics in the nineteenth century, see Sam Bass Warner, *The Private City: Philadelphia in Three Periods of Its Growth*, 2d ed. (Philadelphia: University of Pennsylvania Press, 1987), chap. 5; and Digby Baltzell, *Philadelphia Gentlemen: The Making of a National Upper Class* (Glencoe: Free Press, 1958), pp. 130–41.

19. M. Aiken and P. E. Mott, *The Structure of Community Power* (New York: Random House, 1970).

20. L. H. Seiler, "Community Verticalization: On the Interface between Corporate Influence and the Horizontal Community," paper presented at Annual Meeting of the American Sociology Association, San Francisco, 1975.

21. Roger Friedland and Donald Palmer, "Park Place and Main Street: Business and the Urban Power Structure," in Ralph Turner, ed., *Annual Review of Sociology*, vol. 10 (Beverly Hills: Sage, 1984), pp. 393–416. See also Fred Block, "The Ruling Class Does Not Rule," *Socialist Review* 7 (May/June 1977): 6–27.

22. *Philadelphia Bulletin*, June 7, 1965.

23. Kirk Petshek, *The Challenge of Urban Reform* (Philadelphia: Temple University Press, 1973), esp. chap. 2.

24. Joseph Daughen and Peter Binzen, *The Cop Who Would Be King* (Boston: Little Brown, 1977), p. 154.

25. Ibid., p. 166.

26. Greater Philadelphia Chamber of Commerce, "Report on the Long-Range Planning Committee" (Philadelphia, 1982), p. 2.

27. Greater Philadelphia Chamber of Commerce, "Questions and Answers Regarding Long-Range Plan" (Philadelphia, March 16, 1982).

28. Carolyn Adams, *The Politics of Capital Investment: The Case of Philadelphia* (Albany: State University of New York Press, 1988).

29. Petshek, *Challenge of Urban Reform*, p. 87.

30. Dan Rottenberg, *Philadelphia Inquirer*, February 25, 1989.

31. R. Friedland, F. F. Piven, and R. Alford, "Political Conflict, Urban Structure and the Fiscal Crisis," in D. Ashford, ed., *Comparing Public Policies* (Beverly Hills, Calif.: Sage, 1978).

32. *Philadelphia Inquirer*, April 11, 1987.

33. Ibid., April 13, 1983.

34. Like other American cities, Philadelphia is reviewing and refining its minority set-aside legislation in the aftermath of the Supreme Court's ruling in January 1989 that Richmond's (Va.) set-aside law was unconstitutional.

35. R. P. Browning, D. R. Marshall, and D. H. Tabb, *Protest Is Not Enough* (Berkeley: University of California Press, 1984).

36. For a summary of the literature on this question, see Kenneth Mladenka, "Blacks and Hispanics in Urban Politics," *American Political Science Review* 83 (March 1989): 165–91.

37. Robert Beauregard, "Local Politics and the Employment Relation: Construction Jobs in Philadelphia," in Beauregard, ed., *Economic Restructuring and Response* (Beverly Hills, Calif.: Sage Publications, 1989), pp. 149–79.

38. *Philadelphia Inquirer*, July 13, 1986.

39. Rod Bush, ed., *The New Black Vote: Politics and Power in Four American Cities* (San Francisco: Synthesis Publications, 1984), p. 4.

40. Terry Clark and Lorna Ferguson, *City Money: Political Processes, Fiscal Strain, and Retrenchment* (New York: Columbia University Press, 1983).

41. *Philadelphia Inquirer*, March 15, 1987.

42. Douglas Yates, *The Ungovernable City* (Cambridge: MIT Press, 1978), p. 34.

43. Barbara Ferman, *Governing the Ungovernable City* (Philadelphia: Temple University Press, 1985), p. 211.

Chapter 6

1. Committee for Economic Development, *Modernizing Local Government to Secure Balanced Federalism* (New York: Committee for Economic Development, 1966); National Commission on Urban Problems, *Final Report, Part IV* (Washington, D.C.: Government Printing Office, 1968).

2. Willard Rouse, quoted by Peter Binzen, "Citing a Need for Improved Regional Planning," *Philadelphia Inquirer*, November 24, 1986.

3. Walter D'Alessio, quoted by Thomas Moore, "Wheeling and Reeling in Philadelphia," *Philadelphia Magazine*, May, 1983, p. 158.

4. Julia Klein, "In Two Suburban Contests, Top Democrats Invisible," *Philadelphia Inquirer*, April 8, 1988.

5. Julia Klein, "Republicans in Montco and Delco Increasingly at Odds," *Philadelphia Inquirer*, April 8, 1988.

6. Thomas Luce and Anita Summers, *Local Fiscal Issues in the Philadelphia Metropolitan Area* (Philadelphia: University of Pennsylvania Press, 1987), p. 86.

7. Tanya Barrientos, "Suburban Growth Squeezes Schools," *Philadelphia Inquirer*, July 10, 1987.

8. Vanessa Herron, "A Tale of Two Communities," *Philadelphia Inquirer*, January 12, 1988.

9. Oliver Williams et al., *Suburban Differences and Metropolitan Policies: A Philadelphia Story* (Philadelphia: University of Pennsylvania Press, 1965), p. 71.

10. Ibid., pp. 118ff. Note that the researchers excluded spending on public education from their study.

11. Ibid., pp. 219–20.

12. Ibid., p. 264.

13. Delaware Valley Regional Planning Commission, *Regional Infrastructure Evaluation and Analysis for Southeastern Pennsylvania* (Philadelphia: DVRPC, December 1985).

14. Philadelphia City Planning Commission, *Comprehensive Plan: The Physical Development Plan for the City of Philadelphia* (Philadelphia, 1960).

15. Andrew Cassel, "Closing Gap between Suburban Jobs and City's Seekers," *Philadelphia Inquirer*, September 21, 1987.

16. Pennsylvania Conference of Teamsters, "The Philadelphia Port Mess," *Conference Report* 2 (Spring 1988): 1.

17. Estimate of the Delaware Valley Regional Planning Commission, 1986.

18. Roderick McKenzie, *The Metropolitan Community* (New York: McGraw-Hill, 1933), p. 71.

Chapter 7

1. Susan Warner, "Offices Galore—But Not Tenants," *Philadelphia Inquirer*, May 31, 1989.

2. See Dennis Keating, "Linking Downtown Development to Broader Community Goals," *Journal of the American Planning Association* 52 (Spring 1986): 133–41; on Chicago, see Gregory Squires et al., *Chicago: Race, Class, and the Response to Urban Decline* (Philadelphia: Temple University Press, 1987), pp. 52–53.

3. Hank Klibanoff, "Neighborhoods Explore Tapping Growth Boom Expected in Center City," *Philadelphia Inquirer*, May 22, 1988.

4. M. Dertouzos, R. Lester, and R. Solow, *Made in America* (Cambridge, Mass.: MIT Press, 1989). See also S. S. Cohen and J. Zysman, *Manufacturing Matters: The Myth of the Post-Industrial Economy* (New York: Basic Books, 1987).

5. M. Piore and C. Sabel, *The Second Industrial Divide* (New York: Basic Books, 1984). Also S. Lash and J. Urry, *The End of Organized Capitalism* (Cambridge: Polity Press, 1987); S. Tolliday and J. Zeitlin, eds., *The Automobile Industry and Its Workers: Between Fordism and Flexibility* (Cambridge: Polity Press, 1986).

6. A. J. Scott, "Flexible Production Systems and Regional Development," *International Journal of Urban and Regional Research* 12, no. 2 (1988): 171–85.

7. Figures are from the Philadelphia Board of Revision of Taxes, reported in the *Philadelphia Inquirer*, October 5, 1988.

8. Dan Stets, "Why Big Firms Pay a Small Share of City Business Taxes," *Philadelphia Inquirer*, May 28, 1989.

9. Peter Doeringer et al., *Invisible Factors in Local Economic Development* (New York: Oxford University Press, 1987).

10. A. J. Scott, "Flexible Production Systems," p. 177.

11. Paul Peterson, *City Limits* (Chicago: University of Chicago Press, 1981).

12. *Philadelphia Inquirer*, March 31, 1989.

Index